Coleridge and the Idea of Love

Aspects of relationship in Coleridge's thought and writing

ANTHONY JOHN HARDING

Assistant Professor of English
University of Saskatchewan

CAMBRIDGE UNIVERSITY PRESS

Published by the Syndics of the Cambridge University Press
Bentley House, 200 Euston Road, London NW1 2DB
American Branch: 32 East 57th Street, New York, N.Y. 10022
© Cambridge University Press 1974

Library of Congress Catalogue Card Number 74–80352

ISBN 0 521 20639 1

First published 1974

Printed in Great Britain
by W & J Mackay Limited, Chatham

Contents

This book is dedicated to
LUCY C. FITZWATER
as an affectionate tribute
to her humour and
patience as a teacher

Preface

This book is based on a dissertation prepared for the degree of Ph.D. at Cambridge between October 1969 and March 1973.

The author and publisher are grateful to the following for giving their permission to quote copyright material: Mr Alwyne Coleridge, as copyright-owner, for extracts from the unpublished Coleridge Notebooks; Routledge and Kegan Paul Ltd, for extracts from volumes 1 and 2 of Coleridge's *Notebooks*, edited by K. Coburn; the Clarendon Press, Oxford, for extracts from all six volumes of *The Collected Letters of Samuel Taylor Coleridge*, edited by E. L. Griggs: volumes 1 and 2 © 1956 Oxford University Press, volumes 3 and 4 © 1959 Oxford University Press and volumes 5 and 6 © 1971 Oxford University Press.

My warmest thanks are due to Professor L. C. Knights, for his help, advice and tactful criticism throughout this period. Invaluable help has also been given by Professor Lilian R. Furst and Professor Dorothy Emmet, who patiently guided me through the tenebrosities of certain German philosophers, and by Dr John Beer, whose expert knowledge of the English Romantic poets has been both an incentive and a resource to me. I wish to thank them for their help, and also to thank Professor John D. Jump, Head of the Department of English at the University of Manchester, Professor Brian Cox, and Dr David Pirie, for their guidance and encouragement in the early stages of the work.

I also owe a great deal to the staff of the University Library, Cambridge, and of the British Library, in London; any merit this book may have is in very great measure due to their efficiency and scholarship. And I must record a further debt of gratitude to Mrs Irene Tedder, Assistant Librarian at Jesus College, Cambridge, without whose knowledge of Coleridgeana in Jesus College the work would have been far more difficult, and far less enjoyable.

Any errors, omissions or inadequacies in any part of this book are entirely the responsibility of the author.

1974   A. J. H.

Abbreviations and sources

I list here all the works by Coleridge cited or mentioned in the text, with the abbreviations used after the first reference. I use the letter C as an abbreviation for 'Coleridge' throughout the footnotes. A full bibliography of works by other authors can be found at the end of the book.

In quoting from Coleridge's notebooks I have adopted in the main the conventions used by Professor Coburn. Passages from her edition of the notebooks (of which volumes I and II have now appeared) are reproduced as she prints them; in particular, later insertions by Coleridge are shown in pointed brackets, thus: <word>, and Coleridge's deletions, where legible, thus: ~~word~~. I have not attempted to decipher passages from the later notebooks which have been scored through by Coleridge or a later hand. I have also left his idiosyncratic spellings, especially of Greek, as in the original.

A difficulty arises in the giving of references to the notebooks which have not yet been published in Professor Coburn's edition, or to passages, so far unpublished, in the books of which Professor Coburn has edited parts only. The transcriptions here quoted are based on the photo-facsimiles kept in the Library of Jesus College, Cambridge. These facsimiles are bound in several volumes, each of which contains copies of two, three, four or even five notebooks, and the volumes are foliated *in toto*, not according to the notebook pagination; so that a reference to Notebook 18, folio 152 signifies folio 152 of the volume in which the facsimile of Notebook 18 has been bound. These references are not, therefore, equivalent to references drawn from the originals in the British Museum. Unfortunately, it cannot even be said that the first notebook in each of the Jesus College volumes is foliated similarly to the originals, since although British Museum practice has been followed in the basic

ABBREVIATIONS AND SOURCES

method of foliation, it has been changed in one important respect. Missing pages (of which there are a large number in almost all Coleridge's notebooks) are counted, in the British Museum originals, as if they were still in place; but in the facsimile volumes their absence is ignored, it appears, for purposes of foliation – in other words, the photographic plates, and not the notebook pages as they were in their original condition, are made the basis of the foliation. As soon as a missing page occurs, therefore, the foliation of the facsimile begins to differ from the foliation of the original.

Aids	*Aids to Reflection*, edited by H. N. Coleridge, fifth edition, 2 vols. (London, 1843).
AP	*Anima Poetæ*, edited by E. H. Coleridge (London,1895).
BL	*Biographia Literaria*, edited by J. Shawcross, corrected edition, 2 vols. (London, 1965).
–	*Coleridge on the Seventeenth Century*, edited by R. F. Brinkley (Durham, North Carolina, 1955).
CIS	*Confessions of an Inquiring Spirit*, edited by H. St J. Hart (London, 1956).
CCS	*On the Constitution of Church and State, according to the Idea of each* (London, 1830).
–	'Coleridge's *Dejection: An Ode*', edited by E. de Selincourt, in *Essays and Studies*, vol. xxii (1957), edited by Helen Darbishire pp. 7–25.
–	*Essay on Marriage*, privately printed for T. J. Wise (London, 1919); British Museum C. 57.e.54 and Ashley 2877.
EOT	*Essays on his Own Times*, edited by Sara Coleridge, 3 vols. (London, 1850).
LS	*Lay Sermon (Blessed are ye that sow beside all waters)* (London, 1817).
–	Lecture on the *Prometheus* of Æschylus, in *Transactions of the Royal Society of Literature* vol. ii (1834) pp. 384–404.
Lectures 1795	*Lectures 1795 on Politics and Religion*, edited by Lewis Patton and Peter Mann (Princeton, New Jersey, and London, 1971).
Letters	*Collected Letters of Samuel Taylor Coleridge*, edited by E. L. Griggs, 6 vols. (London, 1956 – 71).
Lit. Rems.	*Literary Remains of Samuel Taylor Coleridge*, edited by H. N. Coleridge, 4 vols. (London, 1836–9).

ABBREVIATIONS AND SOURCES

Miscellaneous Criticism	*Coleridge's Miscellaneous Criticism*, edited by T. M. Raysor (London, 1936).
N	*The Notebooks of Samuel Taylor Coleridge*, edited by K. Coburn (London 1957—), vols I and II (1957, 1961).
Notebooks	Unpublished notebooks, from the photo-facsimiles in the Library of Jesus College, Cambridge. (References to the published notebooks are to Professor Coburn's numbering of the entries, thus: N 1082. Where followed by 'n', thus: N 1082 n, this signifies a reference to Professor Coburn's note on the entry.)
Notes, Theological	*Notes, Theological, Political, and Miscellaneous*, edited by Derwent Coleridge (London, 1853).
Phil. Lects.	*Philosophical Lectures of Samuel Taylor Coleridge*, edited by K. Coburn (London, 1949).
–	'On the Philosophic Import of the Words OBJECT and SUBJECT', *Blackwood's Magazine*, vol. x no. 56 (October 1821, Edinburgh) pp. 247–50.
PW	*Complete Poetical Works of Samuel Taylor Coleridge*, edited by E. H. Coleridge, 2 vols. (London, 1912).
Shakespearean Criticism	*Coleridge's Shakespearean Criticism*, edited by T. M. Raysor, 2 vols. (London, 1960).
SM	*The Statesman's Manual, or, The Bible the best guide to political skill and forethought* (London, 1816).
Table Talk	*Table Talk of Samuel Taylor Coleridge*, &c., with an introduction by Henry Morley (London 1884).
TF	*The Friend*, edited by Barbara E. Rooke, 2 vols. (Princeton, New Jersey, and London, 1969).
–	'Theory of Life', in *Miscellanies, Æsthetic and Literary*, edited by T. Ashe (London, 1885).
The Watchman	*The Watchman*, edited by Lewis Patton (Princeton, New Jersey, and London, 1970).
Two Addresses	*Two Addresses on Sir Robert Peel's Bill*, privately printed for Edmund Gosse (London, 1913).

Introduction

The words 'society' and 'the individual' challenge everyone's conception of what it is to be a person, and all statements about the purpose or the absurdity of human life will be, in one aspect, the statement of some kind of relationship between 'society' and 'the individual'. Most people would agree, however, that 'individualism' is a comparatively recent invention, and like some forms of 'nationalism' is a product of that revolution in European thought which took place between the latter half of the eighteenth century and the middle of the nineteenth, and which is denoted by the term 'Romanticism'. Romanticism, it seems, has taught us to treat 'society' and 'the individual', in our everyday discussions, as heterogeneous quantities. Philosophers and psychologists of course take trouble to show why these quantities are not heterogeneous, why our picture of a society is inevitably also a picture of an individual, and vice versa, but it is rare to find a philosopher whose definition of human fulfilment steps outside this particular polarity (Martin Buber is a notable exception).

Romantic thought is by no means as much dominated by individualism, however, as our presuppositions would have it. It is broadly true that the popular image of the poet as a solitary, anti-social, unapproachable man took root in this era, and Romantic thought, by an illogical but predictable contamination, has come to be seen as the quintessence of individualism. Yet the number of literary friendships that became famous then is itself a warning against taking too much at their face value Romantic legends of the solitary genius.

Far more important, however, in compelling the writers of this age to examine their beliefs about human relationship in all its forms, were the events that followed the fall of the Bastille in 1789. These events ended all merely theoretical discussion of

1

INTRODUCTION

the relative merits of Utopianism, traditionalism and constitutional change. In England in the 1790s, political and ethical issues assumed an immediate, day-to-day importance such as they had not had since the end of the seventeenth century. Burke attacked the Revolution for the destructive effect it had on the most 'sacred' forms of human relationship, marriage and the family, while family loyalty was proclaimed obsolete by many of Godwin's followers. The British Government's increasingly strict laws against the encouragement of sedition, and the large number of outbreaks of popular hysteria against persons suspected of sympathizing with the French, forced many Dissenters to escape to America, where they founded Utopian communities based on democracy, open justice and, sometimes, New Testament Christianity. Coleridge and Southey were themselves intoxicated with their own scheme for such a community, 'Pantisocracy', and Wordsworth, as he says in *The Prelude*,

> began
> To think with fervour upon management
> Of Nations, what it is and ought to be,
> And how their worth depended on their Laws
> And on the Constitution of the State.[1]

Literature itself was seen by some as a cohesive force in society, enabling it to withstand the destructiveness both of revolutionary doctrine on the one hand and of governmental inquisitions on the other. In the period following his disillusionment with the Revolution, described in Books X–XII of *The Prelude*, Wordsworth wrote of the poet as 'an upholder and preserver, carrying everywhere with him relationship and love';[2] the emphasis on continuity and human relationships stands in contrast to the factiousness which both Wordsworth and Coleridge sometimes represented as characteristic of the political demagogue. Wordsworth's tragedy *The Borderers* turns on the poisoning of Marmaduke's compassionate nature by the persuasions of Oswald, an Iago-like figure described by another character as one of the 'Restless Minds',

[1] Text of 1805, edited by E. de Selincourt, revised by Helen Darbishire; Book x, lines 685–9.
[2] *Poetical Works*, edited by Thomas Hutchinson, revised by E. de Selincourt, p. 738

2

Such Minds as find amid their fellow-men
No heart that loves them, none that they can love.[1]

Oswald exemplifies what admiration of nature can become, when
not accompanied by love of human kind.

Godwin and Priestley, the theorists most widely venerated in
the radical circles Coleridge had known at Jesus College, both
taught the interdependence of men and society (as indeed, in a
different sense, did Burke). Godwin's 'Man...holds, necessarily, indispensibly to his species'[2] is a principle from which
none of them would wish to dissent; but *how* man 'holds to his
species', what kind of priority the degrees of his relationship
should have, or whether all such relationships should be dissolved in the universal bonds of human brotherhood, is obviously a question to which there are many possible answers.

This book sets itself the task of analysing Coleridge's work in
so far as it deals with ideas of human relationship. This is not to
deny that other writers of the age – Blake, in particular – did not
have vitally important things to say about love and marriage,
the State, the family and the individual; but the richness of what
Coleridge has to offer makes it difficult to do him justice in a
more general survey. Nevertheless this is not a general study of
Coleridge's thought, nor a contribution to Coleridgean biography. It contains biographical chapters, and a section on the
history of the period, because I believe it would be false to
the spirit of Coleridge's thought to represent his writings as the
work of a remote, solitary thinker untroubled either by political
turbulence or by the intrusions of friend and family. But it should
perhaps be emphasized that biography is always provisional, and
that my aim is to elucidate the ideas actually enunciated by
Coleridge, with only as much biography as will remind the
reader that Coleridge was not insulated from the world.

It will be asked, if the focus of the book is on a particular way
of thinking about the social order, what are my reasons for
selecting Coleridge as a subject of study, rather than (say) a few
texts from the early nineteenth century, among which some
Coleridgean material might be included?

Professor Willey, in *The English Moralists*, identifies three

[1] *Poetical Works*, p. 50.　　[2] *Caleb Williams*, edited by David McKraken, p. 303.

3

stages in the development of modern humanism. The first is the theocentric humanism of Hooker, Milton and Locke: the final stage is the positivist humanism of Comte, Mill and Marx. The intermediate stage, the first step in the 'de-Christianization' of European thought, is 'the man-centred humanism of the eighteenth century, of the Encyclopaedists, of Hume, and of the idealistic romantic poets and philosophers'. Here, 'morality ceases to be dependent upon supernatural sanctions, and becomes either utilitarian – that is, a matter of the consequences of actions in terms of well-being or happiness – or a matter of the Kantian imperative, that is, of obedience to the law of man's own nature.'[1] Coleridge stands at the point of intersection of these three categories, but can be accommodated in none of them, and the complexity of his relationship to 'man-centred humanism' is precisely what makes him a difficult and often disturbing subject of study. As Professor Fruman has very thoroughly shown, Coleridge has been credited with a great deal that is not his own, sometimes because of his own deceitfulness, sometimes because of the partiality of critics, and as a result our picture of the history of European thought at this period must undergo a radical change. But Professor Fruman may also have enabled a new and more objective approach to be made to Coleridge's work. As Dr J. B. Beer has remarked, what Professor Fruman has done is essentially to challenge students of Coleridge to show where his true originality lay.[2] It is to be hoped that this book can be regarded as a small contribution to such an effort; with the proviso that, in order to prove that Coleridge's work repays study, one does not first have to prove that Coleridge the man deserves immortalization.

In the first of his 1901–2 Gifford lectures, William James established a useful distinction between two ways of responding to other people's records of religious experience. One can rest one's claim for the validity of a religious experience on its divine origin; but then a disagreement arises between those who believe that the experience did have a divine origin, and those who attribute it to epilepsy, neurosis or other pathological

[1] Basil Willey, *The English Moralists*, pp. 118–19.
[2] Norman Fruman, *Coleridge, the Damaged Archangel* (London, 1972); J. B. Beer, *The Review of English Studies*, xxiv, 95 (August 1973) (346–53), p. 353.

4

conditions. Or one can disregard origin, and direct one's attention to the independent *value* the experience may be judged to have. As James later shows, John Bunyan's constitution was undeniably psychopathic;[1] but if a man allows this knowledge to prevent him studying the *Pilgrim's Progress*, he has no one but himself to blame for his diminishment.

It will, I hope, become apparent that an essentially coherent idea of human relationship did exist for Coleridge. Its most important manifestations may tentatively be summarized as:

the recognition of personality, rather than conduct, as the starting-point of morality;

the essentiality of love, which is part of the striving of the individual towards the 'one Life';

the origin of self-consciousness, morality and Reason itself in the individual's sense of 'otherness';

and the vital function of religion and the developing social state in breaking through the individual's insular subjectivity and incorporating him into the stream of history.

To all of this the poetry of the great early creative period forms a strange but indispensable commentary, suggesting, through its recurring image of the fountain, that the real sources of love and joy are still mysteries not susceptible of explanation.

[1] *The Varieties of Religious Experience*, pp. 18–19, 157.

I

1795–1803

Ich finde alles eher auf der Erde, so gar Wahrheit und Freude, als
Freundschaft.

Jean Paul Richter*

In this world I can find all things, even Truth and Joy, sooner than I
can find Friendship.

1

Coleridge's friendships were treasured by him to a degree that
made even the slightest threat of a breach intensely painful.
During the period of self-examination that began with the
approach of his thirty-first birthday in October 1803, he could
be so disturbed by the mere arrival of a letter, 'not quite certain
whether it would be affectionate or reproachful, mournful or
happy', that he would keep it for hours before opening it.[1] It was
also during this period of introspection that he wrote, 'My nature requires another Nature for its support, and reposes only in
another from the necessary Indigence of its Being.'[2] Southey,
Poole, Wordsworth and Sara Hutchinson in different ways
served as the buttresses of Coleridge's very shaky self-confi-
dence, and all eventually disappointed him. The demands that
Coleridge made upon them must indeed have been extreme, but
Coleridge's own chief objectives were undoubtedly so far out of
the normal range of human intercourse that, although he would
have found it difficult not to look for similar ideals and standards
in his closest friends, he was certain to be disappointed; yet it
was De Quincey's opinion that 'beyond all men who ever lived,
[Coleridge] found means to engage a constant succession of
most faithful friends'.[3]

* Quoted in *Anima Poetæ*, p. 235.   [1] N 1517.   [2] N1679.
[3] Thomas De Quincey, *Reminiscences of the English Lake Poets*, p. 69.

6

The Pantisocratic scheme, though dismissed in 1809 as 'extravagant' and 'vain', left a legacy of idealism which had its effect on Coleridge's personal life, as well as on his political theory, and he attributed to the same interest and zeal that impelled him towards Pantisocracy his 'clearest insight into the nature of individual man'.[1] It was Southey's failure to show an equivalent idealism that spoiled the first in a series of stormy friendships. Southey charged Coleridge with being 'intoxicated with the novelty of a System', and invited his scorn by abandoning the Pantisocratic scheme in order to study law, giving as his reasons the need to secure a regular income for his family, and the fear that Coleridge's incorrigible indolence would endanger the success of the scheme.[2] Coleridge was incensed less by the unkindness of this charge of 'indolence' than by Southey's betrayal of an ideal which had once appeared far greater than the virtues or vices of any of its adherents. 'How does this [sc. his "indolence"] affect Pantisocracy, that you should reject *it*?' Coleridge wrote indignantly in a long letter of 13 November 1795. He retraces the history of Southey's involvement with Pantisocracy, and his progressive betrayal of its principles, and ends with a painful revelation of the loss he feels himself to have suffered, not from the collapse of the scheme itself so much as from the diminution that Southey had undergone in his esteem.

You have left a large Void in my Heart – I know no man big enough to fill it...never do I expect to meet another man, who will make me unite attachment for his person with reverence for his heart and admiration of his Genius! I did not only venerate you for your own Virtues, I prized you as the Sheet Anchor of mine![3]

That Pantisocracy, in spite of this disappointment, remained at the back of Coleridge's mind for some time, if only as an impossible dream, is evidenced by a letter of January 1800 to Davy, in which he half-jokingly suggests founding a colony to consist of five members: Davy, Tobin, Wordsworth, Coleridge, Southey.[4] But as a recent biographer of Coleridge has pointed

[1] *The Friend*, i p. 224 (no. 11 : 26 October 1809); ii pp. 146–7.
[2] *Letters*, i pp. 169, 171 (no. 93 : 13 November 1795).
[3] *ib*. pp. 171, 173.   [4] *ib*. p. 556 (no. 308 : 1 January 1800).

COLERIDGE AND THE IDEA OF LOVE

out, it never occurred to Coleridge to proceed with the scheme without Southey.[1]

It was the autumn of 1796 before their differences were healed, and even then Coleridge would not submit to calling Southey more than an acquaintance. 'I do not *esteem*, or LOVE Southey, as I must esteem and love the man whom I dared call by the holy name of FRIEND!'[2] Southey, in his function as sheet-anchor, had been replaced by Thomas Poole, whom Coleridge chose as a neighbour by taking a cottage at Nether Stowey, near to Poole's house, in the first days of 1797. Coleridge did not conceal the importance to him of this connection. 'I told [Wordsworth] plainly', he wrote to Poole during his sojourn in Germany, 'that *you* had been the man in whom *first* and in whom alone, I had felt an *anchor*! With all my other Connections I felt a dim sense of insecurity and uncertainty.'[3] And to Josiah Wedgwood, Coleridge wrote of the salutary effect Poole's strength of character and 'manliness', a quality Coleridge was later to admire in Wordsworth, had on his own intellectual enterprises: 'There was some thing both in his understanding and in his affection so healthy and manly, that my mind freshened in his company, and my ideas and habits of thinking acquired day after day more of substance and reality.'[4] Poole took an interest in Coleridge's life and mental history to the extent of eliciting from him a series of five autobiographical letters, and Coleridge evidently warmed to this man who, while possessing no very great talents himself, was seriously interested in poetry and philosophy, and, even more to the point, in the personal history of one who laboured to be both poet and philosopher. For companionship on the intellectual and spiritual as well as on the personal plane, Coleridge could now look to Wordsworth, who after their collaboration on the *Lyrical Ballads* figured very largely in every plan that Coleridge's fertile brain dreamed up. 'You are incorporated into the better part of my being', he wrote to Wordsworth; 'whenever I spring forward into the future with noble affections, I always alight by your side.'[5] In

---

[1] W. J. Bate, *Coleridge*, p. 27.
[2] *Letters*, i p. 294 (no. 170: 31 December 1796).
[3] *ib*. p. 491 (no. 277: 6 May 1799).
[4] *ib*. p. 644 (no. 362: 1 November 1800).
[5] *ib*. p. 453 (no. 268: December 1798).

8

spite of Coleridge's hopes, however, and in spite of the belief, which he confided to Poole, that 'where I live, there [Wordsworth] will live, unless he should find in the North any person or persons, who can feel and understand him',[1] Wordsworth and Dorothy did not settle near Nether Stowey, nor anywhere in the South of England, but moved into Dove Cottage, Grasmere, a few months after their return from Germany. As Coleridge knew, however, Wordsworth's needs were different from his, for Wordsworth did not share Coleridge's 'weaknesses', and had always had a considerable measure of self-sufficiency, or, as Coleridge rather bitterly put it, had 'hurtfully segregated and isolated' himself.[2] The contrast was later to prove fatal to their friendship, but in these early years there was a sufficient sense of shared purpose to counteract the tension it might otherwise have caused.

With the birth of his affection for Sara Hutchinson at the intimate fireside gathering at Sockburn on 24 November 1799, and its gradual transmutation into the deepest passion Coleridge ever knew, Coleridge's loneliness entered a new phase, culminating in the period of intense heartsearching that occupied the last months of 1803. He envied above all the congenial domestic peace that Wordsworth now enjoyed at Grasmere, surrounded by his 'harem' – Mary, Dorothy and Sara. The presence of Coleridge's own wife and children near by at Greta Hall, into which the Coleridge family moved in July 1800, only served to emphasize the contrast between the two households. In a note of September 1801, the importance of which has been recognized by Humphry House, and by Professor Coburn in her edition of the Notebooks,[3] Coleridge juxtaposed the initials 'W.W. M.H. D.W. S.H.' with the description of a placid spring that he had observed near Greta Hall. Professor Coburn interprets the note as signifying that Coleridge 'is not part of the spring, the cone of sand, and the unruffled surface; that is the Dove Cottage circle. He, alas, lives in the angry, spasmodic, painful companionship of Greta Hall.'[4] It is possible too that the special characteristic of the Dove Cottage household which associated it in Coleridge's mind with the tranquil spring was its quiet productivity.

[1] *ib.* p. 491 (no. 277: 6 May 1799).   [2] *ib.*
[3] A. H. House, *Coleridge*, p. 52; and N 980 n.   [4] N 980 n.

Wordsworth was enjoying at this point what Ernest de Selincourt calls his second 'productive period',[1] and it is just this kind of atmosphere that Coleridge may have had in mind when he advised aspiring authors to work in the evenings at home: 'the social silence, or undisturbing voices of a wife or sister, will be like the restorative atmosphere, or soft music which moulds a dream without becoming its object'.[2] It was a privilege which he was to enjoy but seldom, though the evidence of the notebooks shows that there were times when, staying at Dove Cottage, he worked 'hard and successfully' and profited from the advice of his beloved 'Housemates'.[3] Coleridge understood well enough that, as Professor Bald put it, 'incomplete and thwarted achievement is the penalty of isolation.'[4]

Coleridge had always valued domestic fellowship for its own sake, too: in 1795 only the supreme vocation of Pantisocracy could surpass it in importance, and though he insists to Southey that Pantisocracy must override filial and matrimonial duties, he praises 'domestic happiness' in very strong terms indeed.

Domestic Happiness is the greatest of things sublunary – and of things celestial it is perhaps impossible for unassisted Man to believe any thing greater – : but it is not strange that those things, which in a pure form of Society will constitute our first blessings, should in it's present morbid state, be our most perilous Temptations – ! – 'He that doth not love Mother and Wife less than me, is not worthy of me!'[5]

His feelings in this respect have not altered in 1801; he writes to Southey in December of that year, 'What is Life, gangrened, as it is with me, in it's very vitals – domestic Tranquillity?'[6] And to Sara he poured out the tale of his loneliness in the long verse letter of April 1802 (which was to become the 'Ode: Dejection'), speaking of 'those habitual Ills /That wear out Life, when two unequal Minds /Meet in one House, and two discordant Wills.'[7] The note of November 1803 in which he reflects that his nature 'reposes only in another from the necessary Indigence of its Being' is anticipated by many more para-

---

1 Introduction to Wordsworth's *Poetical Works*, p. xxv.
2 BL, i p. 154.   3 N 1829, 1830.
4 R. C. Bald, *Literary Friendships in the Age of Wordsworth*, p. xvii.
5 *Letters*, i p. 158 (no. 87: August 1795).
6 *ib.* ii p. 778 (no. 427: 31 December 1801).   7 See below, p. 75.

graphs in the notebooks and letters. Coleridge's wife, whom Dorothy Wordsworth described as 'a sad fiddle faddler', lacking in sensibility in spite of her skill as a nurse,[1] was shocked into mending her ways by Coleridge's proposal that they should separate. 'For the first time since our marriage', Coleridge wrote to Southey, she 'felt and acted, as beseemed a Wife and a Mother to a Husband, and the Father of her children'.[2] There was no separation at this time. But Coleridge continued to feel acutely the incompatibility of his temperament with his wife's, and matters were exacerbated by Sara Coleridge's disapproval of his attachment to the Wordsworths and Sara Hutchinson.[3] Yet Coleridge's friendships were above all else attempts to find someone who could give him that sympathetic understanding of which Mrs Coleridge was incapable. In May 1802 he wrote,

The unspeakable Comfort to a good man's mind – nay, even to a criminal to be *understood* – to have someone that understands one – and who does not feel, that on earth no one does. The Hope of this – always more or less disappointed, gives the *passion* to Friendship.[4]

Coleridge regarded the marriage bond as indissoluble, however, and indeed to Southey he firmly promised that he would see his wife did not have cause to complain of neglect, in spite of their incompatibility, insisting that it was only weakness on his part which made him demand 'warmth of manner in a female House mate' as well as 'warmth of internal attachment'.[5] Coleridge accused himself of expecting demonstrative affection, without being prepared to return anything but 'general kindness and general Sympathy'.[6] These, however, were self-criticisms that must have owed more to a conscious comparison of his own temperament with that of his correspondent than to any very deep-rooted conviction of his own guilt. His strongest feeling is the simple consciousness of intellectual and spiritual isolation, expressed in the notes of October and November 1803, and in a note made on the Scottish tour: '. . .tho' the World praise me, I have no dear Heart that loves my Verses. . .'[7]

[1] *Early Letters of William and Dorothy Wordsworth*, p. 273 (no. 121 : 27 April 1801).
[2] *Letters*, ii p. 832 (no. 449 : 29 July 1802).
[3] De Quincey, *Reminiscences*, pp. 21–3.   [4] N 1082.
[5] *Letters*, ii p. 929 (no. 491 : 17 February 1803).
[6] *ib.* p. 959 (no. 509 : 1 August 1803).   [7] N 1463.

COLERIDGE AND THE IDEA OF LOVE

With the advent of his thirty-first birthday, the period of five months when his mind had been 'strangely shut up'[1] came to an end, and among the extensive reflections and analyses with which he filled his notebooks in the last months of 1803 there are many passages that evince the growing importance to Coleridge of some ideas on relationship which were beginning to transcend the merely personal.

2

To delve into the subconscious processes of a writer's mind, to search among what is known of his childhood or adolescence for the hidden explanation of the ideas and decisions of his adult life, is more the job of the biographer than of the critic, and even the biographer has to resort to pure conjecture more often than the critic would regard as legitimate. The critic is aware, of course, that subconscious processes must have been at work; but he is generally more interested in the conscious efforts that his author made to understand his own actions, and those of other people, than in the psychological peculiarities which possibly underlay the writer's conscious mind. This is particularly true for the Coleridge critic, when we have evidence that Coleridge thought much about the principles of human conduct, and that, moreover, personal observation and personal experience, often thoroughly analysed, played a very large part in the formation of his total moral and metaphysical outlook. On the other hand, criticism of the moral and metaphysical thought can make the biographer's task more meaningful. George Whalley, in his book *Coleridge and Sara Hutchinson*, has suggested that a major factor in the development of Coleridge's relationship with Sara was his sense of 'the sanctity of the human person' (p. 100). It is an idea that goes back far beyond Coleridge's first meeting with Sara; it is present in one form, for instance, in the essay on marriage as practised among the Germans that begins the third issue of *The Watchman* (p. 89); but it is also true that Coleridge's love for Sara taught him much about the economy of the mind, and intensified his idealism concerning the principles of human conduct and the respect which men owe each other.

1 *Letters*, ii p. 991 (no. 520: 16 September 1803).

When he was a mere freshman at Jesus College, Coleridge read a number of philosophical poems by the Latinist Benedict Stay,[1] and one of them contained a fable which he met with again years later in Drayton's *The Moone-Calf*, though 'most miserably marred in the telling'. It was this fable which he chose to introduce *The Friend*. It concerns a golden age, preserved in the memory of 'the self-dissatisfied Race of Men',

when Conscience acted in Man with the ease and uniformity of Instinct; when Labor was a sweet name for the activity of sane Minds in health-ful Bodies, and all enjoyed in common the bounteous harvest produced, and gathered in, by common effort; when there existed in the Sexes, and in the Individuals of each Sex, just variety enough to permit and call forth the gentle restlessness and final union of chaste love and indivi-dual attachment, each seeking and finding the beloved *one* by the natural affinity of their Beings.[2]

There was a painful discrepancy between the idealism embodied in this myth and the intolerance and narrow moralism of which Southey, Sara Coleridge and Wordsworth were guilty, at least in Coleridge's eyes; indeed even Sara Hutchinson does not escape the charge of 'dyspathy'.[3] Coleridge found that he had increasingly to remind himself of the relative unimportance of *conduct* beside what he was to call the 'original self', and his writings on relationship continually return to this theme. Love and friendship were things too vital to be disturbed by the vagaries and accidental inconsistencies of *conduct*. (It was for something much more serious than a mere error in conduct that he decided he could no longer confer upon Southey 'the holy name of FRIEND':[4] it was for a sin against his true nature, against what Southey was *in himself*.)

In these years, Coleridge not seldom found that he had to have recourse to some such doctrine as the irrelevance of conduct to protect his vulnerable sensibility against the disturbance which even a trivial solecism might cause. During the period of total estrangement from Southey, when he evidently feared the loss of Poole's friendship as well, he wrote to Poole nervously chiding him on no other grounds than that 'you did not leave me so

[1] N 2626 and n. [2] TF, i p. 7 (no. 1 : 1 June 1809); ii p. 11.
[3] N 712. [4] See above, p. 8.

13

affectionately as you were wont to do'. 'The Heart', he wrote,

thoroughly penetrated with the flame of virtuous Friendship, is in a state of glory; but 'lest it should be exalted above measure, there is given it a Thorn in the flesh:' – I mean, that where the friendship of any person forms an essential part of a man's happiness, he will at times be pestered by the little jealousies and solicitudes of imbecil Humanity.[1]

Clearly too much weight should not be put on Coleridge's choice of expression in this letter, nor on the other outpourings of a possibly over-wrought temperament occasioned by, for instance, the quarrel with Charles Lloyd, when Coleridge wrote to Estlin, 'I pray God, that I may sanctify these events; by forgiveness, and a peaceful spirit.'[2] Yet they do show that Coleridge was struggling, against the sufferings of an over-sensitive nature, to establish some kind of equanimity, a resolution of the conflict in which he could value his friends rather for what they were than for what they did, and disregard their occasional lapses into tactlessness or neglect, and even such gross errors of taste as Charles Lloyd's unflattering portrait of him in *Edmund Oliver*. That the perception Coleridge is fighting to preserve is essentially a religious one becomes clear when he implies a contrast between 'imbecil Humanity' and the unsullied state of 'virtuous Friendship', in which only a person's true self, the self only God knows fully, matters.

Even Coleridge's family relationships were subjected to the same test: the measure of esteem he felt capable of granting to each of his relatives for what they were *in themselves*. Except for his sister, and his brother George (who had behaved with considerable generosity towards him during the troubled days of his university career) none came out with any great credit. In spite of his admiration for Burke, for whom the family was the chief repository of moral values and the matrix of social cohesion, Coleridge did not feel inclined to value blood kinship as such too highly. He admitted to Poole in 1801 that he had neglected, and did not love, his family: 'their ways are not my ways, nor their thoughts my thoughts';[3] and Poole himself he

[1] *Letters*, i p. 235 (no. 142: 24 September 1796).
[2] *ib.* p. 407 (no. 245: 14 May 1798).
[3] *ib.* ii p. 756 (no. 411: 7 September 1801).

censured for becoming too constricted by family loyalties; but he makes an interesting *caveat*, excepting the *primary* familial relations, parental, filial and sibling, from his general condemnation.

Poole! I have seen only two defects in your making up, that are of any importance – (let me premise before I write the next sentence that by family attachment I do not mean *domestic* attachment, but merely *family – cousinships*; not Brother, not Sister, not Son – for these are *real* relations; but family, as far as it [is] mere accident). The two defects which I have seen in you, are, 1. Excess of *family* and of *local* attachment, which has fettered your moral free-agency, and bedimmed your intellectual vision... 2. A too great desire and impatience to produce *immediate* good.[1]

Coleridge's own experience of fatherhood (Hartley was five in 1801, Derwent one – Berkeley had died at the age of one while Coleridge was in Germany) obviously goes some way to account for his curiously ambivalent attitude towards the nuclear family, while his sojourn in Germany, as evidenced for instance in the 'Lines written in the Album at Elbingerode',[2] led him to value domesticity even more than he had at the time of the Pantisocracy venture: but the tone of this letter to Poole, even allowing for the degree of candour which Coleridge evidently felt he could safely use with such an intimate friend, is astonishing. Nevertheless, it would not be right to deduce from it that Coleridge was beginning to treat the family and the home from a utilitarian point of view. Rather the opposite, in fact, for he feels himself to have learned the lesson – one that comes to figure increasingly in his moral thought, and even in his theory of poetry – that moral precepts are useless without the kind of affection that a close circle of relationships can foster. His friends were often to be censured for exhibiting the 'love of wisdom' rather than the 'wisdom of love';[3] Hazlitt in particular was prone, Coleridge believed, to this fault, and was characterized in a note of Coleridge's as a 'loveless observer' (an epithet which recalls the fourth stanza of the 'Ode: Dejection').[4] To Greenough, Coleridge wrote

---

[1] *ib.* p. 764 (no. 416: 5 October 1801).   [2] PW, i p. 315.
[3] Coleridge's charge against Schelling: see BL, i p. 105, and p. 33 below.
[4] N 624; PW, i p. 365.

COLERIDGE AND THE IDEA OF LOVE

Amid the dreary Goings on and burthensome Manners of daily Life it might be both pleasant and morally useful to you to dwell awhile with me and Wordsworth and his Sister – for we are in some sort unusual Beings, inasmuch as we have seen a great deal of what is called the World, and acquired a great deal of what is called Knowledge, and yet have formed a deep conviction that all is contemptible that does not spring immediately out of an affectionate Heart.[1]

The period of greatest tension between Coleridge and his wife, which followed on Coleridge's increased intimacy with the Wordsworths and Sara Hutchinson, produced, besides some letters to Mrs Coleridge in which he criticized what he felt to be the defects of her character, a manuscript note that goes further than he dared to go in the letters, linking Mrs Coleridge's notoriously irritable temperament with her coldness in love. 'Coldness' here does not mean sexual frigidity, because Coleridge notes that George Hutchinson, though far from frigid, shared Mrs Coleridge's deficiency in 'tangible [tactual?] Ideas and sensation'. What they both lack is integration of the conscious mind and personality with the body and its sensations, which are not merely momentary sensations, but 'the blending and unifying of the sensations that inhere in the manifold goings on of the Life of the whole man'.[2] Coleridge seems to have in mind here the kind of freedom and spontaneity that Blake was thinking of when he wrote that man has no body distinct from his soul.[3] It is not a moral judgment so much as an intuitive perception, and yet it impinges on the moral sphere, for a lack of spiritual wholeness tends to destroy one's unconscious faith in the promptings of the heart – the expression of the person one truly is – and make one depend overmuch on the opinions and imagined criticisms of others. Sara's fault is this

coldness perhaps and paralysis in all *tangible* ideas and sensations – all that forms *real Self* – hence the Slave of her she creates her own self in a field of Vision and Hearing, at a distance, by her own ears and eyes – and hence becomes the willing Slave of the Ears and Eyes of others. – Nothing affects her with pain and or pleasure as it is but only as other people will *say it is* – nay by an habitual absence of *reality* in her affections I have had an hundred instances that the being beloved, or

[1] *Letters*, ii p. 718 (no. 393: 13 April 1801).   [2] N 979.
[3] *The Marriage of Heaven and Hell, Poems and Prophecies*, p. 49.

the not being beloved, is a thing indifferent; but the *notion* of not being beloved – that wounds her pride deeply.[1]

The note continues as an investigation in psychology; Coleridge generalizes his conclusions, though the immediate object of his analysis is throughout the behaviour and lack of 'real Self' of his wife. These criticisms of her are balanced by the periodic spasms of self-criticism in which Coleridge took himself to task for what he was to call his 'diseased Proneness to Sympathy'.[2] As we have seen, he accused himself to Southey of being too dependent on 'warmth of manner' in others, long before Wordsworth wrote 'Resolution and Independence' as, in part, a gentle corrective to this trait;[3] and vacillation between the two extremes of self-criticism and searching analysis of other people's defects is the salient characteristic of the notes of late 1803 – a period of much speculation on the subject of relationship. Perhaps as a result of Wordsworth's admonitions Coleridge, even in the privacy of his notebooks, was apologetic about his own tendencies; and yet he would rather suffer from this 'medley of good nature, diseased Proneness to Sympathy, and a habit of being *wiser behind* the Curtain than his own actions before it', than from the intolerance and moral pedantry of a Southey. Such harmless flattery as Coleridge did not scruple to apply on occasion was, for Southey, a violation of 'Truth and Sincerity'; and yet Southey would 'publish the harshest censure of men as moralists and as literati, on his simple Ipse dixit.'[4] There is no question which sin of the two Coleridge regarded as venial. One is merely the pathetic refuge of a weak temperament, while the other is the strangulation of the finer human impulses for the sake of a morality of appearances. Sympathy, if constrained, and if we lose the sense of its 'outness', becomes merely 'an inward reverberation of the stifled cry of distress'.[5] Spontaneity, wholeness, the unity of the sensibility with the moral being, is worth preserving, even if it entails the loss of a certain amount of dignity. But it is important not to interpret this belief as an uncritical acceptance of the 'holiness of the heart's affections'. Coleridge agreed with Sir

[1] N 979.   [2] N 1602.
[3] See Stephen Prickett, *Wordsworth and Coleridge: The Poetry of Growth*, pp. 152–6.
[4] N 1602. (I accept Miss Coburn's suggestion that B is Southey.)
[5] AP, p. 23.

17

Thomas Browne that 'I give no alms to satisfy the hunger of my brother, but to fulfil and accomplish the will and command of my God'; God's will was the criterion by which human feelings must be judged.[1]

Coleridge's fascination with what he felt to be of the essence of humanity, stripped of the accretions of code-based moralities, took him occasionally far beyond the personal world of his introspective moments into speculation on such topics as the origins of the incest taboo. In 1803 he read Paley's *Principles of Moral and Political Philosophy*, and strongly disagreed with Paley's argument that the incest taboo must have arisen in order to prevent the early loss of chastity among families forced to live in intimacy. Coleridge's version of the story is rather more imaginative. His interest is in what we may call the sociological and anthropological aspects of the subject, and also, though in a quite different sense from Paley's, in the moral aspects. For Coleridge feels himself to have imaginatively discovered something characteristic of the essential human experience, something which was 'a glorious fact *of* human Nature – the object therefore of religious Veneration to all that love their fellowmen or honor themselves'.[2] Breaking free from Paley's narrowly moralistic view, he praises 'Brotherly and Sisterly Love' not only as precious in itself, but as a vital preparation for wedded love; and in both cases thinks of the love that subsists without physical attraction (whereas Paley's thinking is evidently dominated by his hatred of carnality). Coleridge writes:

By dividing the sisterly and fraternal from the conjugal affection, the human Heart has two loves instead of one, is richer in love – each as strong perhaps in affectionate Natures as it can be – but most certainly as strong as any single affection ought to be, consistently with the performance of our Duties, and the love we owe to our Neighbours etc. ...By the long habitual practice of the sisterly affection preceding the conjugal, this latter is thereby rendered more pure, more even, and of greater constancy.[3]

The *caveat* concerning 'our Duties, and the love we owe to our Neighbours etc.' is significant: Coleridge has not so far abandoned the beliefs of the eighteenth-century moralists concerning

[1] *Miscellaneous Criticism* p. 255: note of 1802 in Browne's *Religio Medici* (II section 2).   [2] N 1637.   [3] *ib.*

18

man's obligations towards society as a whole that he can trust
solely the instincts of the human heart. Yet the thesis he is
propounding is characteristically Coleridgean, with its emphasis
on the value of love, the idealistic view of marriage, and the
faith in sisterly love as an object worthy of 'religious Veneration'. It reappears in one of 'Satyrane's Letters', written from
Germany in 1798 and first printed in *Biographia Literaria*. In a
passage overtly concerned with the meaning of the German
word *Freundin*, Coleridge says that a man and woman can be
more than friends without there being necessarily any sexual
attraction between them; the love of a sister is a step towards the
understanding of this deeper affection, and the man who is
unable to understand it would not be 'capable even of loving a
wife as she deserves to be loved'.[1]

The expression 'religious Veneration' illustrates too the
humanistic bent of Coleridge's religious ideals; Coleridge was
not so far a humanist that he denied the reality of the metaphysical
world, nor so far a theist that he denied the value of human love,
for he asserted that the human race, particularly in its capacity
for love, was the summit of Creation. Because of this, he dis-
liked anything that appeared to constrain or falsify the true
human affections. This might be the effect of the incest taboo, at
least in the hands of unimaginative moralists like Paley. What
began, Coleridge conjectured, as horror of the results produced
by some castes that practised inbreeding, which would be regarded as 'divine Vengeance on the Practice', had now become
a received idea: 'Among common minds, aye, among any but
very uncommon minds, who enquires whether *any* one *can* do
that which no one *does* do [?]'[2]

In a discussion that Coleridge had with Southey on this topic,
however, the question of the value to be put on the brotherly and
sisterly affection was apparently neglected while Coleridge
defended his explanation of the strength and universality of the
incest taboo. Southey was inclined to put it down to the law of
association, and thought it

in the teeth of all analogy that a moral feeling should be traditionary
almost everywhere; and the physical Fact every where forgotten.
This *surprized* me; it seems to me e contra supported by a thousand

[1] BL, ii pp. 146–7.   [2] N 1637.

19

Facts strictly analogous – the dancing round the May pole on May day is a part of the worship of Priapus – the fact is forgotten, the custom, etc. continued.[1]

The anthropological aspects of the problem do not interest Coleridge so much, however, as the idea that fraternal and conjugal affection are both manifestations of the nobility of human nature, since they are something that 'the better part of our nature *feels* – tho' only a few speculative men develop that feeling, and make it put forth its distinctive *form*, in the understanding. – A melancholy task remains – namely to shew, how all this beautiful Fabric begins to moulder, in corrupt or bewildered (*verwilderte*) Nature.'[2]

From what Coleridge writes here of conjugal love, emphasizing the qualities it shares or should share with sisterly affection and insisting that it should not override 'our Duties, and the love we owe to our Neighbours etc.', we should expect to find that Coleridge's idea of marriage was an austere and platonic one. Certainly, though Coleridge did not always regard the *sacrament* of marriage as meaningful, or essential,[3] his respect for the sanctity of the marriage bond was always strong. 'Carefully have I *thought thro'* the subject of marriage', Coleridge wrote to Southey in 1801 – at a time when his own marriage fell far short of any ideal he may have formed – 'and deeply am I convinced of it's indissolubleness.'[4] Yet this respect was far from being a mere acceptance of convention, or even a belief that marriage was a socially useful institution, though this consideration did enter his mind.[5] Coleridge evidently felt that marriage could and should provide, as well as a cohesive influence in society as a whole, a ground for the development of the moral being, the 'real Self', of each partner. Coleridge found himself opposing both the conventional and the newly fashionable on behalf, not of freedom from old institutions, but of the real rewards those institutions could bring in terms of human fulfilment. An interesting early example of this occurs in *The Watchman* when Coleridge attacks the 'routine of etiquette' and '*politesse*' as a falsification

[1] N 1637.
[2] *ib.* For C's use of this note in his Shakespeare lectures see below, p. 99.
[3] *Letters*, i p. 306 (no. 176: 6 February 1797). See below, p. 26.
[4] *ib.* ii p. 767 (no. 417: 21 October 1801).
[5] *ib.* i p. 306 (no. 176: 6 February 1797).

of social relations. Such attacks were of course customary in radical circles; the distinctively Coleridgean note is struck when he goes on to argue that real refinement makes woman the intelligent partner and equal of man, and not an object of mere sensual gratification. The illustration he adduces is the practice of German tribes of the first century A.D. 'The women of Germany', he writes, basing himself on Tacitus' account, 'were the free and equal companions of their husbands: they were treated by them with esteem and confidence, and consulted on every occasion of importance.'[1] But the radicals with whom Coleridge had been fraternising in 1795 held that marriage was the very opposite of 'free and equal' companionship; it was in their eyes an oppressive institution, as outdated as the family loyalty whose abolition Godwin was supposed to have condoned in his *Political Justice*. Coleridge fiercely attacked this kind of argument[2] and indeed assured his audiences at Bristol that family loyalty was essential to the survival of national loyalty, and to the 'general benevolence' which he felt should be the impulse behind all political action. But the institution of marriage was apparently threatened by an influence far more subversive than even that of Godwin: revolutionary France. One of the projects listed in the Gutch notebook is an essay 'On Marriage – in opposition to French Principles';[3] this essay, if written, has not survived (unless the letter written to an anonymous young lady in, probably, June 1821 be a later version of it, which seems unlikely[4]), but Coleridge's views on the subject in the 1790s are nevertheless clear from *The Watchman* and the 'Conciones ad Populum'.

In 1789 the French Government declared that marriage was to be regarded as a civil contract, which like any other civil contract could be broken by the mere agreement of the parties concerned, and in 1792 this principle together with a provision for civil divorce became part of French law.[5] Burke vilified this piece of legislation because, in his view, it 'had not for its object the relief of domestic uneasiness, but the total corruption of all

---

[1] *The Watchman*, p. 91 (no. III 17 March 1796).
[2] *ib.* pp. 98–100.   [3] N 174.
[4] See *Letters*, v p. 152 and below p. 156.
[5] See Alfred Cobban, *A History of Modern France*, i p. 174.

morals, the total disconnection of social life'.[1] James Boulton has argued, too, that Burke's image of Marie Antoinette (in the *Reflections on the Revolution in France*) and his fierce attack on those who were supposed to have maltreated her, owed their strength to his identification of the French queen with familial love and 'natural' emotions, feelings that Burke valued as the ground of all human sympathy, and hence of all social cohesion.[2] Godwin's *Political Justice* (1793) was interpreted by some radicals as authorizing a total disregard of claims of kindred. Since all possible courses of action are to be judged by the quantity of human happiness which they will conceivably contribute to the total sum, and since no man can be allowed special consideration by reason of his happening to be related to the agent, we should be no more ready to protect or help a brother or a father than any other member of the race.[3] Though Godwin later withdrew this argument (in the preface to *St Leon*), some 'Patriots' took advantage of its negative aspect to proclaim the abolition of family loyalty. Coleridge rounded on them.

You have studied Mr Godwin's Essay on Political Justice; but to think filial affection folly, gratitude a crime, marriage injustice, and the promiscuous intercourse of the sexes right and wise, may class you among the despisers of vulgar prejudices, but cannot increase the probability that you are a P A T R I O T.[4]

Coleridge indeed held with Burke that family loyalty, so far from being incompatible with loyalty to the state, was the root from which national loyalty should grow, and his Bristol audiences found themselves being exhorted to look to their family loyalties, and the sympathies which these fostered, for the principle which should guide them in the political sphere. To search here for a principle of action was the very antithesis of Godwinism; but Coleridge's baby-trumpet of sedition, though it should be out of harmony with those of his fellow radicals, was not to be permitted to blast the very institutions which, in his view, nourished the social affections, and that general benevolence without which men are impotent to change society for the better.

---

[1] *Letters on a Regicide Peace*, pp. 42–3.
[2] James Boulton, *The Language of Politics in the Age of Wilkes and Burke*, pp. 129–30.
[3] *Political Justice*, i pp. 128–9; see Stephen, ii p. 230.
[4] *The Watchman*, pp. 98–9.

The searcher after Truth must love and be beloved; for general Benevolence is a necessary motive to constancy of pursuit; and this general Benevolence is begotten and rendered permanent by social and domestic affections. Let us beware of that proud Philosophy, which affects to inculcate Philanthropy while it denounces every home-born feeling, by which it is produced and nurtured. The paternal and filial duties discipline the Heart and prepare it for the love of all Mankind. The intensity of private attachments encourages, not prevents, universal Benevolence.[1]

Both the desire for social improvement and the knowledge of the means by which it is to be achieved originate in the family, for the first is a necessary precondition of the second; one who does not constantly and sincerely desire the happiness of mankind will have no true perception of the means by which it can be realized. Coleridge's quarrel with Godwinism here is a fundamental one, since he questions not only the motives, but the perceptions of the Godwinite. The notion that truth is invisible to all but the man of sincere feeling was later to become axiomatic with Coleridge;[2] its appearance here is a reminder that none of Coleridge's *dicta* on philosophy as a whole, much less on politics, was formulated in a Cartesian vacuum. It also indicates the chief difference between Coleridge's appeal to family relationships in the 'Conciones', and the appeal made by Burke in his *Reflections on the Revolution in France*. There he writes,

We begin our public affections in our families . . . the love to the whole is not extinguished by this subordinate partiality. Perhaps it is a sort of elemental training to the higher and more large regards, by which alone men come to be affected, as with their own concern, in the prosperity of a kingdom so large as that of France.[3]

The young Coleridge adds to this rather tentative claim, while indeed restating and reinforcing it, his own assertion that truth itself, the knowledge of the means towards human happiness, is

[1] *Lectures 1795 On Politics and Religion*, p. 46 ('Conciones ad Populum', Introductory Address).
[2] BL, i pp. xxx, lxiv.
[3] p. 315. The rather different idea that the family is *analogous* to the nation has a longer history: see Aristotle, *Politics*, III, iii, 1; Bacon, *The Advancement of Learning*, p. 72; and C's *Shakespearean Criticism*, ii p. 107.

discoverable only by the man who is endowed with the true philanthropy that is 'produced and nurtured' by family relationships; surely a vitalization, by the introduction of a principle of selflessness, of what might otherwise become a somewhat timid attachment to 'the little platoon we belong to in society',[1] enlightened by no more than a vague feeling of identification with the larger unit, a feeling that our own prosperity is conditional upon that of society. Both Coleridge and Burke start from what they sense to be real in human experience, rather than from a speculative proposition; but Coleridge goes beyond Burke in finding in that experience a source of moral growth.

Different, too, are the two men's views of religion in so far as it relates to family loyalty. Burke argues that, just as there is no escaping the duty of family loyalty, since ties of kindred are established by God's will and not ours, so 'without any stipulation on our own part, are we bound by that relation called our country'.[2] Coleridge knew that such a demand would signify little to the man whom poverty had forced to become selfish. Hartley's philosophy had taught him that our feelings and our moral qualities do not develop in isolation from the influence of our surroundings.

Domestic affections depend on association...how should *he* glow with the charities of Father and Husband, who gaining scarcely more, than his own necessities demand, must have been accustomed to regard his wife and children, not as the Soothers of finished labour, but as Rivals for the insufficient meal![3]

Coleridge's answer is not to say, in the manner of Burke, that unless we are to contravene God's will we have no option but to be loyal to family and to nation. His perhaps more Protestant habit of mind leads him to assert that the Gospel, by directing men's thoughts to their future destiny, releases them from the 'tyranny of the present', as well as teaching them the duties by virtue of which alone they can enjoy the 'rights' claimed for them by the philosopher. To say that the paternal and filial duties are, for Coleridge, 'prescribed by religion', as Professor Colmer

[1] Burke, *Reflections*, p. 135.
[2] *An Appeal from the New to the Old Whigs*; reprinted in *The Debate on the French Revolution*, p. 254.
[3] *Lectures 1795*, p. 45 ('Conciones', Introductory Address).

does,[1] is to distort Coleridge's argument, placing it much closer to that of Burke than it really is. Coleridge's point is that only when the relative unimportance of a man's present state is conveyed to him, can he transcend the selfishness which necessity would otherwise force on him, and bestow on others his sincere affection. Such an argument is easy to criticize, for it is obviously pernicious in one respect; it enables the comfortably-off to ignore poverty altogether, quieting their consciences with the reflection that, as long as the poor have the gospel preached to them, they are assured of happiness in the next world, if not in this. Coleridge spoke in this way not, however, from cynicism, but from the conviction that justice in the state will never be brought about until every member of society learns to direct his life by those principles of sympathy which family relationships, freed from selfishness by Christian teaching, have inculcated. The true patriots whom Coleridge praises in the Introductory Address to the 'Conciones' – men like Joseph Gerrald – are those who act always in the spirit of love, who 'have encouraged the sympathetic passions till they have become irresistible habits'.[2]

Marriage and the domestic affections were not, then, to be classed with the oppressive institutions from which England suffered, such as privilege and the inequality of property. We can only conjecture what it was that struck Coleridge about Milton's phrase for wedded love, 'sole proprietie /In Paradise of all things common else', and made him enter it in the Gutch notebook in 1796,[3] but it seems at least possible that it was its relevance to the attack he believed it necessary to make on Godwinian or 'French' principles, and to his defence of an ideal of marriage which might retain the form of 'proprietie' that was enjoyed in Milton's Eden, one of mutual interest and natural affinity. In 1797, John Thelwall wrote a pamphlet urging the alteration of the law of heredity to enable illegitimate children to claim rights equal to those born within lawful wedlock. Coleridge's criticism of this pamphlet shows not only his distrust of the sacrament of marriage at this point, but also his conviction of the social necessity of marriage as an institution.

[1] *Coleridge, Critic of Society*, p. 13.
[2] *Lectures 1795*, p. 40.   [3] N 79.

COLERIDGE AND THE IDEA OF LOVE

Instead of tacitly allowing that I meant by it [that is, by the innovation Thelwall was proposing] to encourage what Mr B. and the Priests would call licentiousness... I would have shewn that such a law would of all others operate most powerfully *in favor* of *marriage*; by which word I mean not the effect of spells uttered by conjurors, but *permanent* cohabitation useful to Society as the best conceivable means (in the present state of Soc. at least:) of ensuring nurture and systematic education to infants and children.[1]

This, admittedly hesitant and timidly formulated, as intended for the eyes of a staunch radical and unbending social critic, is an austere vision. But his attitude towards sacraments as such was not to remain as sceptical as he here represents it to be. Only months after this letter was written, in July 1797, he wrote in a less confident vein to Estlin 'I cannot as yet reconcile my intellect to the sacramental Rites',[2] a statement which seems to imply that he did expect to become reconciled to them sooner or later. His attitude towards parenthood was also to change as he became a parent himself, and suffered, in 1799, the death of his son Berkeley. He was then much less inclined to evaluate parenthood in terms of its social benefits, much more ready to confess to mystification about its meaning. He wrote to Poole in April 1799, 'A Parent – in the strict and exclusive sense a *Parent*! to me it is a *fable* wholly without meaning except in the *moral* which it suggests – a fable, of which the Moral is God.'[3] This is a strange statement, perhaps susceptible of 'explanation' in terms of a dominant tendency to refer whatever struck him as mysterious in human life to a possible religious signification: it certainly shows how far Coleridge had now moved towards the integration of religious belief into human life.

Yet something was, as we know, seriously wrong with Coleridge's married life, even when he had become a father, and for all his conviction of the indissolubility of the marriage bond he felt acutely the need to break out of the constraints his marriage was putting on him, intellectually, emotionally and spiritually. Three months after his flirtation with Sara Hutchinson he wrote ruefully to Southey,

1 *Letters*, i p. 306 (no. 176: 6 February 1797).
2 *ib*. p. 337 (no. 198: 23 July 1797).
3 *ib*. p. 478 (no. 274: 6 April 1799).

26

Habes quod tibi gratuleris – habes maximum Dei optimi Donum, uxorem carissimam tuæ indoli omnino conformatam et quasi constellatam. Mulier mea purissimæ mentis est, probabili ingenio prædita, et quæ *maternis* curis se totam dat, dicat, dedicat; Indoles veró quotidiana, et Sympathiæ minutiores, meis studiis, temperamento, infirmitatibus eheu! minime consentiunt – non possumus omni ex parte felices esse.[1]

His belief in the value of marriage was not shattered – far from it, for he calls Southey's wife 'maximum Dei optimi Donum' – but he regarded his own case as hopeless, and was already embarked on the course that would lead to his suggestion, in 1802, of a separation.

3

In spite of these indications of Coleridge's high estimate of relationship, both as the source of the rarer moral qualities and as precious in itself, there is another equally important side to Coleridge's early philosophy of life. For Coleridge often averred that he believed intellectual truth – at any rate in its purest form, the deepest insights of religion and philosophy – to be the prerogative of the solitary. In spite of his criticism of Wordsworth,[2] Coleridge believed a measure of segregation to be necessary for the serious thinker. This belief was the impulse behind *The Friend* and *Aids to Reflection*, and the many notes in which he advises the young thinker, 'do not degrade the truth in thee by disputing'.[3] In the early years this instinct took many forms: the criticism of Poole for allowing family attachment to 'fetter' his 'moral free-agency'; letters to friends about the problem, faced by every writer with a young family, of finding somewhere secluded to work; the account of a walking tour undertaken in the company of Southey and Hazlitt, which to Coleridge 'was a mere walk; for I must be alone, if either my Imagination or Heart are to be excited or enriched'.[4] George Whalley writes of Coleridge as 'incurably alone':[5] it is

---

[1] *Letters*, i p. 571 (no. 317: 12 February 1800).   [2] See above, p. 9.
[3] AP, p. 80.
[4] See above p. 15; *Letters*, i p. 584 (no. 330: 31 March 1800); and N 1610.
[5] In *Coleridge and Sara Hutchinson and the Asra Poems*, p. 150.

debatable how much of this loneliness was due to his exceptional powers, and to the fact that he knew no one who was able or willing to follow him in the wildest of his metaphysical speculations (nor to allow his conversational gifts to outweigh the less attractive parts of his character). In some respects it must have been self-imposed, as Coleridge came to value the intellectual freedom that solitude brought, and turned a childhood habit into a conscious, lasting preference. Undoubtedly Coleridge's frequent choice of solitude, in place of the unsatisfactory companionship of his home, or even of Dove Cottage, was the price that must be paid by any poet whose inspiration is that of the visionary. Had Coleridge always walked in the company of friends, mountains and waterfalls would not have spoken to him in the way he describes in this letter, written (according to Professor Griggs) shortly after the composition of 'Kubla Khan':
'My mind feels as if it ached to behold and know something *great* – something *one* and *indivisible* – and it is only in the faith of this that rocks or waterfalls, mountains or caverns give me the sense of sublimity or majesty! – But in this faith *all things* counterfeit infinity! – '[1]

Moreover Coleridge's disposition was an intensely religious one, and if we accept that the religious experience demands, at least in some sense, stability, it becomes clear that a nature as vulnerable as Coleridge's is forced to resort to a degree of solipsism in order merely to preserve the integrity of its vision. This, argues Dr Beer, is one of the major characteristics of the romantic artist.[2] Yet the paradox of Coleridge's nature is that, besides knowing the love of the 'one and indivisible', he also valued 'common human nature' (Dr Beer's phrase) very highly, indeed accorded to some aspects of it, as we have seen, a 'religious Veneration';[3] and in moments of unillumined solitude, feeling the inadequacy of the mind to be its own buttress, he would write of 'the unspeakable comfort...to be *understood*'.[4] The paradox, and its roots in a fundamental dilemma of the Romantic mind, can be seen in a letter to Poole in which Coleridge contrasts Wordsworth's self-sufficiency with his own

[1] *Letters*, i p. 349 (no. 209: 14 October 1797).
[2] J. B. Beer, *Coleridge the Visionary*, p. 17.
[3] N 1637; see above, p. 18.   [4] N 1082.

sense of too great dependence on others. He continues, with what may read like unpardonable arrogance or hypocrisy, 'My many weaknesses are of some advantage to me; they unite me more with the great mass of my fellow-beings – but dear Wordsworth appears to me to have hurtfully segregated and isolated his Being.'[1] In this context it is clear that the 'arrogance' of the statement is quite unconscious, and arises from an acute fear of the possible consequences of romantic 'alienation'. Coleridge is grateful for any traits, however undesirable in conventional terms, that remind him that he is still a member of the human race, and owes a duty to them as well as to himself and to God. Coleridge was not a Nietzsche; the feeling of belonging to what Nietzsche called the many-too-many was for him welcome, even essential, and certainly not something to be despised and 'cured'.[2] The link between this feeling and the tendency towards an apparently contradictory religious and moral idealism – a link which many readers both in his own lifetime and in more recent years have found it hard to understand, or even to recognize – is the moral thought and exhortation set out in *The Friend, Aids to Reflection* and the political essays. Yet there is always a conflict, implicit in George Whalley's description of Coleridge as 'incurably alone': his loneliness was incurable both because he could not, either as man or as thinker, venture into total solipsism, enjoying a permanent visionary state of Nietzschean exaltation, and because his cries for sympathy and understanding were inevitably met by incomprehension on the part of even his closest friends, or (perhaps even more often) by ironic self-administered rebukes, proceeding from what in another man we might have called a sense of proportion.

Even had Coleridge been able to resolve this conflict in some way, however, there would still have been insuperable obstacles in the way of complete communication between him and his friends, or his public. It is not often noticed how distrustful Coleridge was, for a poet and philosopher, of language. A note of 1799, retranscribed and expanded during the turbulent days of October 1803, expresses the incommunicability of all the most prized experiences, whether of pleasure in the forms of a landscape – something Coleridge never felt he could handle, as the

---

[1] *Letters*, i p. 491 (no. 277: 6 May 1799).   [2] *Thus Spoke Zarathustra*, p. 76.

pathetic little drawings that are sprinkled through his notebooks testify – or of the deeper visionary insights.

Without Drawing I feel myself but half invested with language – Music too is wanting to me. – But yet tho' one should unite Poetry, Draftsman's-ship and Music – the greater and perhaps nobler certainly all the subtler parts of one's nature, must be solitary – Man exists herein to himself and to God alone / – Yea, in how much only to God – how much lies *below* his own Consciousness.[1]

Coleridge did undoubtedly appreciate, as many have noted, the role of the subconscious, but at least as important here as the stirrings of the embryonic science of psychology is the observation, common to all mystics, that the conscious mind is incapable of forming any but the most superficial of man's intuitions and perceptions. It is as a result of this belief that Coleridge advises the young philosopher to prefer 'the *sense* of conviction' to 'the passion of proselytism'.[2] Nor is it only revealed religion that Coleridge feels must be fostered in this way, for he advises Godwin himself not to form his opinions in the cut and thrust of open debate, but to mould them in solitude, and to seek nothing from other men but sympathy – this being a peculiarly Coleridgean concession to the spiritual needs of all men. 'You have too soon', he writes, 'submitted your notions to other men's censures in conversation. A man should nurse his opinions in privacy and self-fondness for a long time – and seek for sympathy and love, not for detection or censure.'[3] The emphasis on solitary meditation is characteristic of the thinker who inclines to philosophical realism, and Coleridge's censures of Godwin partake of the realist's common charge against his opponents, that of superficiality. Coleridge particularly scorned Godwin's assertion that it must be possible to trace back all the manifold associations leading to a particular utterance. 'Little reflected he, how much of Eternity there is in each moment of Time!'[4] Another poet of mystic and Platonizing tendencies voiced a similar charge against those he called 'the leaders of the crowd':

---

1 N 1554 (revised from N 524).
2 AP, pp. 80–1.
3 *Letters*, i p. 636 (no. 358: 13 October 1800).
4 N 1563.

How can they know,
Truth flourishes where the student's lamp has shone,
And there alone, that have no solitude?[1]

Coleridge was himself aware, though, that it was not only a devotion to the higher reaches of philosophical speculation that made him prefer the life of the solitary to that of the public figure. In a sense, he never lost his childhood fascination with the products of his own mind, and he wrote to a friend in a mood of amused self-criticism, 'I am far too contented with Solitude. The same Fullness of Mind, the same Crowding of Thoughts, and Constitutional Vivacity of Feeling, w[hich] makes me sometimes the First Fiddle, and too often [a] Watchman's Rattle, in Society, renders me likewise [independent] of it.'[2] The contrast between this kind of self-sufficiency and the strong self-command of a Wordsworth or a Southey – the former produced, if we may adopt a Coleridgean distinction, by power, the latter rather by strength – is evident, and should warn us against the facile assumption that romantic solipsism was, wherever it occurred, basically the same phenomenon. Coleridge never attained the relatively firm moral stance that Wordsworth did, after the troubled years of the Revolution: neither his personal circumstances nor his intellectual adventurousness would permit him to. And the 'Fullness of Mind...and Constitutional Vivacity of Feeling' which made him a voluble talker, and rendered solitary meditation a pleasure, also had its darker side:

Month after month, year after year, the deepest Feeling of my Heart hid and wrapped up in the depth and darkness – solitary chaos – and solitariness – is it not pang and complaint even in sickness and torture how was this every where uppermost /[3]

The unspeakable Comfort to a good man's mind – nay, even to a criminal to be *understood* – to have some one that understands one – and who does not feel, that on earth no one does. The Hope of this – always more or less disappointed, gives the *passion* to Friendship.[4]

Years later, an older and perhaps wiser Coleridge repudiated and condemned the desire for external confirmation of our 'very

[1] W. B. Yeats, *Collected Poems*, p. 207.
[2] *Letters*, ll pp. 1021–2 (no. 529: 5 December 1803).
[3] N 1670.   [4] N 1082.

selves'. His relation to friends of either sex, and also, perhaps, to what Goethe first called 'das ewige Weiblich', has changed considerably.[1] He is writing about the Spanish play of *Don Juan*, and is particularly interested in the ambivalent attitude towards womankind which the story of Juan enshrines.

To be so loved for my *own self*, that even with a distinct knowledge of my character, she yet died to save me!. . . it is among the miseries, and abides in the dark ground-work of our nature, to crave an outward confirmation of that *something* within us, which is our *very self*, that something, not made up of our qualities and relations, but itself the supporter and substantial basis of all these. Love *me*, and not my qualities, may be a vicious and an insane wish, but it is not a wish wholly without a meaning.[2]

This is the voice of self-criticism, now objectivized into a general proposition concerning those archetypes of the romantic experience, Don Juan and Satan. Coleridge's desire for one who could understand had become transmuted by time into an intenser form of what Locke called 'uneasiness', directed towards some 'absent good', a phenomenon that Professor Willey equates with 'divine discontent'.[3] It appears, indeed, in the chapter of the *Biographia* on Christian belief, the foundation of which Coleridge holds to be the sense 'in the soul of each Believer of [Religion's] exceeding *desireableness*'[4] – merging with that 'primal palpable anxiety'[5] with which all religious experience begins.

4

The great importance of solitude and self-determination to Coleridge's genius, however, does not invalidate the many proofs we have that Coleridge derived immense benefit, intellectually and imaginatively as well as spiritually, from the experience of relationship, and indeed associated some of his most exciting endeavours with the inspiration of a particular friendship, or with his love for Sara Hutchinson. 'Love', he

---

[1] See *Faust*, Part II Act v, scene 7.   [2] BL, ii p. 188.
[3] Basil Willey, *The English Moralists*, pp. 211–12; John Locke, *An Essay concerning Human Understanding*, p. 143 (Book II, chapter 21).
[4] BL, ii p. 215.
[5] Professor McFarland's phrase; see *Coleridge and the Pantheist Tradition*, p. 233.

wrote, '[is] to all the Passions and Faculties, as Music to all the varieties of sound',[1] and this is an observation which is certainly borne out by some of his own projects. It is a philosophy which spans his entire career, though it evidently took on a rather different meaning when he met Sara, and indeed each new friendship brought with it an upsurge of interest in a field of knowledge dear to the friend, or a revival of lost vitality in Coleridge's own intellect. In its general form the philosophy is first stated in the 1795 political address, where its importance has rightly been emphasized by Professor Emmet.[2] 'The searcher after Truth must love and be beloved...'[3] The context of this statement, admittedly, limits its applicability, for Coleridge had in view a particular kind of philosophical radicalism. In later writings, however, it developed into a belief in the interdependence of feeling and intellect which coloured almost every opinion Coleridge offered: even Schelling is censured, in the *Biographia*, for exhibiting 'the love of wisdom rather than the wisdom of love'.[4] It is common to find writers on Coleridge representing his vacillation between the logical but 'atheistic' philosophy of Spinoza and the Christian faith in a knowable, personal God as the conflict between a philosophy of the 'head' and a philosophy of the 'heart': but it is clear that, although the expression 'the heart' is used by Coleridge himself as virtually synonymous with 'the moral nature', this by no means authorizes the use of the word 'emotional' as an adumbration of its salient characteristics.[5] Coleridge, as we have seen,[6] does not assert that undisciplined emotion is a trustworthy source of philosophical insight, but rather seeks to illuminate the sense and the understanding by infusing into them the light of a moral principle not deriving directly from either of them, and which certainly has more in common with the conviction that elicited Dante's 'En la sua volontade e nostra pace' than with Reason as it was understood by Locke and Hume. This however does not mean that it is

[1] N 1229.
[2] In 'Coleridge on the Growth of the Mind', *Coleridge: A Collection of Critical Essays*, edited by K. Coburn, p. 171.
[3] See above, p. 23.   [4] BL, i p. 105.
[5] See Thomas McFarland, *Coleridge and the Pantheist Tradition*, p. 220; G. M. McKenzie, *Organic Unity in Coleridge*, p. 4.
[6] Above, p. 17.

'emotional' in origin. As J. H. Muirhead has pointed out, Reason was not to Coleridge the remote, independent faculty that it was for Jacobi, but rather 'the completion of thought, returning to the intuitiveness of sense with all the richness and variety which its passage through the prism of the reflective mind had given it'.[1] So the moral nature, or heart, is continually tested and re-shaped by the Reason. It is in this sense that Coleridge writes, 'a metaphysical Solution, that does not instantly *tell* for something in the Heart, is grievously to be suspected as apocry[p]hal'.[2] Professor McKenzie, who presents this as evidence that Coleridge was 'desperately trying to reconcile two fundamentally opposed elements', comments 'so much the worse for intellect'; but the problem was never one of simple opposition between head and heart, or intellect and emotion. What is remarkable is, not that Coleridge should have given the 'heart' a primary role as the criterion by which metaphysical systems were to be judged (if only in the sense that a system which did not speak to the heart, as well as to the intellect, was untrustworthy); but that the experience of human relationship, rather than any *rêveries du promeneur solitaire*, should have been the acknowledged source of so much that was, in Coleridge's eyes, essential to the 'moral nature'. In a margin note on Sir Thomas Browne's well-known declaration, 'I have loved my friend as I do virtue, my soul, my God', Coleridge comments approvingly, 'The great business of real unostentatious virtue is – not to eradicate any genuine instinct or appetite of human nature; but – to establish a con-cord and unity betwixt all parts of our nature, to give a feeling and a passion to our purer intellect, and to intellectualize our feelings and passions.'[3] Dr Beer has pointed out the links that this idea of the interfusion of head and heart may have with Cabbalistic lore, through Boehme's *Aurora*:[4] but as is often the case with Coleridge's most characteristic themes, it begins in the earlier years with predominantly personal affirmations, as in certain of the letters written from Germany, and only later rises

1 'Coleridge – Metaphysician or Mystic?', in *Coleridge – Studies by Several Hands*, p. 192.
2 *Letters*, ii p. 961 (no. 510: 7 August 1803).
3 *Miscellaneous Criticism*, p. 255: note of 1802 on *Religio Medici* (II, 5).
4 J. B. Beer, *Coleridge the Visionary*, p. 61.

into a more generalized and almost philosophical perception, as in the margin comment on Browne.

One remarkable instance of the more personal statement is contained in a letter of March 1799, written from Göttingen. 'I am deeply convinced that if I were to remain a few years among objects for whom I had no affection, I should wholly lose the powers of Intellect – Love is the vital air of my Genius.'[1] There is little reason to doubt the sincerity of this, at least as regards Coleridge's feeling about his own needs. It is remarkable, too, how often a new friendship could be the beginning of an addition to Coleridge's immense range of interests. To Davy he writes 'You know how long, how ardently I have wished to initiate myself in Chemical science... I would fain sympathize with you in the Light of Knowlege';[2] and a similar desire to know another through shared knowledge and shared delight, though more intense, of course, by as much as the passion of love was more intense than that of friendship, is revealed in many notes relating to Sara Hutchinson.[3] There is another sense too in which the experience of relationship contributed significantly to Coleridge's intellectual development. Questions of pyschology, and particularly of the relation between the subconscious and the moral nature, deeply interested him, and the self-observations which he made in this field gave clarity and even conviction to his moral thought. Basic to all Coleridge's observations on this subject is the feeling that the mind's economy can be shown to be an organic whole, not a collection of different functions; that the imagination can originate emotions and moral propensities, though itself unimpelled by any evident emotions, and without regard even to the presence or absence of the object of the emotions; and that the irruption into the mind of so strong a feeling as love has, conversely, a vitalizing effect on even the strictly intellectual faculties. The earliest form of this observation occurs in the Gutch notebook: 'Love transforms the soul into a conformity with the object loved.'[4] Here it is more speculative than serious; even if we believe the word 'soul' to have

1 *Letters*, i p. 471 (no. 272: 10 March 1799).
2 *ib*. ii p. 671 (no. 378: 3 February 1801).
3 For instance, N 984, 1356, 1451.
4 N 189 (and AP, p. 2).

had real dialectical meaning for Coleridge at this point, the tenor of the statement suggests more a stray thought written down for the sake of its verbal felicity than the product of rigorous self-analysis. Yet the epoch of his most intense passion saw a resurgence of the same idea and the same experience, in a form that he believed it worthwhile to set down. Sara's face was before him, but though invisible in the darkness, it was yet apparent to him as a 'spectrum', so vivid that 'it had almost all its natural sense of *distance* and *outness* – except indeed that, feeling and all, I felt her as *part* of my being – 'twas all spectral'.[1] Again we are mistaken if we categorize this kind of observation as indicative of belief in the primacy of 'emotion', for Coleridge knew that this kind of phenomenon had to do with forces a good deal more recondite. Just over a month after making this entry, he wrote to Southey, 'That to be in love is simply to confine the feelings prospective of animal enjoyment to one woman is a gross mistake – it is to associate a large proportion of all our obscure feelings with a real form.'[2] This passage admittedly partakes more of the psychological than of the mystic, for Coleridge compares the lover's state with that of the miser, the poet and the scientist; but it contains a thought which also sustains many more general psychological observations in *The Friend* and *Biographia Literaria*. Had Coleridge not observed in himself the power of love to call up phantoms in the mind, and to intensify or channel the moral feelings, his view of the function of literature and, indeed, of the human mind as a whole, would have been very different. He writes of the 'imperishability' of thoughts, as contrasted with the 'perishability' of things,[3] and the perception is used in the *Biographia*, where he defends the poetic consciousness from the vantage-point of this favourite psychology.

Where the ideas are vivid, and there exists an endless power of combining and modifying them, the feelings and affections blend more easily and intimately with these ideal creations than with the objects of the senses; the mind is affected by thoughts, rather than by things; and only then feels the requisite interest even for the most important events

[1] N 985.
[2] *Letters*, ii p. 768 (no. 417: 21 October 1801).
[3] N 1575.

and accidents, when by means of meditation they have passed into *thoughts*.[1]

It would be wrong, however, to conclude from this and similar passages that Coleridge based his conception of the moral nature entirely on the observation of the effect of love on the human mind. There was a converse lesson to be learned, and a note in which Coleridge analyses this paradox sets out succinctly the thesis and antithesis of Coleridge's thinking about relationship, and brings us to perhaps the most important single insight which Coleridge's experience of relationship gave him, and which is foremost in the crowded, anxious thoughts that Coleridge set down in the autumn of 1803. The problem with which we are to be concerned is the nature of the individual self, and the note which summarizes the two poles of the problem dates from October, 1830:

'As if their whole vocation
Were endless imitation'

Two things we may learn from little children from 3 to 6 years old –

. . . The first lesson, that innocent Childhood affords me, is – that it is an instinct of my nature to pass out of myself, and to exist in the form of others.

The second is – not to suffer any one form to pass into *me* and to become a usurping Self in the disguise of what the German Pathologists call a *fixed Idea*.[2]

We are close here to the Coleridgean concept that Whalley has referred to as 'the sanctity of the human person'.[3] In at least one of its aspects it embraces a notion that it is hard to fit into any complex of thoughts even remotely adumbrated by the term 'moral', and yet this notion is of major significance for Coleridge as a moral thinker. The notion is that of an 'original' or 'real' Self, and it occurs in a complex and strangely disturbing notebook entry of the summer of 1803.

The entry begins with an attempt at psychological analysis which already foreshadows the arrival at an 'original Self' by

---

[1] BL, i p. 20.
[2] Notebook 47, fols. 193–4. (See note preceding the Bibliography, p. viii). Part of the entry here quoted was printed by D. P. Calleo in *Coleridge and the Idea of the Modern State*, pp. 84–5.
[3] *Coleridge and Sara Hutchinson and the Asra Poems*, p. 100.

putting the question, 'How far is Habit congenerous with Instinct?'[1] If Habit, in the sense Coleridge gives – 'the desire of a desire' – is *not* congenerous with Instinct, if there are recurring impulses which precede the establishment of the desire of a desire, then the conception of an original Self, capable of desiring something outside itself without the desire becoming perpetually internalized and feeding only on itself, is feasible. If, on the other hand, Habit *is* congenerous with Instinct, and the human constitution knows no desires which do not perpetually create pale replicas of themselves; if, that is, it is incurably solipsistic even in its desires; then even to imagine an 'original Self', which might reach out to another being in simple love for it, is impossible. The question resolves itself into the difficulty which threw a shadow over Coleridge's life, given as he was – perhaps to an unhealthy degree – to introspection and self-analysis, though increasingly in search of 'all the natural man'. Is love the refuge of the selfish and self-fearing man, 'desiring to desire', but in reality trapped by this eternally reduplicating demand within himself, unable ever to break the cycle of self-centredness, or is it a real reaching-out, a self-transcending act which can be free of all taint of egotism? The answer is vital for the future orientation of Coleridge's moral philosophy, and deeply significant for the student of the phenomenon of Romanticism. Coleridge in effect affirms the second, but in the process he reveals a deep-seated fear of the possible truth, and the consequences, of the first. His repudiation of Don Juan-ism, and of Juan's 'vicious and insane' desire to be confirmed in his 'very self', is another facet of this fear: Coleridge abjured the selfish aspiration of the archetypal romantic, not because it was alien to him, but because he had perceived what its consequences would be, and perhaps suffered them, in some way, throughout his own life. These complexities will possibly become clearer as we examine the process by which Coleridge rejects the first, 'self-inspired', definition of love, and opts for the second.

Having posed his question, Coleridge speculates on the ramifications of the theory of self-communing desire, envisaging that the 'Desirelet, a' would 'so correspond to the Desire, A, that the latter being excited may revert wholly or in great part to its

---

[1] N 1421.

exciting cause, *a*, instead of sallying out of itself toward an external Object, B'.[1] Coleridge reflects that this form of association may account for 'the marvellous velocity of Thought and Image in certain full Trances'; but then he continues the former train of thought, to speculate on the form of consciousness that we may know after death, and reveals that he has at least dreamt of this as a possible road to union with Sara. He is repelled, however, by the picture of eternal, ever-internalizing selfhood that his theories of the after-life present to him, and chooses at this moment the other theory of love, or rather, reveals that he longs for it to prove true.

Connect with this the state after Death, Death being taken as the removal of the outward excitements of Desire – Must not the Soul then work eternally inwards, Godward, or Hellward – will it not be all Habit? and what is the Law of its Increase? –

There is one thing wholly out of my Power. I cannot look forward even with the faintest pleasure of Hope, to the Death of any human Being, tho' it were, as it seems to be, the only condition of the greatest imaginable Happiness to me, and the emancipation of all my noblest faculties that must remain fettered during that Being's Life. – I dare not, for I can not: I cannot, for I dare not. The very effort to look onward to it with a stedfast wish would be a suicide, far beyond what the dagger or pistol could realize – absolutely suicide, cœlicide, not mere viticide. –

But if I could secure you full Independence, if I could give too all my original Self healed and renovated from all infirm Habits; and if by all the forms in my power I could bind myself more effectively even in relation to Law, than the Form out of my power would effect – then, *then*, would you be the remover of my Loneliness, my perpetual Companion?[2]

The form of the final appeal, the fact that it is couched as a question and no answer is proposed, epitomizes its hopelessness, and yet brings out a fundamental belief of Coleridge's: that there must exist in each of us an 'original Self', free from the accidents of vice and virtue too, capable of loving absolutely and without selfishness, much as the inhabitants of the ideal country which was eventually ravaged by the Madning Rain had no need of either virtue or vice, for they formed attachments with each

[1] N 1421. [2] *ib.*

other, through 'the natural affinity of their Beings', and 'Conscience acted in Man with the ease and uniformity of Instinct'.[1]

Of course the note of August 1803 expresses more a reaction from the insoluble problems that Coleridge was facing at this time than a fully thought-out philosophy, and solitude remained dear to him – on the Scottish tour he undertook in September (initially with Wordsworth and his sister, though he parted from them at Arrochar), he conceived the idea of a poem which would celebrate 'Solitude, Nature, Liberty – the Solitude free and natural, the Nature unmanacled and solitary, the Liberty natural and solitary – / – I feel here as if I were here to wander on the winds, a blessed Ghost, till my Beloved came to me / go back with her and seek my children.'[2]

Yet the free, 'original' self that Coleridge longed to return to was evidently not an egoismus of the type adumbrated by Fichte, but was on the contrary associated primarily with those whom he 'loved indeed', to borrow a phrase from 'The Pains of Sleep' (composed in September and October 1803).[3] That poem reflects the strongest wish to escape from himself, from the 'Desire with loathing strangely mixed', and the fearful sense of wrongs suffered or done being one and the same. What we have here in Coleridge's work has no parallel in English Romanticism, except perhaps in the work of Emily Brontë. For her, writes a recent critic, 'all suffering derives ultimately from isolation. A person is most himself when he participates most completely in the life of something outside himself.'[4] But the deep, almost mystic intermingling of souls which she represents Catherine and Heathcliff as experiencing, and which impels Cathy's anguished cry 'I *am* Heathcliff', had no counterpart in Coleridge's life; nor could 'nature', so completely over-against mankind as it was in Coleridge's eyes,[5] answer his need; and Coleridge's ideas of the after-life were not such as promised what Emily Brontë looked for, 'an infinite subjectivity which is at last a full possession of the self'.[6] Coleridge could find no way out which was not an infinite reduplication of selfhood, no way to 'participate completely in the life of something outside himself'.

[1] TF, i p. 7.   [2] N 1504.   [3] PW, i pp. 390–1.
[4] J. Hillis Miller, *The Disappearance of God*, p. 172.
[5] R. F. Brinkley (editor), *Coleridge on the Seventeenth Century*, p. 214.
[6] Miller, p. 173.

A similar idea to that of the 'original Self' occurs in further notes of October 1803, and this time belongs more certainly to a moral dialectic. Coleridge reflects on the mistakes he has made in condemning others, particularly Southey, and he joins to the intuition of an 'androgynous' mind, that what men are matters more than what they do, the Gospel message, 'judge not, that ye be not judged', making a moral axiom that, if difficult for one as sensitive as Coleridge to observe, indicates nevertheless the kind of choice he held to be important.

Prodigious Efficacy in preventing Quarrels and Interruptions of Friendship among Mankind in general, but especially among young warm-hearted men, would the habitual Reflection be, that the Almighty will judge us not by what we *do*, but by what we *are*; and in forbidding us to judge each other has manifestly taught us by implication, that we cannot without hazard of grievous error and without hazard of grievous Breach of Charity deduce the latter from the Former. – Apply this now to my former Quarrel with Southey. – [1]

He was wrong, he feels, to condemn Southey for certain *actions*: such a thing contradicts the ideal of free communication and mutual acceptance that had been one goal of the Pantisocratic scheme, and which Coleridge later met with in Schiller: 'Warum kann der Lebendige Geist dem Geist nicht erscheinen? SPRICHT die Seele, so spricht ach! schon die SEELE nicht mehr.'[2]

Coleridge's attempt to see men as they really are, and not as their conduct represents them, was, in part, a reaction against the heavy emphasis that had been placed on conduct by some eighteenth-century moral philosophers, and the attempt of Jeremy Bentham to become the Newton of the moral world and 'introduce a mathematical calculation on subjects of morality'.[3] Yet it was difficult for Coleridge to step entirely out of this dialectic, much as he longed for freedom from the eighteenth-century modes; he could not quite assert with Blake's confidence that man has no body distinct from his soul. Kant's subjective–objective distinction provided him with a possible answer, and in *The Friend* he used it to separate jurisprudence, and the

---

[1] N 1605.

[2] N 1063. 'Why cannot the living Spirit appear to the Spirit? If the Soul *speaks*, as it speaks, it is no longer the *Soul*.'

[3] Quoted by Leslie Stephen, *The English Utilitarians*, vol. i p. 179.

punishments inflicted by the State for its own preservation, from morality, which he conceived to be entirely subjective, in the sense that it is the motive that justifies or condemns, and only God can know a man's true motives. Bentham, by contrast, worked from a background of legal training and questions of jurisprudence to the wider question of individual morality, and so, according to Leslie Stephen, fell into the error of ignoring motives altogether.[1] It cannot be claimed that Coleridge found a satisfactory answer to this problem, however; both in *The Friend* and in later works, he was happier in speaking of the inward discipline and the importance of faith than in justifying society's prerogative of punishing malefactors.

It is clear that Coleridge put these observations on the primacy of 'being' over 'doing' to good use, for we find him, shortly after writing them, appending to them a note on envy and 'personal uncharitableness', the latter term standing for the kind of resentment that is felt when a man we despise does something to merit our approbation. Coleridge felt guilty at envying a friend – whom Professor Coburn conjectures to be Wordsworth – when a poem the friend had written turned out to be a success. The passage shows a renewal of the desire to clear the fog of misunderstanding and jealousy, and return to the truth of the friendship.

Deeplier than ever do I see the necessity of understanding the whole complex mixed character of our Friend – as well as our own / of frequently, in our kindest moods, reviewing it – intensifying our Love of the Good in it, and making up our mind to the Faulty – it would be a good Exercise to imagine and anticipate some painful Result of the faulty part of our Friend's character – fancy him acting thus and thus to you – when it would most wound you / then to see how much of the wound might not be attributed to some lingering Selfishness in one's self.[2]

In view of this stern self-admonition, carried to the verge of moral pedantry, it is ironical to find the question asked by a recent critic, 'Was Coleridge capable of loving anybody *as a person?*'[3] From the evidence that Coleridge himself provides,

[1] TF, i p. 95; Leslie Stephen, *The English Utilitarians*, vol. i p. 258.
[2] N 1606.
[3] George Whalley, *Coleridge and Sara Hutchinson and the Asra poems*, p. 108.

we can see that he did indeed believe himself to love his friends, or at least to be capable of loving them, as persons, as they were in themselves. Yet the very fact that these notes exist, with their painful representation of the process of self-analysis, proves also that in common with most sensitive natures Coleridge found almost insuperable difficulties, and not least the all-vitiating Selfhood, to lie in the way of the frank expression of this love.

5

What follows does not pretend to be a complete 'reading' of some poems of Coleridge. In particular, it tries to avoid the tempting but problematical aim of investigating or approaching Coleridge's mind. The notions which we may find embedded in certain passages of Coleridge's poetry are interesting not as evidence of introspection, nor as clues to the labyrinth of one man's mind, but as assertions about the nature of humanity and the human response to the world. The mind, as Coleridge wrote in an article in *Blackwood's*, '*knows* itself, and may be inferred by others; but...cannot appear';[1] and we are warned in *Biographia Literaria* against treating poetic language, the product of 'an unusual state of excitement',[2] as we would treat a prose discourse.

This should help us to avoid too exclusive an emphasis on the 'subjectivity', or 'solipsism', which is so often found to be the distinguishing characteristic of Romantic poetry. Dr Beer is right to contrast the situation of the Renaissance poet, who had a relatively stable moral universe on which to base his models of conduct, faith or passion, with that of the Romantic, who is (as Dr Beer puts it) 'a lonely, diminished figure', his intellectual position always precarious, his works the result of a fine balance between self-involution and self-alienation.[3] But we are reminded, in many of the poetic statements Coleridge makes – especially in his 'conversation poems', which I believe Dr Beer

[1] 'On the Philosophic Import of the Words OBJECT and SUBJECT', *Blackwood's Magazine*, vol. x, 56 (October 1821) (247–50), p. 249.
[2] BL, ii p. 56.
[3] *Coleridge the Visionary*, pp. 18–20.

COLERIDGE AND THE IDEA OF LOVE

and Professor Willey underrate[1] – that not even the Romantic artist exists entirely to himself and to his own visions. Wordsworth spoke of the poet as 'an upholder and preserver, carrying everywhere with him relationship and love'.[2] The relevance of this dictum to 'Christabel' and 'The Ancyent Marinere' may at first sight seem small; but let us begin with one or two of Coleridge's earlier poems.

> My pensive Sara! thy soft cheek reclined
> Thus on mine arm, most soothing sweet it is
> To sit beside our Cot, our Cot o'ergrown
> With white-flower'd Jasmin, and the broad-leav'd Myrtle,
> 5 (Meet emblems they of Innocence and Love!)
> And watch the clouds, that late were rich with light,
> Slow saddening round, and mark the star of eve
> 8 Serenely brilliant (such should Wisdom be)
> Shine opposite! How exquisite the scents
> Snatch'd from yon bean-field! and the world so hush'd!
> The stilly murmur of the distant Sea
> Tells us of silence.[3]

The poise achieved in these lines is remarkable. There is no straining of the rhythm, which rides over the line endings, these being balanced and reduced in importance by strong midline cæsuras; no intellectual pressure makes itself felt, warning us that the poet might be about to extract a moral lesson from the contemplation of nature; sounds, scents and the evening light contribute harmoniously to the picture of conjugal serenity. Coleridge was surely wrong to omit line 5 and line 8 in the 1803 edition. They should not, in their context, strike the reader as sententious: the point about the harmony these lines establish, and their tone (to which the definitions 'Effusion' and 'Conversation Poem' hardly do justice), is that such things can be said. The poet's perceptions mirror the inner assurance he feels, and there is harmony between the love which sustains his inner life, symbolized by the myrtle, Venus's flower, and the wisdom which he contemplates, symbolized by the evening star, Venus's planet. His home is almost literally a part of the natural world –

[1] See Basil Willey, *Nineteenth Century Studies*, p. 34.
[2] *Poetical Works*, edited by Thomas Hutchinson and E. de Selincourt, p. 738.
[3] 'The Eolian Harp', lines 1–12, PW, i p. 100.

44

'our Cot o'ergrown /With white-flower'd Jasmin' – and nature
is in turn almost a living being, accommodating herself to his
mood, and speaking to him of peace – 'The stilly murmur of the
distant Sea /Tells us of silence.' In this context, the idea of
wisdom is bound to appear as almost a natural outgrowth from
the stillness and harmony of nature, in spite of the famous lines
of speculation about 'organic Harps diversely fram'd'. We should
remember that the lines on the 'one Life within us and abroad'
were not added to the poem until the publication of *Sibylline
Leaves* in 1817, when they appeared in the errata, so that the
poem as originally published contained only five lines of 'theological speculation'.[1] These lines are the ones usually given
prominence today, thanks to the recent upsurge of interest in
Coleridge's theological development; but it cannot be said that
in the original (1796) version of the poem they outweigh his
promise to 'be lowlie wise':

> For never guiltless may I speak of him,
> The Incomprehensible! save when with awe
> I praise him, and with Faith that inly *feels*;
61   Who with his saving mercies healèd me,
62   A sinful and most miserable man
> Wilder'd and dark, and gave me to possess
> Peace, and this Cot, and thee, heart-honour'd Maid![2]

Lines 61 and 62 could almost be from one of Wesley's hymns;
they certainly suggest the poet's firm personal faith, which is so
far in harmony with the life evoked by the poem's first few lines
that he can end by attributing his present happiness to God's
special providence, in spite of the speculative notions about Godhead that 'Philosophy's aye-babbling spring' may have brought
in its train. To read these lines, with Albert Gérard, as the
expression of a sense of 'intellectual impotence', with a 'Sunday-
school undertone of abject self-abasement in the phrasing',[3] is, I
believe, to impoverish the poem's meaning by imposing on it a
popular archetype, that of the Defiant Infidel. Humility before
God is itself an intellectual stance. Nor can I accept that the

[1] PW, i p. 101, note.
[2] Lines 58–64. PW, i p. 102.
[3] A. Gérard, 'The Systolic Rhythm: The Structure of Coleridge's Conversation
Poems', *Essays in Criticism*, vol. x no. 3 (July 1960) (307–19), pp. 313, 315.

poem fails to deliver what it promises when the five lines
beginning 'And what if all of animated nature /Be but organic
Harps diversely fram'd...?' are followed by 'But thy more
serious eye a mild reproof /Darts, O beloved Woman!' Here,
says Mr Watson, speaking of the poem's 'unfortunate close',
'the poem seems on the point of authoritative utterance, and it is
only the return of the poem to its starting point . . . [ll. 49–50
quoted] that proves the weak link in what would otherwise have been a poem that elegantly solved the early romantic
dilemma of a poetry without an audience.'[1] The presence of
Sara, Mr Watson finds, is a 'nuisance', and the initial address
to her 'has no greater function than the humiliating necessity of
finding some audience, however inapt, to release the "aye-
babbling spring" of Philosophy'. But if the opening twelve lines
are successful in the way I have suggested, and if we do not
cling too tenaciously to the assumption that Coleridge must have
been perpetually voyaging through strange seas of thought,
alone, the poem's real coherence emerges. It is not, and is not
meant to be, a true picture of Coleridge's relationship to his
bride; it is not pure autobiography, or rather, like most autobiography, it contains a certain element of myth-making. The
lowly cottage, and the meekness which the poet praises in his
wife, are the myth's main resting-points, and these have more
in common with Book Four of *Paradise Lost* than with the higher
pantheism. The bower of Adam and Eve, before the Fall, was
shaded by myrtles and laurels, and hedged about with jasmin,
roses, and irises;[2] Coleridge pictures himself as an Adam in
reverse, one who first suffered the Fall and the guilt of sin, and
then, 'Wilder'd and dark', was granted his Eden of innocence
and love.

The myrtles and jasmin flowers figure also in 'Reflections on
having left a Place of Retirement', but the tense of the description is now the past, and the scene is as it were distanced, a
'Valley of Seclusion'. No serpent threatened this Paradise; the
poet's exile from it is a voluntary one, accepted because of his
conviction that no man can erect barriers between himself and a
suffering world without turning his Eden into a place of cowar-

---

[1] George Watson, *Coleridge the Poet*, p. 66.
[2] *Paradise Lost*, Book IV, lines 694–700.

dice and sloth. The ego cannot be preserved in isolation from the feelings and demands of other men. Of course, even cold beneficence is better than none, but 'he that works me good with unmoved face, /Does it but half: he chills me while he aids'.

> Ah! quiet Dell! dear Cot, and Mount sublime!
> 44   I was constrain'd to quit you. Was it right,
> 45   While my unnumber'd brethren toil'd and bled,
> That I should dream away the entrusted hours
> On rose-leaf beds, pampering the coward heart
> With feelings all too delicate for use?
> Sweet is the tear that from some Howard's eye
> Drops on the cheek of one he lifts from earth:
> And he that works me good with unmov'd face,
> Does it but half: he chills me while he aids,
> My benefactor, not my brother man![1]

G. M. Harper's analysis of this poem as (1) quiet description, (2) a flight of imagination, and (3) a return to the starting-point, obscures the point of the poem's opening and closing lines, for (by contrast with 'The Eolian Harp') the myrtle-entwined cottage and its surroundings are given to us as a separate, secluded world, not as a present recipient of Nature's beneficent forces; yet as the concluding lines tell us, the image of the dell remains as a spiritual reality, an inner reminder of the innocence and 'wiser feelings' which all men might possess were they not ravaged by poverty, or, like the 'wealthy son of Commerce', overburdened with material riches.[2] But it is mere selfishness to keep oneself enclosed in such a paradise.

> Yet oft when after honourable toil
> Rests the tir'd mind, and waking loves to dream,
> My spirit shall revisit thee, dear Cot!
> Thy Jasmin and thy window-peeping Rose,
> And Myrtles fearless of the mild sea-air.
> And I shall sigh fond wishes – sweet Abode!
> Ah! – had none greater! And that all had such![3]

Since Joseph Cottle recorded that Coleridge's real motive in

---

[1] Lines 43–53, PW, i p. 107.
[2] 'Coleridge's Conversation Poems', *Quarterly Review*, vol. 244 (April 1925) (284–98) p. 289.
[3] Lines 63–9. PW, i p. 108.

leaving Clevedon was to be nearer the Bristol Library it is easy enough to be contemptuous of Coleridge's 'bombastic phraseology', as Gérard puts it, about 'Science, Freedom, and the Truth in Christ'[1] – though one could point to Coleridge's 1795 Lectures as witnesses for his defence – but our concern is not with whether Coleridge was sincere, but with the poetic transformation of whatever feelings gave rise to these lines. Here we must, I think, go part of the way with M. Gérard, and agree that the declaration of brotherly feeling for humanity in lines 44–62 does not carry conviction. It sweeps too glibly from personal statement – 'I was constrain'd to quit you' – to the universal condition of humanity – 'While my unnumber'd brethren toil'd and bled' (line 45) – so that the disproportion between the colossal sum of suffering that the poet declares war on, and the trivial action which he takes, that of moving house, is too great. Perhaps only Wordsworth succeeded in reconciling humanitarian declarations of this kind with poetic decorum, in passages such as Book XII, lines 69–111 of *The Prelude* (1805) – too long to quote here. But whether or not the poem as a whole is flawed, I believe it is important to recognize that it steps outside the idyllic but circumscribed scene of 'The Eolian Harp', and admits the impossibility, in a fallen world, of human self-sufficiency. This is more than admitting the ego to be 'but the starting-point of poetic meditation', which is what M. Gérard shows;[2] it involves the far more radical perception that the ego cannot be humane without permitting its own hallowed precincts to be invaded. It is easy enough to be vaguely philanthropical: but the real brother of mankind has no spiritual plot which he may call his own. He is not like Johnson's Abyssinian princes, who merely 'passed their lives in full conviction that they had all within their reach that art or nature could bestow, and pitied those whom nature had excluded from this seat of tranquillity as the sport of chance and the slaves of misery.'[3] He and his kind have, in Coleridge's words, 'encouraged the sympathetic passions till they have become irresistible habits, and made their duty a necessary part of their self-interest.'[4]

[1] 'The Systolic Rhythm', p. 315.   [2] *ib.* p. 317.
[3] *Rasselas*, edited by A. J. F. Collins, p. 4 (chapter 2, paragraph 11).
[4] *Lectures 1795*, p. 40.

Richard Haven interprets the 'Reflections' in a similar way to
G. M. Harper, as a movement out and back; a visionary climax
followed by a 'return to the conventional world'. His key phrase,
in treating of other poems of Coleridge as well as the 'Reflections', is 'mental traveller'. Yet, he says, the poem fails because
the 'vision of omnipresence' depicted in lines 26–42 is 'pleasant
but useless': it does not compel assent, as the Ancyent Marinere's tale does.[1] Let us examine closely what Coleridge says of
the landscape.

> It seem'd like Omnipresence! God, methought,
> Had built him there a Temple: the whole World
> Seem'd *imag'd* in its vast circumference:
> No *wish* profan'd my overwhelmèd heart.
> Blest hour! It was a luxury, – to be![2]

What Coleridge sees here is very unlike what the Ancyent
Marinere saw. For him, we remember, 'So lonely 'twas, that
God himself /Scarce seemèd there to be':[3] but here we are given
sunny fields, seats, and lawns, and cots, and hamlets, and the
faint city-spire; moreover Coleridge, unlike the Marinere, is in
complete harmony with the prospect, in a state of 'negative
capability' – 'No *wish* profan'd my overwhelmèd heart'.
Coleridge has 'travelled' nowhere, but describes a state in which
England appears to him like God's temple, and himself its
blessedest inhabitant, desiring nothing, his only pleasure that
of simple existence. Then follow the lines I have already quoted,
expressing the fear that such feelings are 'all too delicate for
use'. Like Rasselas in the Happy Valley, Coleridge must voice
his discontents, and is compelled to sacrifice his tranquillity in
order to retain his humanity.

In the 'Ode to the Departing Year', a new element of conflict enters: that of guilt, but a guilt which is not confined to the
poet. As stanzas VII and VIII of the Ode make clear, the guilt
is England's. Mercifully protected by the sea from the wars that
have periodically ravaged Europe, England has abused the
privilege thus given her, carrying warfare, slavery and commercial exploitation into all parts of the world.

[1] *Patterns of Consciousness*, pp. 50–3.
[2] Lines 38–42, PW, i p. 107.
[3] Lines 599–600, PW, i p. 208.

Abandon'd of Heaven! mad Avarice thy guide,
At cowardly distance, yet kindling with pride –
Mid thy herds and thy corn-fields secure thou hast stood,
And join'd the wild yelling of Famine and Blood![1]

It is hard not to believe that in speaking of England's 'valleys, fair as Eden's bowers', and her lucky seclusion as an 'Island-child' of Ocean, Coleridge had in mind the well-known lines that Shakespeare puts into the mouth of John of Gaunt, picturing England as 'this other Eden, demi-paradise', protected by the sea against infection and the hand of war.[2] But unlike old Gaunt, Coleridge is unable to point to a single cause of England's ills: in the Pindaric language suitable to his form, he explains that though he cannot see to what eventual good the dreadful events of recent history can tend, he is called upon to 'solemnize' the passage of the year; and in the second strophe (as the footnote added in 1803 rather superfluously explains) he 'calls on men to suspend their private Joys and Sorrows, and to devote their passions for a while to the cause of human Nature in general.'

From every private bower,
And each domestic hearth,
Haste for one solemn hour;
And with a loud and yet a louder voice,
O'er Nature struggling in portentous birth,
Weep and rejoice![3]

The phrase 'Weep and rejoice!' is admittedly a rather unsatisfactory poetic gesture towards the turmoil of feelings which a philanthropist might have experienced in 1796, rather than a successful evocation or description of such feelings; but the poem does make one thing clear. As in the 'Reflections', what has changed Coleridge's Happy Valley, or rather what has called his possession of it into question, is not a visionary moment, or a journey of the imagination, but a moral awakening. In this respect, it is all one whether the Eden which the poet possesses is an internal one, as in the 'Reflections', or that state of conjugal serenity which is celebrated in 'The Eolian Harp', or the tranquil prosperity which England has enjoyed for so many years of

[1] Lines 135–8, PW, i p. 167
[2] Lines 123, 130, PW, i pp. 166–7. *Richard II*, Act II, scene 1.
[3] Lines 27–32, PW, i p. 161.

privilege: the lesson is the same in all these cases: to persist in being inward-looking and self-sufficient is to pervert God's gifts to evil uses, and invite an appropriate punishment. If we compare Coleridge's lines with those in which Wordsworth recalls his reaction to the British Government's declaration of war on France, the difference that immediately strikes us is that Wordsworth describes a feeling of total estrangement from his countrymen, whereas Coleridge seems overpowered by a sense of shared guilt. Coleridge, in the 'Ode to the Departing Year', *is* England: Wordsworth, in *The Prelude*, Book X, is a stranger in his own country.

> I only, like an uninvited Guest
> Whom no one own'd sate silent, shall I add,
> Fed on the day of vengeance yet to come?[1]

Yet Wordsworth suffered, as he tells us, a period of intense mental anguish, feeling that he had lost the moral foundation of his life: Coleridge, having prophesied, recentres his mind 'in the deep Sabbath of meek self-content'.[2] The image of Eden, and of what man might be, is still with him, but the concluding strophe of the 'Ode', like the second half of the 'Reflections', is not successful, and for a similar reason – there is a disproportion between the apocryphal vision of the poem's central stanzas, and the closing picture of the poet's personal life with its 'daily prayer and daily toil'.

'Fears in Solitude' is much more successful in blending 'oratory' (Coleridge's term)[3] with an image of the poet's self as the meditative and sympathetic philanthropist. It is the poem which more than any other of Coleridge's reminds us how dangerous are generalizations about the relationship of the Romantic poet to his audience. Professor Abrams has shown, simply by contrasting a statement of Wordsworth with one of Keats and one of Shelley, that there was no question of all poets after 1790 suddenly deciding to write for themselves alone.[4] 'Fears in Solitude' manages to combine, in a quite remarkable way, private meditation with concern for the fate of the country. It also portrays the 'spirit-healing' ministrations of nature in a way which –

[1] (1805) Book x, lines 273–5.   [2] Line 159. PW, i p. 168.
[3] *ib.* p. 256 note 1.   [4] *The Mirror and the Lamp*, p. 26

in view of the fact that the poem was written nine months after
the arrival of William and Dorothy Wordsworth to live near the
Coleridges at Alfoxden[1] – it is hard not to attribute to the opportunities Coleridge would have had to discuss such thoughts with
Wordsworth. ('Frost at Midnight', in which Coleridge expresses the hope that his first child will enjoy the ministrations
of a beneficent nature, also dates from this period).[2] Yet this
'Wordsworthian' theme is quietly combined with the themes
we have seen at work in earlier conversation poems, and with
the 'English Eden' theme of the 'Ode to the Departing Year'.
Some in authority, Coleridge says, call all those who refuse to
worship national idols 'enemies to their country'.

> Such have I been deemed. –
> But, O dear Britain! O my Mother Isle!
> Needs must thou prove a name most dear and holy
> To me, a son, a brother, and a friend,
> A husband, and a father! who revere
> All bonds of natural love, and find them all
> Within the limits of thy rocky shores.
> O native Britain! O my Mother Isle!
> How shouldst thou prove aught else but dear and holy
> 184   To me, who from thy lakes and mountain-hills,
> Thy clouds, thy quiet dales, thy rocks and seas,
> Have drunk in all my intellectual life,
> All sweet sensations, all ennobling thoughts,
> All adoration of the God in nature,
> All lovely and all honourable things,
> Whatever makes this mortal spirit feel
> 191   The joy and greatness of its future being?
> There lives nor form nor feeling in my soul
> Unborrowed from my country! O divine
> 194   And beauteous island! thou hast been my sole
> And most magnificent temple, in the which
> 196   I walk with awe, and sing my stately songs,
> Loving the God that made me! – [3]

England's natural beauty is here pictured not only as the creator
of spiritual beauty (lines 184–91), but as a temple which

[1] The Wordsworths arrived in July 1797; C dated 'Fears in Solitude' 20 April
1798. See W. J. Bate, *Coleridge*, p. 38, and PW, i p. 263.
[2] PW, i p. 242.   [3] Lines 175–97. PW, i pp. 262–3.

spiritual beauty in turn sanctifies, and which therefore in some sense receives enhanced beauty and holiness in return for its ministrations (lines 194–6). England is also revered as the vessel of 'all bonds of natural love', and is thus doubly holy, both as the family home, as it were, and as the precinct of the poet's own self, an Eden 'possessed' by him as he possessed the cottage at Clevedon. Coleridge is very far from feeding on the day of vengeance yet to come. As in the 'Ode to the Departing Year', Coleridge *is* England, and the threat of an invasion is almost like the threat of a profanation of that *sanctum sanctorum*, the inner self. It is a punishment of 'retributive Providence' (line 126), like the inner anguish suffered by a guilty man. But precisely because Coleridge insists on the fact that we are members one of another, and preaches an extension of sympathies beyond the self and its immediate attachments (though not relinquishing either), the prospect of an invasion, whether or not it is in the name of 'Liberty', must appear as a threat to the individual psyche. And the guilt is again a shared guilt.

> My God! it is a melancholy thing
> For such a man, who would full fain preserve
> His soul in calmness, yet perforce must feel
> For all his human brethren – O my God!
> It weighs upon the heart, that he must think
> What uproar and what strife may now be stirring
> This way or that way o'er these silent hills –
> Invasion, and the thunder and the shout,
> And all the crash of onset; fear and rage,
> And undetermined conflict – even now,
> Even now, perchance, and in his native isle:
> Carnage and groans beneath this blessed sun!
> We have offended, Oh! my countrymen!
> We have offended very grievously,
> And been most tyrannous. From east to west
> A groan of accusation pierces Heaven!
> The wretched plead against us; multitudes
> Countless and vehement, the sons of God,
> Our brethren![1]

One doubts whether any Frenchman, incensed by Coleridge's

[1] Lines 29–47. PW, i pp. 257–8.

description of the French nation as 'cruel' and 'impious', would have been much mollified by the lines which call England to repentance for her great crimes: but it can also be said that the sentiments here expressed are hardly what would in this century have been called 'patriotic'. 'Patriotic' in the sense then current they may be, though I do not think the poem presents an identifiable political point of view; nor that it is as much a product of sheer anger as George Watson implies in writing of it as 'evidently written in a white heat of patriotic indignation against the degradation of English public opinion during the French wars'.[1] National egotism is certainly represented as being as great a moral evil as individual egotism. But, in contrast with the 'Ode to the Departing Year', these elements of private and public guilt are held in tension to the end of the poem, in spite of a quietening of tone. The poet is homeward bound, leaving the 'green and silent spot' which for a time has been the scene of his lonely meditation, when he is confronted by a panoramic view of the Somerset hills. A Somerset landscape, especially in summer, would not be present to the eye alone. Dorothy Wordsworth wrote of 'that noiseless noise which lives in the summer air',[2] and in 'Frost at Midnight' Coleridge remarked on the 'strange and extreme silentness' of an icebound landscape, which actually disturbs meditation, as it hushes 'all the numberless goings-on of life', so creating an unnatural stillness.[3] The landscape Coleridge now describes, as in the 'Reflections on having left a Place of Retirement', is made to speak to him, not of his own isolation, nor of mankind's sufferings, but of 'society'; it is not a departure from our everyday world, but a joyful opening-out to it. And – again as in the 'Reflections' – the place departed from remains with the poet, a kind of mental sanctuary, but not as the refuge for a tender sensibility. It is its fountainhead, the spring from which wells upwards and outwards the poet's concern for his own soul, and his loved ones, his nation, and humanity as a whole: 'a circumference continually expanding through sympathy and understanding', not 'an exclusive centre of self-feeling'.[4]

[1] *Coleridge the Poet*, p. 71.
[2] *Journals*, edited by E. de Selincourt (2 vols), i p. 4 (23 January 1798).
[3] PW, i p. 240.   [4] J. H. Muirhead, *Coleridge as Philosopher*, p. 229.

And after lonely sojourning
In such a quiet and surrounded nook,
This burst of prospect, here the shadowy main,
Dim-tinted, there the mighty majesty
Of that huge amphitheatre of rich
And elmy fields, seems like society –
Conversing with the mind, and giving it
A livelier impulse and a dance of thought!
And now, beloved Stowey! I behold
Thy church-tower, and, methinks, the four huge elms
Clustering, which mark the mansion of my friend;
And close behind them, hidden from my view,
Is my own lowly cottage, where my babe
And my babe's mother dwell in peace! With light
And quickened footsteps thitherward I tend,
Remembering thee, O green and silent dell!
And grateful, that by nature's quietness
And solitary musings, all my heart
Is softened, and made worthy to indulge
Love, and the thoughts that yearn for human kind.[1]

It is I think relevant here that Cain, the arch-criminal of man-kind, who has sinned against the light, is represented by Coleridge as seeking darkness and solitude. 'The Wanderings of Cain' begins with a reminiscence of the opening speech of Samson in Milton's *Samson Agonistes*:

A little onward lend thy guiding hand
To these dark steps, a little further on.

Enos (speaking to Cain):

'A little further, O my father, yet a little further, and we shall come into the open moonlight.'

... 'Lead on, my child!' said Cain; 'guide me, little child!'[2]

But Cain longs for that darkness and solitude which is inflicted on Samson as a punishment for his weakness of spirit, a solitude which is not the possession of selfhood, but in truth the negation of it. (A similar point is made in the poem 'The Dungeon', which

[1] Lines 213–32. PW, i p. 263.
[2] *Samson Agonistes*, 1671 edition, p. 9. 'Cain': PW, i p. 288.

was excerpted from Coleridge's tragedy *Osorio* and printed in the *Lyrical Ballads*.) Cain speaks thus:

'O that a man might live without the breath of his nostrils. So I might abide in darkness, and blackness, and an empty space! Yea, I would lie down, I would not rise, neither would I stir my limbs till I became as the rock in the den of the lion, on which the young lion resteth his head whilst he sleepeth.'[1]

In Milton's poem the Chorus addresses Samson:

> Which shall I first bewail,
> Thy Bondage or lost Sight,
> Prison within Prison
> Inseparably dark?
> Thou art become (O worst imprisonment!)
> The Dungeon of thy self; thy Soul
> (Which Men enjoying sight oft without cause complain'd)
> Imprison'd now indeed,
> In real darkness of the body dwells,
> Shut up from outward light
> To incorporate with gloomy night;
> For inward light alas
> Puts forth no visual beam.[2]

Whether it is sought as a refuge, or inflicted as a punishment – if in fact we can distinguish between these two cases at all[3] – to become immured in one's own selfhood is clearly both for Coleridge and for Milton a godless and fearful state: and one senses that both poets had experienced it, for what is Coleridge's assertion that Wordsworth's taste was too 'austerely pure and simple to imitate the Death of Abel' but a hint that his own 'taste' was more suited to this sombre task?[4] As Humphry House points out, it can be seen as very unflattering to Wordsworth to represent him as hopelessly outstripped in a composition-race.[5] But if the real contrast Coleridge is thinking of here

---

1 PW, i p. 289.
2 (1671) p. 17; lines 153–65.
3 'To sin against God is to punish oneself'. Kierkegaard, *The Last Years: Journals 1853–1855*, translated by R. Gregor Smith, p. 182.
4 PW, i p. 287.
5 *Coleridge* (*The Clark Lectures 1951–1952*), p. 22.

is the contrast between his own uncertain and guilt-ridden thought and Wordsworth's outwardly simpler moral outlook, the passage makes better sense. One also notes at this time the beginnings of a change in Coleridge's use of the idea of 'wisdom'. In 'The Eolian Harp', wisdom appeared to be a quality that the poet already possessed, or at least was capable of possessing: we have noted in that poem the apparent harmony between the nuptial bower, with its jasmin and myrtle flowers, and the serene brilliance of the evening star, which is compared to Wisdom itself. Wisdom is in harmony with Innocence and Love. But in the concluding stanzas of 'The Rime of the Ancyent Marinere' wisdom is associated with quite different qualities. The Wedding-Guest is left 'sadder and wiser', and 'turned from the bridegroom's door'. The word 'sadder' here seems to have at least some of the connotations of its older meaning – 'more steadfast, grave, serious' rather than simply 'joyless' – and this marks a distinct change from the Wedding-Guest's earlier manner, which is that of the reveller bent on mirth and japes – 'Nay, if thou'st got a laughsome tale, /Marinere, come with me.'[1] It indicates too that the wedding-feast framework to the tale is not merely a conventionally festive setting. Innocence and Love, if these qualities are what is represented by the nuptial feast from which the Wedding-Guest turns away, are treated as incompatible with wisdom. What is wrong with these things, that the Marinere's tale makes it impossible for the Wedding-Guest to participate in them?

Richard Haven says of the poem's last lines – ignoring I think the richness of meaning that is in the word 'sadder', with its implication of greater maturity – 'whether the wisdom was worth the sadness is a question the poem does not answer', and also that the Marinere 'does not understand and cannot interpret his tale'. The tale itself Haven sees as a journey to the limits of consciousness, where the boundaries of subject and object are fluid; the Marinere, having experienced this terrifying journey, chooses the church rather than the marriage feast because 'the depths of the self are known not in social relations but

---

[1] PW, i p. 187, note, and p. 209 (lines 618–25). Here and throughout the following discussion I refer to the first (1798) version of the poem: I have not the space for a full analysis of C's 'second thoughts' concerning it.

in relation to the universe and to "God" '.[1] Most other critics are agreed on at least one point; that the meaning of the Marinere's tale is left obscure, though some believe that the Marinere himself does understand it, some (with Haven) deny this. The Marinere's experience and subsequent visitations are treated by many critics as some form of psychological abnormality, and his state is seen as one of alienation from his fellow men. Dr Beer is one of those who believe that the Marinere does understand his tale. He sees the Marinere as suffering the punishment of a Platonic vision, in which 'all human beings are in communion with God and therefore in harmony with one another'; and after his return from the voyage the Marinere has to undergo the anguish of a 'dual consciousness', which draws him away from everyday experience.[2] George Whalley suggests that the compelling quality of the Marinere's tale is a result of its closeness to Coleridge's own sufferings: 'it brings us, with Coleridge, to the fringes of madness and death'.[3] Professor Coburn, emphasizing that the poem's 'supernatural' elements are not there as embellishments, but as part of 'a story which...treats of mental states and spiritual phenomena, amalgamated uncannily with a vivid physical world', sees the Marinere as an individual overpowered by circumstances, 'whose connections with life are snapped'.[4] For George Watson, the Marinere's return is analogous to the Wordsworthian sad return to scenes once the source of joy and inspiration, which inevitably brings a sense of loss: it is 'a spectre vision of... that infinite loss mourned or celebrated by other Lyrical Ballads: the loss of appetite and youth'.[5] Robert Penn Warren finds numerous examples of Christian symbolism in the poem, of which the central one is the murder of the Albatross, symbolizing the Fall, and he ends by comparing the lonely, wandering Marinere to the figure of the *poète maudit*[6] (an approach which

[1] R. Haven, *Patterns of Consciousness*, pp. 28, 33.
[2] J. B. Beer, *Coleridge the Visionary*, p. 165.
[3] 'The Mariner and the Albatross', *University of Toronto Quarterly*, vol. xvi (July 1947) (381–98) p. 381.
[4] 'Coleridge and Wordsworth and "the Supernatural"', *University of Toronto Quarterly*, vol. xxv (January 1956) (121–30), pp. 124, 129.
[5] *Coleridge the Poet*, p. 104.
[6] 'A Poem of Pure Imagination', *Kenyon Review*, vol. viii no. 3 (Summer 1946), pp. 391–427.

E. E. Stoll scathingly attacks as a mere mystification).[1] D. W. Harding is cautious of interpretations which rely too heavily on symbolism, though he has in view not Christian symbolism but the symbolism used in certain forms of psychoanalysis. He contrasts the 'bold independence' with which the Marinere sets out – an independence which is only a step from the 'outrageous self-sufficiency' the Marinere displays in killing the Albatross – with his state of mind on returning from the journey, 'the sense of being a worthless social outcast'. The Mariner's recovery 'leads on to reunion with the very simple and humble kinds of social life', and he finds a source of love in religious worship; but it is not a complete recovery, since he has to content himself with 'submissive sociability', in place of his earlier buoyancy of spirit, which was what led him to that wilful act of destruction which began all his sufferings.[2]

D. W. Harding's essay was, in part, an answer to an earlier essay in *Scrutiny* by Eugene Marius Bewley, and Bewley's criticism of the poem – that it suffers from 'an ambiguity of motive, of creative purpose', and that in the moralizing stanza, 'He prayeth best, who loveth best', Coleridge 'for a small effect debases a universe'[3] – is I believe fairly representative of the line of attack against which the critics I have cited are defending the poem. Irving Babbitt is often cast in the role of Coleridge's arch-inquisitor; he is sometimes misquoted as having said that 'the Mariner is relieved of the burden of his transgression by admiring the colour of water-snakes', which appears to be a rather arrogant attempt to ridicule the poem on the ground of the triviality of its central action. According to the arguments of Coleridge's defenders, the poem is vindicated from these charges if it can be shown that the Marinere's voyage in some way teaches him about 'the deeps of the mind', in Professor Knights's phrase,[4] and about the mysteries of the universe, of which he was, in his original state, culpably ignorant. This knowledge is generally represented as having a radical effect

[1] 'Symbolism in Coleridge', *PMLA*. vol. LXIII (March 1958) (214–33).
[2] *Experience into Words*, p. 64.
[3] 'The Poetry of Coleridge', *Scrutiny*, vol. VIII (March 1940) (406–20), pp. 406, 411.
[4] 'Taming the Albatross', *New York Review of Books*, 26 May 1966, p. 12.

on the Marinere's psyche, either breaking his independent spirit or severing him from human ties and condemning him to a life of exile (alternatives which are not necessarily irreconcilable). There is thus no contradiction between the moral seriousness which the poem is generally agreed to lay claim to and the fantastic events of the poem's central sections, for the fantastic events, including the Marinere's sudden act of blessing the water-snakes, are taken as the metaphorical or symbolical equivalents of psychological experiences, or of some form of visionary or imaginative reorientation. The embarrassing 'moralizing stanza' itself is difficult to fit into this interpretation as it stands. It may be taken as indicative of the Marinere's incomprehension of his experiences – he can respond to them only with this vulgar platitude, which is therefore dismissed as irrelevant to our interpretation of the main body of the poem. Or it may be seen as an apology for a moral: how can the Marinere summarize the knowledge gained through such terrifying and outlandish events? – therefore this sententious statement is merely a sign that there is a moral to the Marinere's story, but it is far too profound to be crammed into the confines of a four-line stanza. Either way, the moralizing stanza has little or nothing to do with the wisdom that makes the Wedding-Guest 'sadder', and his change – to return to our starting-point – remains unexplained.

But Irving Babbitt does not dismiss the stanza as irrelevant; he takes it entirely seriously. His criticism of the poem – which he actually allows to be successful in a limited way, as a study of the isolation brought about by an intense emotion – is based on the charge that it confuses the involuntary gush of love, which impels the Marinere to bless the water-snakes 'unaware', with the awakening of Christian charity, which to work the Marinere's salvation would really have had to be a much deeper and more significant spiritual experience. The blessing of the water-snakes is not intrinsically a trivial act, but the fact that it is done involuntarily makes it another thing altogether from the willed self-giving which is the true Christian charity recommended in 'He prayeth best, who loveth best'. The poem does not, therefore, illustrate its own moral. Babbitt's argument *in extenso* is this:

The Ancient Mariner actually has a moral ('He prayeth best, who loveth best,' etc). Moreover, this moral, unexceptionable in itself, turns out, when taken in its context, to be a sham moral. The mode in which the Mariner is relieved of the burden of his transgression, symbolized by the albatross hung about his neck – namely, by admiring the color of water-snakes – is an extreme example of a confusion to which I have already alluded: he obtains subrationally and unconsciously ('I blessed them *unaware*') the equivalent of Christian charity. Like many other works in the modern movement, the poem thus lays claim to a religious seriousness that at bottom it does not possess.[1]

We do not need to enter into the question of what precisely is Christian charity – a question to which every theologian would undoubtedly have his own answer – to see that the idea of it here implied by Babbitt is greatly at variance with what we know to have been Coleridge's idea of 'charity' at this time. George Watson is fairer to the 'Christian' interpretation of the poem than most critics, but I believe he draws too firm a line, which Coleridge would never have allowed, between received Christian doctrine and permissible philosophical and psychological speculation. He eventually, however, dismisses the 'Christian' interpretation of the poem in a similar way to Irving Babbitt (though for different reasons): 'The Mariner,' he writes, 'is simply not felt to be morally responsible, as he would be in any ordinary Christian parable.'[2] We should recall here the description in Coleridge's 1795 Lectures of the true philanthropist as one who has 'encouraged the sympathetic passions till they have become irresistible habits'. This is not the expression of a facile sentimentalism; it implies that the will is involved in the awakening of Christian charity, not through the sudden production of affection to order, as it were, but in a permanent effort to realign the deepest human feelings, so that acts of charity stem from him as naturally as fruit or flowers from a plant, and to reshape the consciousness of self, so that the self is no longer exclusive but inclusive, and radiates the love whose origin is found in God alone:[3] that 'omnipresent Love', as Coleridge expressed it in 'Religious Musings',

---

[1] 'Coleridge and Imagination', *On Being Creative and other Essays*, pp. 115, 118–19.
[2] G. Watson, *Coleridge the Poet*, p. 97.
[3] See M. H. Abrams, *The Mirror and the Lamp*, pp. 173–4.

Whose day-spring rises glorious in my soul
As the great Sun, when he his influence
Sheds on the frost-bound waters.[1]

But the corollary of this is that if God closes off the fount of his love to any man it is only by a return of God's grace that it can be re-activated; otherwise we should have to claim that the human will was itself the source of love. The Marinere's penance is solitude, not only in the sense of his total deprivation of human company, but also in that Christ himself turns away his face.

Alone, alone, all, all alone,
Alone on the wide wide sea;
And Christ would take no pity on
My soul in agony.[2]

In recalling this part of his penance in his closing words to the Wedding-Guest, the Marinere says:

O Wedding-Guest! this soul hath been
Alone on a wide wide sea:
So lonely 'twas, that God himself
Scarce seemèd there to be.[3]

What is so striking about this central part of the poem (Part IV) is that the Marinere's state is shown to be both a punishment and a crime. He sins by hating himself and the 'thousand thousand slimy things' that he sees; but his heart is 'as dry as dust', so he can hardly be capable of either love or prayer.[4] His state is like that of Cain, whom God punished by 'drying up' his heart: and Cain is trapped in a barren selfhood, and also desires death, or oblivion – the negation of self. 'O that I might be utterly no more! I desire to die – yea, the things that never had life, neither move they upon the earth – behold! they seem precious to mine eyes...the Mighty One who is against me speaketh in the wind of the cedar grove; and in silence am I dried up.'[5] This is the state of Life-in-Death, which is so much more horrible than death itself that death is longed for and sought out as a blessed release. But its changelessness, or 'fixed-

---

[1] Lines 415–18. PW, i pp. 124–5.   [2] Lines 232–5. PW, i p. 196.
[3] Lines 597–600. PW, i p. 208.   [4] Lines 238, 247. ib. p. 197.
[5] ib. pp. 288–9.

ness' as Coleridge's later gloss has it, and the complete paralysis of the will which it inflicts on the victim, can be broken only by an act of grace. So far is it from being true that the Marinere earns his salvation in any way, that Coleridge emphasizes the very opposite, the act of grace which enables him to love and pray again.

> O happy living things! no tongue
> Their beauty might declare:
> A spring of love gushed from my heart,
> And I blessed them unaware:
> Sure my kind saint took pity on me,
> And I blessed them unaware.[1]

What is granted the Marinere here is not a sudden insight into the fact that even water-snakes are part of the divine plan: the moment is not in this sense a 'visionary' one, but a spiritual one. To put it another way, it is not the recipients of the blessing who are important, but its divine origin, and the fact that the 'spring of love' enables the Marinere to transcend his selfhood for the first time. It does not matter whether the object of his love is water-snakes, stars or Polar Spirits; the important thing is that God, acting perhaps through some 'kind saint', has made the Marinere's self a centre and source instead of an enclosing defensive wall, and so enables it to resemble God himself a little more, for (to draw one further conclusion from this argument, which however now enters the realm of speculative inference) what ultimately matters about Christian charity may be not its beneficial effects on mankind and the animal world in general, but the fact that whoever achieves it is thereby brought a very little closer to resembling God's own nature. We can now better reconcile the Marinere's redemptive experience with the 'moralizing' stanza which so troubled Irving Babbitt. 'Commonplace' as a sentiment it may be, but there is no law against poets or theologians pointing to the commonplace as a source of deeper truths; or rather, there was none in the age of Wordsworth.

The whole point of the Wedding-Guest framework to the story is, it seems to me, to bring out the uncomfortable truth

[1] *ib.* p. 198. Lines 282–87.

that 'sociability' is not the same as love, and that the jolly party
to which the Wedding-Guest was bound is one of those ego-
worlds which can be inward-looking, exclusive, and therefore a
misuse of gifts not in themselves evil. At the beginning of the
poem the Wedding-Guest attempts to draw the Marinere into
the party, and when he refuses, threatens to use his stick to rid
himself of this persistent stranger:

> 'The Bridegroom's doors are opened wide,
> And I am next of kin;
> The guests are met, the feast is set:
> May'st hear the merry din.'

> But still he holds the wedding guest –
> There was a Ship, quoth he –
> 'Nay, if thou'st got a laughsome tale,
> Marinere, come with me.'

> He holds him with his skinny hand –
> Quoth he, there was a Ship –
> Now get thee hence thou greybeard Loon!
> Or my Staff shall make thee skip.[1]

But the Marinere's powers of compulsion have their way, and
it is clear that his choice of audience has not been at random:

> That moment that his face I see,
> I know the man that must hear me:
> To him my tale I teach.

Moreover the Marinere predicts the effect that his narrative
will have on the Wedding-Guest:

> Listen, O listen, thou Wedding-guest!
> 'Marinere! thou hast thy will:
> For that, which comes out of thine eye, doth make
> My body and soul to be still.'

> Never sadder tale was told
> To a man of woman born:
> Sadder and wiser thou wedding-guest!
> Thou'lt rise to-morrow morn.[2]

So we are three times shown that the Marinere knows his man,

---

[1] Lines 5–8 and note. PW, i p. 187.
[2] *ib*. pp. 201, note, and 208, lines 588–90.

and it is clear from the poem's first four stanzas what kind of man the Wedding-Guest is: one who will brook no rude interruption of his social pleasures. After concluding his story, the Marinere hears some sounds, which seem to represent three quite different worlds; the noise of the party, the singing of the bride and her bridesmaids, and the ting of the vesper bell.

> What loud uproar bursts from that door!
> The wedding-guests are there:
> But in the garden-bower the bride
> And bride-maids singing are:
> And hark the little vesper bell,
> Which biddeth me to prayer![1]

The Marinere has learnt that the power to love is not altogether ours to use as we wish, but comes from God, and so is a gift which may not be misused without unpleasant or even terrifying consequences. The easy sociability of the wedding party, and even the paradisaic innocence of the 'garden-bower', can both become in the end prisons which trap love within an artificially enclosed world. Human love must exclude no living thing – for no other reason than that God's love does not. No wonder the Wedding-Guest was 'sadder', and 'turned from the bridegroom's door', for his Eden has been shown to be a prison, and he has had to accept not only that already disturbing truth, but the realization that the outside world may be capable of showing love towards him. The albatross, we are told, loved the Marinere; there is no need to add (as D. W. Harding does) that the bird 'represented in a supernatural way the possibility of affection in the world'.[2] The Marinere has positively killed a living being that loved him; the symbolical interpretation, if my reading of Part IV is correct, is unnecessary. If, as I have suggested, part of the Marinere's lesson is that love is of God – and the albatross is at first welcomed 'in God's name' – it becomes as ungodly an act to reject love when it is offered as to withhold it when it is needed. In both cases the ego is defending its own precincts. Every man would desire, if it were possible, to 'preserve his soul in calmness' (the phrase used by Coleridge at the beginning of 'Fears in Solitude'). This need not preclude the

[1] Lines 591–6. PW, i p. 208.   [2] *Experience into Words*, p. 57.

enjoyment of love, marriage, friendship and the sense of identity with one's country that is depicted in 'Fears in Solitude' and elsewhere. In fact these things are all part of any selfhood that is not merely the negation of self, like Cain's, or Samson's, which emit no rays of spiritual light, and receive none.[1] But any of these Edens, once it excludes knowledge of and concern for the larger sphere, and has no centre out of itself, suffers a terrible change: it becomes a prison, and the prospect of remaining alive and sentient in it is so sickening that one desires nothing but darkness and death. Individuality, as Coleridge understood it, is 'a force which reaches out and makes new connections and relations. The greatest individuality is that which has the greatest degree of organization, the largest quantity of relations.'[2] To be entire and self-sufficient, to 'preserve one's soul in calmness', is impossible, or only momentarily possible. Each man has to be prepared to forfeit his Eden, or – which is infinitely more frightening – to open it up to something that seems completely alien.

'Christabel' is if anything a still more tempting ground for speculation than 'The Rime of the Ancyent Marinere', not only because it is unfinished, but because even the fragment that we have is full of ambivalences and shadowy recollections. Unconventional interpretations abound. Gerald Enscoe suggests that the hooting of the owls after what he calls the 'deflowering' of Christabel represents 'a jubilant rejoicing' and 'tumultuous celebration' by the forces of nature,[3] in spite of the general convention of Gothic writing that owls are sinister and Coleridge's apparent acceptance of such a convention in other poems – in the 'Rime', for instance:

> 'When the ivy-tod is heavy with snow,
> And the owlet whoops to the wolf below,
> That eats the she-wolf's young',

and the 'owlet Atheism' in 'Fears in Solitude'.[4] Dr Beer does not go quite as far as Enscoe, but still believes that 'the owls . . . represent good forces . . . they are minimal agents of good.'[5] The

---

[1] See above p. 55.
[2] G. M. McKenzie, *Organic Unity in Coleridge*, p. 44.
[3] *Eros and the Romantics*, pp. 50–1.   [4] PW, i pp. 207, 259.
[5] *Coleridge the Visionary*, p. 181.

identity of Christabel has often been debated, and it must be
admitted that it is a fascinating question; Carl Woodring, noting
the close resemblances between parts of 'Christabel' and parts
of Dorothy Wordsworth's Alfoxden journal reviews the likeli-
hood of Christabel being a combination of Dorothy Wordsworth and Sara Hutchinson: but he then sides with the critics
who believe that Christabel is actually S. T. Coleridge.[1]

However my concern is not to offer a comprehensive 'reading'
of the poem, but to point to one element in it which I think has
been overlooked. With Enscoe, we may begin by recalling
Derwent Coleridge's explanation of the character of Geraldine,
who was not intended to be a 'witch or goblin, or malignant
being of any kind, but a spirit, executing her appointed task with
the best of good will'.[2] This makes her similar to the Polar
Spirit in the 'Rime', or even to the Mariner himself in his relation to the Wedding-Guest. But Christabel appears to possess
that very charity and generosity which the Wedding-Guest
lacks: she brings Geraldine home 'in love and in charity',[3] and
offers to share her bed with her. Nor are there grounds for believing that Christabel is any wiser after her night with Geraldine; and unless we regard the narrator's interruptions at the
end of Part I and throughout Part II as heavily ironical, it is
difficult to imagine that Christabel has been an accomplice in
some kind of crime. Woodring suggests that Christabel's
succumbing to the 'evil' latent in Geraldine means that she herself is not wholly innocent;[4] but if that is the case we must read
irony into the lines,

> Yea, she doth smile, and she doth weep,
> Like a youthful hermitess,
> Beauteous in a wilderness,
> Who, praying always, prays in sleep.
> And, if she move unquietly,
> Perchance, 'tis but the blood so free
> Comes back and tingles in her feet.
> No doubt, she hath a vision sweet.
> What if her guardian spirit 'twere,

---

[1] 'Christabel of Cumberland', *Review of English Literature*, vol. VII (1966) (43–52),
p. 46.
[2] See H. House, *Coleridge*, p. 127: G. Enscoe, *Eros and the Romantics*, p. 40.
[3] Line 277, PW, i p. 225.   [4] 'Christabel of Cumberland', pp. 47–8.

What if she knew her mother near?
But this she knows, in joys and woes,
That saints will aid if men will call:
For the blue sky bends over all![1]

– which do not seem to invite an ironical interpretation. Moreover, if, as Derwent Coleridge's comment indicates, Geraldine herself is not an evil spirit, but the reluctant agent of some higher power, there seems no reason to impute guilt to Christabel on account of her collaboration with Geraldine. Enscoe suggests the opposite interpretation: for him Christabel is innocent to begin with, but has to learn that innocence is a denial of nature, and therefore experiences in Geraldine's caresses a sexual liberation which for the time being renders her incapable of normal speech. 'Christabel's pious innocence is not enough', Enscoe argues; 'she must be corrupted in order to exist in the corrupt world.'[2] According to Enscoe, therefore, Geraldine's entry into the castle is the entry of life and fertility into a pious, but barren and death-centred world, and the singing of the owls is a kind of epithalamium; Geraldine is an ambivalent figure because Coleridge's attitude towards sex was itself ambivalent. This interpretation seems to me to detract from the poem's richness of meaning: Christabel, after all, is not only pious, but actively charitable; she is chaste, but not coldly so, since she has a betrothed lover; and she is hardly liberated or made sexually mature by her night with Geraldine, since she has recurring visions of Geraldine's horrible scaly bosom, and is under a powerful spell which prevents her from speaking of her experience. It also imposes on these lines (describing the moment after Christabel has had one of her awful visions), a forced sense:

> The touch, the sight, had passed away,
> And in its stead that vision blest,
> Which comforted her after-rest
> While in the lady's arms she lay,
> Had put a rapture in her breast
> And on her lips and o'er her eyes
> Spread smiles like light![3]

[1] Lines 319–31. PW, i p. 226.   [2] *Eros and the Romantics* pp. 57–8.
[3] Lines 463–9. PW, i p. 230.

This, read in conjunction with the passage to which it refers, gives a picture of piety troubled but not yet overthrown: her 'All will yet be well!' is much more like an expression of faith than one of sorrowful resignation. Yet though 'devoid of guile and sin', she is clearly subject to some power in Geraldine, and it is hardly consonant with the appearances of this power which Coleridge describes to classify it merely as a sexual ascendancy.[1] Moreover if Christabel's innocence at the beginning of the poem is meant to be seen as limited or inadequate – if we accept G. Wilson Knight's description of Christabel's world as 'religious' and 'mother-watched' in some pejorative sense[2] – we must read as ironical Geraldine's effort to reassure Christabel:

> 'All they who live in the upper sky,
> Do love you, holy Christabel!
> And you love them, and for their sake
> And for the good which me befel,
> Even I in my degree will try,
> Fair maiden, to requite you well.'[3]

If then it is not our impression that Christabel is culpable in any way, either in being too innocent or in not being quite innocent enough, must we see Geraldine's invasion of her world as an enactment of some irrational and nightmarish fear from which Coleridge suffered? This is G. Wilson Knight's feeling about the poem: 'Some hideous replacing of a supreme good is being shadowed, with an expression of utter surprise, especially in the conclusion to Part I, that so pure a girl can have contact with so obscene a horror...The poem expresses fear of some nameless obscenity.'[4] But if Christabel is made to suffer for no reason, other than the inscrutable cruelty of an amoral Providence, or if the poem is merely 'a story of sexual molestation and terrorism' which 'seems to accept without irony the serious task of chilling the reader's spine',[5] it is difficult to see why Geraldine should be reluctant to undertake her task, and why she should reassure Christabel in the words above quoted. There is a reason for Christabel's suffering, I believe, but it is not to be found in any sin or inadequacy of her own. She is made to expiate not her own

---

[1] Lines 583–612. *ib.* pp. 233–4.   [2] *The Starlit Dome*, p. 82.
[3] Lines 227–32, PW, i p. 223.   [4] *The Starlit Dome*, p. 83.
[5] George Watson, *Coleridge the Poet*, p. 113.

guilt but her father's. Perhaps, had the poem been completed, we would also have been shown how Christabel's sufferings worked for the weal of her lover, who is 'exposed to various temptations in a foreign land', this being part of the basis of the story according to Gillman's account.[1] This is not to say that Christabel actually chose martyrdom, as Yarlott puts it: 'Christabel's sufferings. . .were contracted voluntarily since, for the "weal" of her absent lover, she chose deliberately to undergo a martyrdom.'[2] There is surely no evidence in the poem as it stands to suggest that Christabel chose martyrdom in this way; indeed, if she had done so it would arguably have detracted from her innocence. She would have had to be seen as succumbing to the temptation put before Becket, in T. S. Eliot's play, by the Fourth Tempter. Yarlott is right, however, to point to the godlessness already present in the castle, its origin being Christabel's father, whose 'neurotic obsession with death implies an incapacity for vital living relationships'.[3] The aura of death and gloom that surrounds the castle, and spreads its baleful influence 'from Bratha Head to Wyndermere', emanates not from Christabel's piety but from Sir Leoline's decree of lifelong mourning.

> Each matin bell, the Baron saith,
> Knells us back to a world of death.
> These words Sir Leoline first said,
> When he rose and found his lady dead:
> These words Sir Leoline will say
> Many a morn to his dying day!
>
> And hence the custom and law began
> That still at dawn the sacristan,
> Who duly pulls the heavy bell,
> Five and forty beads must tell
> Between each stroke – a warning knell,
> Which not a soul can choose but hear
> From Bratha Head to Wyndermere.

And Bracy, who next to Christabel herself is the inmate of the

[1] See A. H. House, *Coleridge*, p. 126.
[2] Geoffrey Yarlott, *Coleridge and the Abyssinian Maid*, p. 179.
[3] *ib.* p. 185.

castle who most makes for life, reflects that the bell seems to call up an answer from the ghosts of other 'sinful sextons'.

> Saith Bracy the bard, So let it knell!
> And let the drowsy sacristan
> Still count as slowly as he can!
> There is no lack of such, I ween,
> As well fill up the space between.
> In Langdale Pike and Witch's Lair,
> And Dungeon-ghyll so foully rent,
> With ropes of rock and bells of air
> Three sinful sextons' ghosts are pent,
> Who all give back, one after t'other,
> The death-note to their living brother;
> And oft too, by the knell offended,
> Just as their one! two! three! is ended,
> The devil mocks the doleful tale
> With a merry peal from Borodale.[1]

Dr Beer sees Sir Leoline's proposal to crush the snake which threatens Christabel – or rather, as the Baron sees it, Geraldine – as a 'reliance on force' which 'recalls Bœhme's Cain', and the poem's heroine is thus the embodiment of a redeeming principle, doomed to suffer the misdirected blow meant for the serpent, and thereby to teach the ungodly that man is powerless to redeem himself by his own will, and can be saved only by entrusting everything to God.[2] I would wish to add to this that Sir Leoline's sins begin long before he leads Geraldine out of his 'presence-room'. His religious observance is not a genuine turning to God in humility as the source of all love, but an obsessive attachment to private grief. He loves his daughter, admittedly, but in all other ways he is presented as a self-willed and proud man, trusting not even his daughter nor his best friend. Coleridge insisted on the vital importance for friendship of complete trust, even beyond what seems prudent;[3] but Sir Leoline has put his own pride before his friendship, and listened to the 'whispering tongues' that can 'poison truth'.[4] He now declares his repentance, but remains as proud as ever. Geraldine,

---

[1] Lines 332–59. PW, i p. 227.
[2] See *Coleridge the Visionary*, pp. 122, 193.
[3] See Notebook 13, fol. 271.
[4] Line 409. PW, i p. 229.

or the authority for which she works, has chosen an appropriate means of punishing Sir Leoline. As Yarlott says, 'he is so wrapped up in self-centredness and the feelings Geraldine's nearness excites in him, that he rides roughshod over his daughter's feelings.'[1] Like the Ancyent Marinere in the seven days of his agony, or Coleridge himself in the nightmare experiences of 'The Pains of Sleep', Sir Leoline undergoes a punishment which is also a crime: he distrusts his beloved daughter, and transfers his love to an impostor, putting her in his daughter's place. The dove which he used to call by his daughter's name is now a symbol for Geraldine, and she also takes the place of Christabel's dead mother. Geraldine drives the mother's protective spirit away from Christabel's room with 'Off, woman, off! this hour is mine', and in the Conclusion to Part I Geraldine, sleeping with Christabel in her arms, is likened to 'a mother with her child'. Christabel's childlike trustfulness as she succumbs to the spell put on her by this surrogate mother is the real obscenity in the poem, if obscenity there is. But Christabel is not 'corrupted', or even abandoned by the saints, as the Mariner for a time was. In spite of her involuntary passive imitation of Geraldine's 'look of dull and treacherous hate', she is still capable of prayer; her faith and heart are untouched, but she is 'o'ermastered by the mighty spell'.[2] If the idea of this seems terrifying, it is no less so than Milton's 'Evil into the mind of God or Man /May come and go, so unapprov'd, and leave /No spot or blame behind.'[3] The spell is necessary, and not just a 'Gothic' embellishment to the tale, for Christabel must be estranged from her father in order that he may be punished, but she herself must remain untouched and blameless. She tries to warn Sir Leoline; then the narrator intervenes.

> Why is thy cheek so wan and wild,
> Sir Leoline? Thy only child
> Lies at thy feet, thy joy, thy pride,
> So fair, so innocent, so mild;
> The same, for whom thy lady died!

[1] *Coleridge and the Abyssinian Maid*, p. 187.
[2] Lines 569–71, 211, 301, 606, 388, 462, 614, 620. PW, i pp. 233, 223, 226, 234, 228, 230, 234.
[3] *Paradise Lost*, Book v, lines 117–19.

O by the pangs of her dear mother
Think thou no evil of thy child!
For her, and thee, and for no other,
She prayed the moment ere she died:
Prayed that the babe for whom she died,
Might prove her dear lord's joy and pride!
    That prayer her deadly pangs beguiled,
        Sir Leoline!
And wouldst thou wrong thy only child,
    Her child and thine?[1]

The situation resembles that in the famous 'chapel scene' of *Much Ado About Nothing*, when Leonato (is the similarity of names entirely coincidental?) is tricked into believing that his daughter is an approved wanton, and spurns her the more violently by reason of the intensity of his former love for her. The sentiment of love – as the Conclusion to Part II points out – can sometimes so much resemble other passions in their 'giddiness' that it speaks in their voice, and Sir Leoline is too deeply enmeshed by Geraldine to heed Bracy's warning, or even his own daughter's:

Within the Baron's heart and brain
If thoughts, like these, had any share,
They only swelled his rage and pain,
And did but work confusion there.[2]

It is probably true in some sense that Coleridge could not finish the poem because of the difficulty of keeping Christabel innocent, while enabling her to overcome the power exerted by Geraldine. Dr Beer argues that Coleridge's chief problem was how to incorporate evil into the true angelic nature, and that this would have had to take place through Christabel's subconscious mind, a project which has obvious difficulties.[3] I feel that it is not so much 'evil' which has to be incorporated into Christabel's innocence – nor even that she is 'innocent' in any way which implies mere limitation – but the equally terrifying truth which Blake's Thel learns from the clod of clay: 'O beauty

[1] Lines 621–35. PW, i p. 234.
[2] Lines 636–9. PW, i pp. 234–5.   [3] *Coleridge the Visionary*, pp. 195–6.

of the vales of Har, we live not for ourselves.'[1] The mysterious horror that 'Christabel' embodies is not some kind of cruel sexual initiation, but the equally humbling idea that a man cannot do as he likes with his own, even when he has the strongest apparent justification to 'preserve his soul in calmness'. Christabel's innocence is no more a protection against this knowledge than is her father's pride.

I have said that the chief characteristic of both the Marinere's punishment and Sir Leoline's is that it is also a crime. The fountain of joy which makes the ego a source and centre rather than a circumference is cut off, and the result is a dryness and dereliction which no human efforts can cure. As is by now well enough known, in the 'Ode: Dejection' Coleridge expressed his sense that a punishment of this kind was inflicted upon him; but the received text of the poem – the version published in *Sibylline Leaves* in 1817 – camouflages the confession which is clearly made in the original version, addressed to Sara Hutchinson. The recurring theme of this first version is not so much the poet's loss of the imaginative and creative power, but his sense that the desiccation of his inner self is destroying his capacity to love, and spreading a baleful influence around him, rather as the bell at Langdale Hall tolled a message of hopelessness and gloom to all the surrounding valleys. To take one instance: in the received version, the lines

> But oh! each visitation
> Suspends what nature gave me at my birth,
> My shaping spirit of Imagination,

are followed immediately by

> For not to think of what I needs must feel,
> But to be still and patient, all I can;
> And haply by abstruse research to steal
> From my own nature all the natural man –
> This was my sole resource, my only plan:
> Till that which suits a part infects the whole,
> And now is almost grown the habit of my soul.[2]

[1] 'The Book of Thel', iii line 10. *Poems and Prophecies*, p. 40.
[2] Lines 84–93. PW, i pp. 366–7.

This implies that Coleridge has undergone an etiolation of the creative power, as a result of having turned to abstruse studies in order to inure himself to mental suffering: it is a statement, in other words, about the psychology of the individual creative mind. The published version thus supports such interpretations as that of Professor Abrams, who finds the poem to be a record of 'the utter loss of the reciprocating power of the mind' and of 'the dependence of nature's life on the inner life of man'.[1] There is more to it than this, however, as we may be warned by the fact that Coleridge does not, like Wordsworth, end by finding 'Strength in what remains behind... /In years that bring the philosophic mind.'[2] The individual mind, in 'Dejection', is if anything a form of penance. The great virtue of joy is precisely that – as Coleridge phrased it in his *Philosophical Lectures* – 'in joy individuality is lost'.[3] But a hostile environment can soon dry up the 'day-spring' of that love which, at the time of 'Religious Musings', Coleridge had confidently described as 'omnific, omnipresent'; and this affects not only the poet's creative powers, but also his very capacity to care for others. After the phrase 'My shaping spirit of Imagination', in the original version, there follows a passage in which Coleridge laments that he cannot offer Sara the sympathy and comfort which she deserves, because of the harsh unsympathetic atmosphere in which he is forced to live, and which drives him to the soul-deadening activity of 'abstruse research'.

> I speak not now of those habitual Ills
> That wear out Life, when two unequal Minds
> Meet in one House and two discordant Wills –
> This leaves me, where it finds,
> Past Cure, and past Complaint, – a fate austere
> Too fix'd and hopeless to partake of Fear!
> But thou, dear Sara! (dear indeed thou art,
> My Comforter, a Heart within my Heart!)
> Thou, and the Few we love, tho' few ye be,
> Make up a World of Hopes and Fears for me.
> And if Affliction, or distemp'ring Pain,
> Or wayward Chance befall you, I complain

---

[1] *The Mirror and the Lamp*, p. 67.
[2] 'Ode: Intimations of Immortality'; *Poetical Works*, edited by T. Hutchinson, p. 462.   [3] *Phil. Lects*, p. 179 (Lecture v).

Not that I mourn – O Friends, most dear! most true!
    Methinks to weep with you
Were better far than to rejoice alone –
But that my coarse domestic Life has known
No Habits of heart-nursing Sympathy,
No Griefs but such as dull and deaden me,
No mutual mild Enjoyments of it's own,
No Hopes of its own Vintage, None O! none –
Whence when I mourn'd for you, my Heart might borrow
Fair forms and living Motions for it's Sorrow
For not to think of what I needs must feel,
But to be still and patient all I can;
And haply by abstruse research to steal
From my own Nature, all the Natural man –
This was my sole Resource, my wisest plan!
And that, which suits a part, infects the whole,
And now is almost grown the Temper of my Soul.[1]

Stephen Prickett argues that there is an analogy between the blessing of the water-snakes in Part IV of the 'Rime', and Coleridge's blessing the Lady at the end of 'Dejection'. Each manifestation of love follows a period of deadness, but in the 'Rime', 'insight and new development grows out of an experience of utter dereliction and loss', while this does not appear to happen in 'Dejection'. Prickett concludes that there is a difference between those moments which 'through affliction, assert our community with our fellow-creatures, be they water-snakes or men, and those which only increase the isolation of the individual'.[2] This distinction seems to me a little artificial. Certainly the isolation which the Marinere experiences can reasonably be compared to the 'grief without a pang' described in 'Dejection', but (as I have stated above) I can see no grounds for holding that the 'spring of love' which the Marinere experiences is strictly the result of his isolation, or of any 'insight' which that isolation gives him. The feeling of 'community with our fellow-creatures, be they water-snakes or men', as Prickett phrases it, comes from God's grace, and there is no other reason to suppose that the Marinere's isolation 'differed' from Cole-

---

[1] 'Coleridge's *Dejection: An Ode*', edited by E. de Selincourt, *Essays and Studies* vol XXII (1937) (7–25), p. 23. See also H. House, *Coleridge*, pp. 157–65.
[2] S. Prickett, *Wordsworth and Coleridge: the Poetry of Growth*, pp. 155–6.

ridge's because it ends in a different way. Furthermore, in 'Dejection' Coleridge analyses an overwhelming sense of personal guilt, for in addition to his sins of omission he confesses to a sin of commission, in that his very dependence on Sara for comfort has sapped her strength, and brought her physical as well as mental suffering. He seems to be condemned to spreading unhappiness around him, as well as suffering it himself. These lines form part of a passage of about 130 lines entirely omitted from the version published in 1817. In this passage, Coleridge admits that even the thought of Sara herself, watching the same night sky, now moves him very little; but then he pictures Sara thinking of him, and recalls a time when she and her sister gave him their affection and comfort.

> Ah fair Remembrances, that so revive
> The Heart, and fill it with a living Power,
> Where were they, Sara? – or did I not strive
> To win them to me? – on the fretting Hour
> Then when I wrote thee that complaining Scroll,
> Which even to bodily Sickness bruis'd thy Soul!
> And yet thou blam'st thyself alone! And yet
> Forbidd'st me all Regret!
>
> And must I not regret, that I distress'd
> 120 Thee, best belov'd, who lovest me the best?
> My better mind had fled, I know not whither,
> For O! was this an absent Friend's Employ
> To send from far both Pain and Sorrow thither
> Where still his Blessings should have call'd down Joy!
> I read thy guileless Letter o'er again –
> I hear thee of thy blameless Self complain –
> And only this I learn – and this, alas! I know –
> That thou art weak and pale with Sickness, Grief, and
>   Pain –
>
> And *I*, – *I* made thee so!
>
> O for my own sake I regret perforce
> Whatever turns thee, Sara! from the course
> Of calm Well-being and a Heart at rest!
> When thou, and with thee those, whom thou lov'st best,
> Shall dwell together in one happy Home,
> One House, the dear *abiding* Home of All,
> I too will crown me with a Coronal –

77

Nor shall this Heart in idle Wishes roam
  Morbidly soft!
No! let me trust, that I shall wear away
In no inglorious Toils the manly Day,
And only now and then, and not too oft,
Some dear and memorable Eve will bless
Dreaming of all your Loves and Quietness.[1]

The poetic merit of these lines, as George Watson says,[2] is not
equal to that of the shortened version, but I have quoted them at
length because I believe they, and the poem of which they are
a part, mark the end of that theme in Coleridge's poetry which
we have traced in its various manifestations from 'The Eolian
Harp' and the 'Reflections' to 'Christabel'. Coleridge's pathological sense of isolation – of being 'a wither'd branch upon a
blossoming Tree' – is expressed in numerous powerful and
austere poems from later years, such as 'The Blossoming of the
Solitary Date-Tree', which begins with a line from the unpublished version of 'Dejection' (line 120 above, reading 'The' for
'Thee'), and ends with the famous cry 'Why was I made for
Love and Love denied to me?' On occasion there is even a
renaissance of the kind of feeling Coleridge had for Sara and her
sister, as in the poem 'To Two Sisters' (addressed to Mary
Morgan and Charlotte Brent). But the upsurge of 'Love, omnific, omnipresent Love, /Whose day-spring rises glorious in my
soul' never again appears. Coleridge has found that if joy cannot
be held within the confines of a single soul, neither can grief,
guilt or despair: they lay their shadows over other beings, and
the soul which is deprived of the divine source which should
sustain it must feed, like a caterpillar, on other lives – the fearful
vision of human life embodied in the seven-line poem written in
1808, 'Psyche'.[3]

> The butterfly the ancient Grecians made
> The soul's fair emblem, and its only name –
> But of the soul, escaped the slavish trade
> Of mortal life! – For in this earthly frame
> Ours is the reptile's lot, much toil, much blame,
> Manifold motions making little speed,
> And to deform and kill the things whereon we feed.

[1] 'Coleridge's *Dejection: An Ode*', pp. 19–20.
[2] *Coleridge the Poet*, pp. 74–5.   [3] PW, i pp. 397, 124–5, 412.

II

1804–1813

There is a power upon me which withholds,
And makes it my fatality to live, –
If it be life to wear within myself
This barrenness of spirit, and to be
My own soul's sepulchre.

Byron*

– Ah! Seigneur! donnez-moi la force et le courage
De contempler mon cœur et mon corps sans dégoût!

Baudelaire†

1

When he was at length compelled to see and acknowledge the true state of the morals and intellect of his contemporaries, his disappointment was severe, and his mind, always thoughtful, became pensive and almost gloomy: for to love and sympathize with mankind was a necessity of his nature. Hence, as if he sought a refuge from his own sensibility, he attached himself to the most abstruse researches, and seemed to derive his purest delight from subjects that exercised the strength and subtlety of his understanding without awakening the feelings of his heart.[1]

Coleridge's self-portrait in the character of 'Satyrane' has in it a measure of self-justification, and for precisely that reason helps us to understand why the years following his return from Malta produced so little finished work besides a few *Courier* essays, some lectures, and of course *The Friend* itself. It goes some way towards answering the question that puzzled De Quincey, who saw that Coleridge 'burrowed continually deeper into scholastic subtleties and metaphysical abstractions; and…lived

* *Manfred* Act i scene 2. (*Poetical Works*, OUP 1959, p. 393.)
† 'Un Voyage à Cythère', *Les Fleurs du Mal*, edited by Antoine Adam, Garnier, Paris 1961, p. 138.
[1] TF, ii p. 187 (no. 14: 23 November 1809).

chiefly by candlelight',[1] but could not reconcile this spectacle of voluntary incarceration with the outwardly sociable and friendly milieu of Grasmere. De Quincey felt that some mysterious power – other than opium – must be at work, as Coleridge's domestic life became more and more difficult to shore up, until it virtually collapsed following the quarrel with Wordsworth in the autumn of 1810. 'Satyrane' reveals that – rightly or wrongly – Coleridge felt betrayed, even before the tension between him and the Wordsworths became an open breach; and this betrayal did not reside in any one particular act or declaration on the part of his friends. They had failed him, it appeared, in what was to Coleridge a much more serious way, by betraying their own nature, failing to live up to the high moral ideals of which they had seemed to be the incarnation. 'Satyrane', by his own declaration, 'had derived his highest pleasures from the admiration of moral grandeur and intellectual energy.'[2] Now the preoccupations and even the conceptions of those who had seemed the embodiment of moral grandeur sank into pettinesses, and 'Satyrane' turned more and more to the moral grandeur of ideas, philosophies and metaphysical systems. Yet his writings repeatedly urge that religion does not call upon men to renounce their humanity, but to realize it; that noble passions and faculties do not exist only in exceptional men, or even only in civilized men, but are an essential part of human nature itself, however deeply they may be buried under the rubble of superstitions and selfishness. Man was a fallen creature, but not the brute that Hobbes had pictured, nor yet the self-concerned, if 'enlightened', creature conceived by Paley and his disciples. And Coleridge also knew that, however well he understood what man was, and what things were necessary for salvation, his own salvation depended, not on the depth of his understanding, but on what he in himself was; and solitude and illness served only to increase his sense of self-disgust.

2

The student of Coleridge's love poetry has opportunities for a

---

[1] *Reminiscences of the English Lake Poets*, p. 54.
[2] TF, ii p. 186 (no. 14: 23 November 1809). Compare *Shakespearean Criticism*, ii p. 119 (Lecture VIII).

closer acquaintance with his author than is possible with almost any other poet. His reputation as a poet of love rests not only on work in print during his lifetime, but on the fragments, unfinished poems, first drafts and prose sketches that have been preserved in his letters and notebooks; and these sources provide an incomparable means of chronicling the biographies of Coleridge's poems *ab ovo*. With some poets, of course, it is unhelpful, not to say impossible, to treat their poems other than as mature progeny who can be allowed to speak for themselves. The origins of their work are better left obscure, or perhaps have no separate existence apart from the attractions of the form, or of a striking image, or a well-turned phrase, or a clever conceit. It seems clear that Coleridge's love poetry was not of this kind, but was always felt along the heart, and (perhaps for this reason) was not usually abandoned to its own devices, but kept in a mental anthology to be quoted, revised, and meditated upon as the occasion arose. This is not to suggest that Coleridge had only to utter his feelings in metre to produce poetry of lasting value, but only that each finished or half-finished poem was an attempt to idealize and unify the thoughts and feelings that distressed his mind, and in doing so not to escape from them, but to give them permanence and the power of the uttered word. Like other solitaries, Coleridge became in some sense a connoisseur of his own passions. A note of autumn 1808 about his own ashen dullness as contrasted with Sara's radiant coldness is followed by the memorandum, 'N.B. – This put in simple and elegant verse, as an imitation of Marini...'[1] He declared (apropos of the 'Soother of Absence') that he felt an 'utter want of Sympathy' with most of the love poetry of previous ages, since he was unable to love without the 'knowlege of being loved in return – or even with the knowlege of the contrary'.[2] Sara, it is clear, either returned his love at one time, or at least appeared to him to do so.

The study of Coleridge's love poetry is rendered both more fascinating and more difficult by the fact that so much of it is part of a continuing dialogue, carried on largely by himself,

---

[1] Notebook 13, fol. 245.

[2] N 2062. (I take it to mean: he was unable to love as certain poets professed to love, without knowing if their love was returned, even sometimes being certain it was not).

with occasional intrusions on the part of other people. This dialogue merges, at one extreme, into the rueful, often bitter comments on Wordsworth, Dorothy, Sara and the rest of the Grasmere circle, which Coleridge confided to his notebooks, and with which we are not primarily concerned; and at the other extreme, into the metaphysics that Coleridge hoped would anæsthetize his tormented mind. Yet a metaphysic, of a kind, mingles with all Coleridge's work as a poet of love, and gives it its peculiar quality of psychological surrealism, recaptured best in this century by T. S. Eliot.

> This form, this face, this life
> Living to live in a world of time beyond me

If, however, we accept Professor Wilson Knight's view that Eliot's 'poetic self' was not 'wholly, or even mainly, Christian', and adduce 'Marina', as he does, as evidence for this judgment[1] – then we must approach Coleridge's love poetry circumspectly. For it is no more overtly Christian than 'Marina', and yet is not out of harmony with Coleridge's religious beliefs, indeed often springs from the same sources; it informs and intensifies his beliefs, and is informed and intensified by them, to use Eliot's phrase. In particular, Coleridge found that his belief in a 'real Self', an essential non-personal being, abstracted from outward circumstances and even from personal vices or virtues, was corroborated by his own psychological experience in dreams and meditation. The dress, the expression and facial features of the beloved counted for nothing in the realm of dreams; far more vivid and frequent than the vision of these things was the pure sense of the other person's presence, somehow depersonalized like the 'blessed face' of Eliot's poem, so that a purely spiritual communion was achieved – for it was of the essence of this experience that individuality was transcended, and lover, friend, children appeared to partake of one and the same soul. One such experience, occurring during the stay in Malta when Coleridge's long absence from England had impelled his subconscious mind into troubled activity, inspired these lines:

[1] 'T. S. Eliot: Some Literary Impressions', in *T. S. Eliot, The Man and the Work*, edited by Allen Tate, p. 261.

All Look or Likeness caught from Earth,
All accident of Kin or Birth,
Had pass'd Away: there seem'd no Trace
of Aught upon her brighten'd Face
Uprais'd beneath the rifted Stone,
Save of one Spirit, all her own /
She, she herself, and only she
Shone in her body visibly.[1]

But as well as being enjoyed as the remarkable verbal ikon which it undoubtedly is, this poem can be seen as part of a tapestry of thought, part of the ceaseless inner dialogue of Coleridge's mind; indeed it was used by Coleridge in this way, for when he wrote the version here quoted he was not composing, but quoting from himself (and a slightly different version of the lines occurs again, as part of a quite different argument, some years later).[2] Like the mystic face in the blue flower of Novalis's story, it promised not merely friendship or love, but spiritual completion. Coleridge's deep need for such 'completion' went almost wholly unanswered in this period of his life, and was exacerbated by the rift with Wordsworth. Throughout the period, he recorded the symbols of barren isolation and productive companionship that he came across; some, such as the story of the solitary date-tree that produced fruit only when a branch from a distant tree was grafted on to it, became the materials of finished or near-finished poems.[3] A favourite symbol – never used in a completed poem – was that of 'the huge Organ Pipe at Exeter larger than that at Haarlem – but *dumb*! Green determined to make it speak / tried all ways and means in vain / till at last he made a second Pipe precisely alike, and placed it by it / – then it spoke.'[4] But for most of his life Coleridge was denied any chance of 'completion'; 'whirled about', in his own phrase, 'without a center...a vortex without a center',[5] only rarely, outside the world of dreams, did he achieve the repose of silent communion with another person.

On the first awakening of his love, he had been aware that his

---

[1] N 2441 (in the original, written as a piece of continuous prose). Compare PW, i p. 393; AP, p. 120, and Notebook 23, fols. 3–4.
[2] Notebook 23, fols. 3–4.   [3] See PW, i pp. 395–6.
[4] N 1972 (March 1804: see AP, p. 67, and N 2998).
[5] Notebook 14, fol. 322 (dated 29 October 1810).

imagination had its own Sara, which nevertheless merged and 'coadunated' with her real form as the two images received by the eyes merge to create a single picture in the mind.[1] But in the silent companionship which he sometimes enjoyed with Sara in later years, during his residence at Keswick, this *visual* image of coadunation was replaced by a pervading *sense* of the beloved's presence, like that experienced in his dream.

> I most commonly do not *see* her with my imagination – have no visual image / but she is present to me, even as two persons at some small distance in the same dark room / they know that the [? one] is present, and act and feel under that knowlege – a subtler kind of sigt [sic] seems to confirm and enliven the knowlege.[2]

Silence was vital for the subsistence of such 'knowledge'; words destroyed the ambience in which two separate identities could for a time remain in perfect accord with each other, perhaps because words necessarily engaged the conscious mind, the discursive reason. This state has much in common with the receptive, pre-verbal state that Keats named 'negative capability', for it includes one element which is the very opposite of a dream-life, 'the sense and substance of intensest Reality'. This is no escape from knowledge, but the experience of a deeper knowledge than full consciousness can provide.

> I fear to speak, I fear to hear you speak – so deeply do I now enjoy your presence, so totally possess you in myself, myself in you – The very sound would break the union, and separate *you-me* into you and me. We both, and this sweet Room [...] its' books, its' pictures, and the Shadows on the Wall slumbering [...] with the low quiet Fire are all *our* Thoughts [...] harmonious Imagery of Forms distinct on the still substance of one deep Feeling, Love and Joy – – A Lake – or if a stream, yet flowing so softly, so unwrinkled, that its' flow is Life not Change – / – That state, in which all the individuous nature, the distinction without Division, of a vivid Thought is united with the sense and substance of intensest Reality.[3]

'Distinction without Division': the state here experienced shares important qualities with the state of æsthetic pleasure as Coleridge later defined it – beauty being in his definition 'the unity of the manifold, the coalescence of the diverse' (his

---

[1] N 2994.   [2] Notebook 17, fol. 111 (dated 26 June 1810).
[3] Notebook 17, fol. 84; and see below, pp. 119–21.

phraseology here being borrowed, however, from Schelling[1]). 'To be wise', he wrote, 'I must know all things as *one*; to be knowing I must perceive the absolutely indivisible as infinitely distinguishable.'[2] Yet it is evidently seen as the outcome, not of lonely meditation, still less of opium intoxication, but of 'confident Love', and this perhaps startling juxtaposition throws light both on Coleridge's fear of spiritual isolation, which, we can see, would inevitably threaten the very sources of his most urgent beliefs, and on his fondness for a form of spiritual monism. I use this term to refer to the notion that the soul is not the exclusive property of one individual, but just one manifestation of a spirit shared by all men, though not recognized in our usual state of awakened consciousness. (This is what Heraclitus seems to have understood by the word 'soul'[3]). Shaftesbury gave currency to this notion with his argument (in the *Exercises*) that the 'particular mind', ordering and directing the individual's affections and imaginings, is part of a 'general mind' which animates all men.[4] For Coleridge, its appropriateness lay not so much in its accordance with the ideal of 'general benevolence' as in its corroboration of his own feelings of deep unity with other souls.

These feelings had at first to encounter and supersede a somewhat too simple psychology of perception. As we have seen, he compared the 'coadunation' of his first mental image of Sara and her 'real form' with the mind's unification of the eyes' two images; though even before his Malta experiences he found a symbol for the untroubled communion of souls in the quiet spring, with its pulsating cone of sand, seen near Dove Cottage. The interest in mental 'images', and the vocabulary of associationism, could not outlast the dream experiences of the Malta years, however. In particular, they were inadequate to cope with the pervasive, irreducible sense of another person's presence that these dreams often brought to him.

Remember my repeated Memoranda – Dorothy, myself, etc, in my Red Cottle Book. Does not this establish the existence of *a Feeling* of a

---

[1] 'On Poesy or Art', BL, ii p. 257 and note, p. 318.
[2] Notebook 21¼, fol. 277.   [3] See Philip Wheelwright, *Heraclitus*, pp. 58–9.
[4] See L. L. Whyte, *The Unconscious Before Freud*, p. 97; and Stephen, *History of English Thought in the Eighteenth Century*, ii p. 26.

Person quite distinct at all times, and at certain times *perfectly separable* from, the Image of the Person?...I seem to see, tho' darkly, that the Inferences hence are many and important / [1]

These hints of a vaster world of the spirit yet to be discovered were closely allied with another dominant interest of Coleridge's, the interest in Instinct, the power that somehow induces the stag-beetle, before its metamorphosis, to make its case half as long again as itself, in order to leave room for its horns. For Coleridge, such a manifestation of pre-rational intelligence was necessarily part of an all-pervading life-spirit, the higher levels of which were shared by humanity; children, especially by their uncanny propensity to reproduce unwittingly their parents' characteristic traits and affections, proved that an inexplicable unity underlay the discrete conscious minds of human beings. Wordsworth had represented children's gifts of mind and feeling as an indication of their being possessed, or haunted, by an 'eternal mind';[2] for Coleridge, the application was at once more personal and – through its link with the idea of the one Soul, differently manifested in several beings who had a common bond of love – more immediate. From a theory not far removed from Wordsworth's, if couched in more prosaic language – 'To deduce instincts from obscure recollections of a pre-existing State' – Coleridge proceeded to affirm his belief in that essential unity in the spirit which is not contradicted by apparent disunity, and division into 'personality', 'character' and so on.

Ey! have I said, when I have seen certain tempers and actions in Hartley, that is *I* in my future State / so I think oftentimes that my children are my Soul. / that multitude and division are not (o mystery) necessarily subversive of unity. I am sure, that two very different meanings if not more lurk in the word, *one*.[3]

It is in a similar context to this that Coleridge saw the poem 'Phantom', with which our investigation began. Far from being a piece of whimsy, conceived quite apart from the normal traffic of Coleridge's thought, it was at the start deeply meaningful to him, and even gained in meaning as time went on; for as he thought more about the ethereal quality of the face seen in

---

[1] N 2061; compare N 2078.
[2] 'Ode: Intimations of Immortality', line 113. *Poetical Works* p. 461.
[3] N 2332.

dreams, the necessary indistinctness of the love object, and hence its apparent closeness to the universal Soul, so the poem itself acquired importance as his most distinct memory of the dream-experience which first prompted these reflections. Some few weeks after writing the note just quoted (in December 1804), Coleridge set down his further thoughts on this subject, quoting the poem 'Phantom' in illustration of the belief that when the feeling of love enters a dream, 'a certain indistinctness, a sort of *universal-in-particularness* of Form, seems necessary'. The vision, as in the case of the 'individual Babe and mine' who was yet neither Sara, nor Derwent, nor Berkeley, is so closely identified with the feeling of love that individual facial features are of no importance.[1] The 'abstract Self' seen in the dream is a 'Universal personified'; and its inseparability from the feeling of love proves that feeling to be of a different kind from other moral impulses. It shows love to be 'a *deeper* Feeling, and of such intimate affinity with ideas, so to modify them and become one with them, whereas the appetites and the feelings of Revenge and Anger co-exist with the Ideas, [...] not combine with them; and alter the apparent effect of the Forms not the Forms themselves.'[2] The notion that love is a more powerful inhabitant of the psyche than anger again recalls the optimism of Shaftesbury, and his belief that the particular mind is not naturally insular, but is part of a ubiquitous general mind – a belief which in the form of the thesis 'una est anima intellectiva in omnibus hominibus' Coleridge also came across in Meiner's life of Pico della Mirandola.[3] And yet Coleridge's use of the idea lacks the confidence of Pico's and Shaftesbury's; it is tentative and personal where theirs was considered and reflective. Though Coleridge had recourse to the idea in other contexts, its deepest meaning remained for him in the realm of relationship. In Italy, for instance, he noted the feeling of community awakened among the English sailors by the arrival of a convoy from home; but continued the thought by reflecting upon the unity-in-the-spirit of parted friends: 'My Friends are indeed my Soul'. At a time when he believed his relationship with Sara to be at an end (June 1806), he wrote, 'O my Children, my Children! I gave you life

[1] N 2441.   [2] *ib.*; and see AP, p. 120.
[3] N 374 and n: see G. N. G. Orsini, *Coleridge and German Idealism*, p. 129.

once, unconscious of the Life I was giving / and you as unconsciously have given Life to me.' A letter to Allston contained the same sentiment: 'I gave Life to my Children / and they have repeatedly given it to me.'[1]

The most complex and longest-lasting manifestation of the idea of spiritual unity, however, is in the succession of notes relating to Sara Hutchinson. In these – in four of them in particular, two dating from 1805 and two from 1810 – Coleridge resolved the tension between the two contradictory impulses which he was to describe in 1830 as the impulse to 'pass out of myself' and the opposite impulse 'not to suffer any one form to pass into *me* and to become a usurping *Self*'.[2] Coleridge appears to discover a new level of consciousness at which this distinction is meaningless; for where love seems to reveal unity in the spirit through the 'consummation' of two souls in each other,[3] the question of the integrity of the self is really transcended. The beloved *'verschiedene Eine'* no more usurps the self of the lover than sunlight usurps the self of the eye which received it. Each is necessary to the other.[4] In love – in the love that Coleridge knew – the individual soul still exists, but only to be transformed into something higher, less 'personal', by its admiration for something outside itself. 'Love is most nearly itself /When here and now cease to matter' – the 'here and now' of personality cease to matter in that state of knowledge and mutual affirmation which lovers experience.[5] Yet this brings no emotional stability, for it has to do with that level of the psyche which emotions do not touch. Coleridge's months away from England, the strange behaviour of his troubled mind, and his long hours of introspective thought had encouraged his awakening sense of the unity which can underlie two apparently separate minds in the mysterious realms of sleep and imagination; and it now began to incorporate into itself elements of his religious beliefs – proof, if it were needed, that Coleridge was describing what he believed to be significant realities, not merely interesting dream-phenomena. 'The flux of Things

---

[1] N 2410 (AP, p. 115); N 2860; and *Letters*, ii p. 1173 (no. 620: 17 June 1806). Compare N 2554.
[2] Notebook 47, fols. 193–4.   [3] N 2540.
[4] Notebook 23, fol. 116 (dated 1810 by E. H. Coleridge; AP, p. 233).
[5] See T. S. Eliot, *Collected Poems*, p. 203.

without' has yet, as Coleridge put it, a *forma efformans* of feelings and images within'. The permanent pattern of this Heraclitean stream is spiritual, inhabiting what would be called in Kantian language the subjective sphere: it is not only real, in Coleridge's eyes, but of the deepest reality. 'Scripture speaks of the Spirit as praying to the Spirit – the Lord said to my Lord/ etc.'[1] It appears that, as love similarly to religion reveals the permanent inner pattern, and calls the individual self out of itself to be re-created in a higher form, love can be not only analogous to religious experience but an advancement of it. Coleridge boldly developed this thought in one of the Malta notebooks.[2]

The best, the truly lovely, in each and all is God. Therefore the truly Beloved is the symbol of God to whomever it is truly beloved by! – but it may become perfect and maintained lovely by the function of the two / The Lover worships in his Beloved that final consummation <of itself which is> produced in his own soul by the action of the Soul of the Beloved upon it, and that final perfection of the Soul of the Beloved, <which is in part> the consequence of the reaction of his (so ammeliorated and regenerated) Soul upon the Soul of his Beloved / till each contemplates the Soul of the other as involving his own, both in its givings and its receivings, [. . .] and thus still keeping alive its *outness*, its *self-oblivion* united with *Self-warmth*, and still approximates to God! Where shall I find an image for this sublime Symbol <which ever> involving the presence of Deity, yet [. . .] tends towards it ever![3]

Despite what has been said about the undoubted reality to Coleridge of the 'forma efformans', it may be a question here whether he has not so far spiritualized the love relation as to lend weight to the charge that he could not love anyone 'as a person'.[4] Certainly this passage, with its philosophy in part borrowed from Berkeley,[5] its bold description of the love object as a 'symbol of God', and its idealization of the love relation almost as a process of spiritual education, would be a strange way of attempting to declare love, if that is what it were. But it proceeds from two assumptions: that the highest in each of us is God, as he shows himself in human lives; and that, when we love another, it is the 'highest' in him which we love, and not

[1] N 2550.   [2] Notebook 17.
[3] N 2540; see AP, p. 133.   [4] See above, p. 42.
[5] On 'outness' see *Principles of Human Knowledge* chapter I, section 43.

that amalgam of the good and the bad which make him what he outwardly is. Our phrase, to love someone as a person, is itself called into question by these two assumptions. If the person is merely the sum of his attributes, then Coleridge's thinking can be seen as idealistic, in a derogatory sense of the word, and subtracts from the love relation its essential quality of acceptance of the whole person in a fruitless attempt to prove that love is allied to religion. If, on the other hand, there is in each man and woman something 'truly lovely', truly worthy of love, which is substantial and not accidental, a ground of personality which can make them a symbol of God to a lover, Coleridge's emphasis on the spiritual nature of love is a revelation of love's deeper significance. Upon our conception of the 'person', particularly upon our acceptance or rejection of the notion that there is a 'best' in each man and woman which the lover sees and loves, permanent and quite independent of all 'qualities', depends our attitude to this note of Coleridge's.

In the autumn of 1808, when for a brief period Coleridge believed he really had won Sara's love, he spoke a language which was still very similar to that of the Malta notes. In the excess of joy, it was still the language of the spirit that came most naturally to him; and some of these passages are among the most eloquent and untroubled prose that Coleridge ever wrote, full of a sense of wonder at the new world of feeling which has opened for him, yet retaining also elements of the strange Coleridgean humility, which seems to turn away from the highest joys of this life towards a life free of the sheer burden of bodily existence.

Love unutterable fills my whole Spirit, so that every fibre of my Heart, nay, of my whole frame seems to tremble under it's perpetual touch and sweet pressure, like the string of a Lute – with a sense of [. . .] vibratory Pain distinct from all other sensations, a Pain that seems to shiver and tremble on the threshold of some Joy, that cannot be entered into while I am embodied – [1]

But in spite of the exhilaration of this writing, it is still imbued with doubt as to the suitability of words themselves for such a theme. All words, being (in Coleridge's phrase) 'generalities',

[1] Notebook 13, fols. 278–80 (reversed) (dated 9 September 1808).

involve associations with other words, but 'that, which I see, must be felt, be possessed, in and by its' sole self!'[1] Qualities, physical attributes, may be affirmed, but if we do believe that over and above these things there is a 'very Self', something in each person which is of God (and perhaps immortal), words become less than adequate, and through the associations which the purest of writers cannot avoid may even be in danger of blaspheming the Spirit in man.

The main theme of 'The best, the truly lovely, in each and all is God', however – the treatment of the interaction of minds as a process of 'amelioration' and 'regeneration', bringing the soul of each lover closer to God – is central to Coleridge's thinking about relationship. It lies behind his violent disagreement with Wordsworth over the nature of love, when Wordsworth argued that love was a combination of various other passions, including that of animal lust as well as more conventionally admirable feelings, and Coleridge insisted that it was *sui generis*.[2] It also points to the unifying tendency in all Coleridge's thought. Coleridge does not insist on retaining a dichotomy between human affections and religious faith, as does T. S. Eliot;[3] he affirms that human affections can be prompted by that in us which is of God, and moreover that they lead us towards God, and are not merely 'intensified' or 'elevated' by religious faith, which was Eliot's belief. Human love, 'involving the presence of Deity, yet tends towards it ever!' Coleridge could transcend the disunity of the divine and the human in ways which were closed to Eliot.[4]

Further thought rather strengthened than weakened Coleridge's trust in the unique powers of love. In October 1810, some months after the decease of *The Friend*, and (apparently) following the rift with Wordsworth, Coleridge, once more alone, wrote

My love of ‚κθγ [5] is not so much in my Soul, as my Soul in it. It is my whole Being wrapt up into one Desire . . . God is our Being, but thro' his works alone doth he reveal himself – and that for which all other

---

[1] *ib.* fol. 254.   [2] See below, pp. 107–8.
[3] In a letter to Bonamy Dobrée; see *T. S. Eliot, The Man and the Work*, edited by Allen Tate, p. 81.
[4] See also *Letters*, iii p. 485 (no. 922: April 1814).
[5] C's cipher for Sara Hutchinson, 'Asra'.

objects have a [? visual] meaning [? ...] force or attractions are desired or avoided – that of which all other Objects are but a copious language of epithets and synonymes – that is God appearing to one – in that he reveals himself – and in that I love and adore him – I hold it therefore neither impiety <on the one hand> nor superstition on the other that you are the God within me, even as the best and most religious men have called their Conscience the God within them. But you, tho' existing to my senses, have ever abode within me – you have been, and you alone have been, my Conscience – in what form, with what voice, under what modification can I imagine God to work upon me, in which *you* have not worked?[1]

Thus the works of love are shown in the moral as well as in the spiritual; indeed it would have been impossible for Coleridge to keep his overwhelming passion wholly apart from his moral life, since the tendency to 'idealize and to unify' dominated all his thought, and not only his view of poetical creation. David Hume had desired to see an end to the artificial separation of the passions from reason.[2] Their unification was experienced by Coleridge, at least for a time, when he found 'all the Hopes and Fears, Joys and Sorrows, all the Powers, Vigor and Faculties of [his] Spirit abridged into <one> perpetual Inclination'.[3] Yet this joyful feeling of unity inevitably changed, following the estrangement from Wordsworth (and hence from all the Grasmere circle), leaving a numbing sense of 'incompleteness' – a word used in another note which dates probably from October 1810.[4] For when the 'advantages and favorable accidents of Nature, or Fortune' have been valued, not for themselves, but as part of the wages of a world of mirth in which love is supreme, and when that love has made one person 'the symbol of God' to the lover, its death makes other things not merely worthless, but 'insulting remembrancers of misery'. Other things were enjoyed only through love, as light is enjoyed through the eyes; loss of love is 'loss of the sole organ thro' which <we> could enjoy them'. Not even the oblivion of Duty, which he had found such

---

[1] Notebook 13, fols. 320–1. (After an account of C's journey to London, 18–26 October 1810).

[2] *A Treatise of Human Nature*, edited by L. A. Selby-Bigge, p. 415 (Book II, Part iii section iii).

[3] Notebook 13, fol. 320.

[4] Notebook 23, fol. 116. (See above, p. 88, note 4.)

a compelling call in 1805,[1] was now left to him, for he had already realized that the weakness of human nature could never embrace Duty without its calling up all the painful associations with sublunary tragedies that were, supposedly, irrelevant to the high dedication of the pure life of the Spirit. If human love merges into religious experience, the converse is also true, and the religious life does not remain immune from the 'weakness' of human sorrows and regrets.

The very Duty must for ever keep alive feelings, the appropriate Objects of which are indeed in another world; but yet our human nature cannot avoid at times the connection of these feelings with their *original*, their first, the [sic] mistaking forms and objects – and so far therefore from removing the scar, will often and often make the wound open and bleed afresh / – but still we know that the feeling is not *objectless* – that the counterfeit has a corresponding *Genuine* – and this is the comfort. – 1808.[2]

A greater theologian than Coleridge, Søren Kierkegaard, stated the essence of the matter with a terrifying clarity: Christianity has to do with 'the single person', and that which is in human terms an object of envy and admiration, the happy marriage, is the very antithesis of everything that the true Christian desires.[3] But Coleridge, refusing to make such a strict dichotomy in what he believed to be the one world of the Spirit, paid the penalty; and his keen sense of 'incompleteness' is a melancholy theme in many of his writings about religious faith.

3

Despite the personal anguish which he underwent in these middle years – despite also the brief periods of joy and hope – Coleridge was working out some of the ideas of relationship which would contribute so significantly to *The Friend*, the 1811–1812 Lectures, and the 1825 'Essay on Faith'. Ever unwilling to adopt the severe Kierkegaardian stance of renunciation, he still insisted, as in the 'Conciones' of 1795, on the great importance of human love; and a concept not unlike the Goethean concept

---

[1] N 2537.   [2] Notebook 25, fol. 153.
[3] *The Last Years: Journals 1853–55*, pp. 79, 92–4, and elsewhere.

of the *ewige Weiblich* has its place in much of his thought, though he does not, of course, use the phrase itself. He had private reasons for trusting such a concept; he knew how the 'woman-soul' – symbolized in the 'brighten'd face' of the poem, or personified in Sara's presence – had the power of drawing his mind on to further and greater efforts, even of making him, as he unequivocally admitted, 'very much a better man'. One note describes how Sara's presence worked like a conscience within him, inducing 'Horror of whatever is base...fervent aspirations after Good, and great, honorable, and beautiful things'. Sara's influence strengthened his resolution, bestowed on him 'the power of uttering abstrusest Truths as from the mouth of Childhood', and even preserved him from moral dangers. The almost talismanic quality of the woman's face seen in a 'heavenly Vision...as the guardian Angel of my Innocence and Peace of mind' had made Coleridge unwilling, indeed, quite resolved not to tolerate any alteration in Sara's 'angel countenance'. It was as if Sara's physical presence owed it to her spiritual manifestation not to betray, with 'unbecoming' accoutrements, that symbol of her spiritual being, her face.[1] 'Symbol', here, may be read in the strictly Coleridgean sense of that which 'is characterized by the translucence of the eternal through and in the temporal...[and] partakes of the reality which it renders intelligible.'[2] Ideas such as the eternal and the universal could never, in Coleridge's eyes, be grasped unless the understanding began with the particular. Benevolence, 'goodwilldoingness', however strongly felt, seemed to need an actual object, a real relationship, if they were to be anything more than temporary impulses. The sense of 'outness' seemed to be vital for the increase of 'active benevolence'.[3] So, although still believing that the thinker must 'love [human nature] in order to understand it,'[4] Coleridge insisted in *The Friend* that such a love must begin with the love of particular persons. Those thinkers who made much of their solitude, like Rousseau, were reproached; while those whom Coleridge particularly admired were praised for their participation in a community – of intellect, if not of actual

[1] N 2495; N 2536; Notebook 13, fols. 249, 256 (dated 22 October 1808), 322.
[2] *The Statesman's Manual*, pp. xviii–xiv.
[3] N 2495.   [4] Notebook 13, fol. 277.

persons: thus Rousseau, in Coleridge's judgment, suffered from 'Constitutional Melancholy pampered into a morbid excess by solitude', while Luther, by contrast, profited by sharing in the healthy dialogue of a flourishing intellectual community. It is a matter open to dispute how far these pictures are accurate – it was Bacon's view, for instance, that Luther, finding no intellects in his own age deep enough to second his battle against the degeneracy of Rome, turned to the classics merely 'to make a party against the present time'.[1] But Coleridge held that the isolation of great thinkers, their existence in 'all time' rather than in an age, was an illusion created by their great stature; in fact their genius would be found to have developed 'in a circle defined by human affections'.[2] This sense of the constant inter-play and cross-fertilization of minds, which he held to be so important if thought was not to become fanatical or strident, is peculiar to Coleridge, and undoubtedly has its roots in his own sad experience. Yet Coleridge does not only declare the impor-tance of human love in the realm of thought, but also judges and analyses the particular effects of certain kinds of love in the moral sphere. The sixteenth issue of *The Friend*, for instance, contained a digression upon the possibility of platonic love between the sexes – 'there is a sex in our souls as well as in our bodies...and he who does not feel it, never truly loved a Sister'.[3] But the most sustained treatment of platonic love and the *ewige Weiblich* occurs in those of the 1811–1812 Lectures which took as their subject 'Love and the Female character as displayed by Shakespear'.[4]

Coleridge's idea of conjugal happiness retains elements at least of Milton's description, in *Paradise Lost*, of the happiness shared by Adam and Eve, when 'in thir looks Divine / The image of thir glorious Maker shon'.[5] We know that Coleridge thought the description of the love of Adam and Eve in Paradise to be 'of the highest merit': 'it is', he writes, 'the sentiment of one rational being towards another made tender by a specific differ-ence in that which is essentially the same in both; it is a union of

---

[1] *The Advancement of Learning*, p. 23.
[2] TF, ii pp. 113–14 (no. 8: 5 October 1809); p. 323 (no. 24: 15 February 1810).
[3] TF, ii p. 209 (no. 16: 7 December 1809); also printed in BL (ii, p. 147).
[4] *Letters*, iii p. 353 (no. 844: 7 December 1811).
[5] Book iv, lines 291–2.

opposites, a giving and receiving mutually of the permanent in either, a completion of each in the other.' And it is significant that in one of the Shakespeare lectures Coleridge gave the opinion that Shakespeare had been excelled by no poet in his portrayal of woman, except perhaps Milton in his delineation of Eve.[1] From what we had already learned of Coleridge's views on relations between the sexes, we might perhaps have anticipated this judgment; but as so often in Coleridge's criticism, the critical judgment is surrounded and sustained by an expression of its moral implications. The premise on which Coleridge's high valuation of Shakespeare and Milton rests, in this respect, is that man combines a heavenward tending potentiality with an indolent, earth-bound nature. With an oblique reference to Plato's argument in *The Symposium* that through the successive gradations of love man is drawn to higher and still higher realms of consciousness, Coleridge refers love to that insatiable desire for 'completion' which attracts men towards the spiritual. In this way, Providence has made that 'which is necessary to us a step in our exaltation to a higher and nobler state'.

Love is a desire of the whole being to be united to some thing, or some being, felt necessary to its completeness, by the most perfect means that nature permits, and reason dictates'... Who shall dare to stand alone, and vaunt himself, in himself, sufficient? In poetry it is the blending of passion with order that constitutes perfection: this is still more the case in morals, and more than all in the exclusive attachment of the sexes.[2]

Coleridge has discovered in poetry – not in its subject-matter, but in its very nature – a principle which is analogous to the aims of morality itself, the blending of passion with order. The point will gain in clarity if we refer to a notebook entry (which seems to have been the source of this part of the lecture), for the notebook entry is concerned only with the effect of love on the individual, not with its final cause. Love, especially the sorrow it brings, can bestow a poet's eloquence on every lover – 'Love will vent his inmost and veriest Griefs in sweet and measured

[1] *Miscellaneous Criticism*, pp. 164–5; *Shakespearean Criticism*, ii p. 106 (Lecture VIII).
[2] *Shakespearean Criticism*, ii pp. 106–7 (Lecture VII).

sounds.'[1] Even in expressing sorrow, the lover creates beauty, for aesthetic pleasure is an earthly shadow of celestial happiness. Or perhaps it could be said (and this is the seed of the seventh Shakespeare lecture) that since love unites passion with reason, it naturally expresses itself through the intellect, which in a poet is what gives order to the poetic impulse, as well as in the passions.

Is it that – a divine Joy being its end it will not utter even its woes and weaknesses, sorrows and sicknesses, except in some form of pleasure? pleasure the shadow and sacramental Type of that Joy (which by union fit and et facit et creat et creatur) or is it rather, that its essence being a divine synthesis of highest order reason – and passion vehementest Impulse, it must needs the soul in its two faculties, or perhaps of the two souls, vital power of Heat, and Light of Intellect – attract and combine with poesy, whose essence is passionate order.[2]

When these thoughts were made part of the Shakespeare lecture, however, their scope was widened; instead of applying them simply to the individual, Coleridge introduced considerations of the final cause of love. If in the individual man love were a manifestation of the spiritual, its ultimate purpose in man viewed as a race must be as high above the mere propagation of the species as divine joy is above concupiscence. Its end must, in short, be a moral one, in the Coleridgean sense of the phrase. Men who falsely declare themselves sufficient unto themselves lack the one thing necessary for human development: human love, and the unceasing education provided by conjugal and domestic life. 'All the operations of mind, in short, all that distinguishes us from brutes, originate in the more perfect state of domestic life.'[3]

This interest in the progressive improvement, or what would later be called the 'cultivation', of man was the impulse behind many of Coleridge's arguments in the Shakespeare lectures. In the first lecture, he had argued that man was in part his own creation, for 'by the improvement of the faculties bestowed upon him by God, he not only enlarges them, but may be said to bring new ones into existence'.[4] Poetry is analogous to religion (as is

---

[1] N 3092. C deleted 'sounds' as here shown, without substituting any word.
[2] N 3092.
[3] *Shakespearean Criticism*, ii p. 107 (Lecture VII).
[4] *Shakespearean Criticism*, ii p. 36 (Lecture I).

clearly stated in Lecture VIII[1]), for it is the function of religion to effect those reconciliations in life which poetry effects in the realm of art, the reconciliation of passion with order, of intellect with emotion. In all that Coleridge says about poetry, there is the added weight and significance of a deep moral and religious concern – concern not so much with what man has been as with what he might become. Coleridge's thinking about poetry, like the thinking of many Old Testament writers, is heavy with the burden of the presence of God.

It is so evident that Providence intended man...to be the master of the world, that marriage, or the knitting together of societies by the tenderest, yet firmest ties, seems ordained to render him capable of maintaining his superiority over the brute creation. Man alone has been privileged to clothe himself, and to do all things so as to make him, as it were, a secondary creator of himself, and of his own happiness or misery: in this, as in all, the image of the Deity is impressed upon him.[2]

This may now seem a rather cumbersome way of introducing a brief discussion of *Romeo and Juliet*, yet the moral issues raised by a consideration of the play were so important, to Coleridge's mind, that they had to be placed in the right perspective before the play could be understood and evaluated. The prime moral question that presented itself was simple enough: if Romeo was purportedly already in love with Rosaline when the play began, was he not shown to be no better than a weathercock when he succumbed to a new passion for Juliet? Coleridge's answer is that Romeo's vaunted love for Rosaline is only a symptom of his state of 'incompleteness', the resolution of which is only found in Juliet – though who is to say whether even Juliet could for long satisfy the spiritual craving which – *pace* Plato – was thus awakened? But love 'leads us, not to sink the mind in the body, but to draw up the body to the mind'.[3] Physical love is only a part, if a necessary part, of a ceaseless process of amelioration and regeneration of the race and of the individual, tending ever away from the physical towards the spiritual. *Romeo and Juliet* portrays the middle stages of this process in the individual, the onset and fulfilment of what Coleridge elsewhere called 'Love to

[1] *Shakespearean Criticism*, ii p. 111.
[2] *Shakespearean Criticism*, ii p. 107 (Lecture VII).   [3] *ib.* p. 108.

some *verschiedene Eine* of our own kind'; they are necessary stages, for without them the spiritual would be debased and eventually sink itself in the physical – the 'lewd Idolatry of Paphian Priestesses'.[1] Woman is not only *phusis*, and the object of physical love, but the symbol of something more; and the precise excellence of Shakespeare's portrayal of woman is that it conveys that most important attribute of womankind, the reconciliation of 'the real and of the ideal,'[2] making woman not only the recipient of sexual homage, but also the symbol of the highest joy that exists, union with the Divine.

It is important to notice how this treatment of sexual love as a symbol of the Divine differs from the strictly Platonic view of love. In Plato, to love is essentially to long for something which one does not possess – quite naturally, since Beauty and Goodness, the higher objects of Eros in Plato's *Symposium*, cannot be conceived of as returning love in any sense. But the essence of a Christian's love of God (as Professor Passmore points out in a lucid comparison between the Platonic and the Augustinian ideas of perfection) is that it *is* reciprocated – indeed it is only because God first loves mankind that men are enabled, by grace, to worship him, and to love other men.[3] The fact that Romeo's love for Juliet is reciprocated, therefore, need not be in any way troublesome as regards Coleridge's wish to see in Romeo a symbol of the human spirit yearning for union with the Divine. On the contrary, the mutual character of their love renders it a more suitable symbol of the interpenetration of human and divine love.

In a continuation of the discussion in the eighth lecture, Coleridge pressed into service the notebook entry of 1803 where he wrote of the beneficial effects of sisterly love.[4] (The theme was a favourite one with Coleridge; it had already made its appearance in *The Friend*.) By the action of various taboos, derived from various sources, children are taught that brothers and sisters do not 'marry': but a sense of difference, of similitude in dissimilitude, has already been awakened through

[1] N 3154.
[2] *Shakespearean Criticism*, ii p. 94 (Lecture vi).
[3] John Passmore, *The Perfectibility of Man*, pp. 79, 96.
[4] N 1637; see above, p. 18.

brother-and-sister affection, purified of any sexual element –
indeed it is exactly this purity which gives it value in Coleridge's
eyes. Here the course of his argument changes somewhat, as he
returns to the theme of 'incompleteness'. If the individual remains alone, he forgoes all share in the excellences which distinguish the opposite sex; he remains incomplete, like one
unsupported half of a great arch.

> The individual has . . . learned the greatest and best lesson of the human
> mind – that in ourselves we are imperfect; and another truth, of the
> next, if not of equal, importance – that there exists a possibility of
> uniting two beings, each identified in their nature, but distinguished in
> their separate qualities, so that each should retain what distinguishes
> them, and at the same time each acquire the qualities of that being
> which is contradistinguished. This is perhaps the most beautiful part
> of our nature.[1]

His fascination with this aspect of relationship – as involving not
loss of self but the mutual strengthening and purification of two
selves – was the inspiration behind the note 'The best, the truly
lovely, in each and all is God.' Its relevance here is that *Romeo
and Juliet* appears to him to be proof that Shakespeare understood, more clearly than any other poet, the process of mutual
'amelioration'. Coleridge praises the 'moral grandeur' and
'philosophical penetration' with which Shakespeare conceived
Romeo and Juliet's relationship; Romeo is an admirable creation precisely because his feelings trace out the path which man's
moral nature always follows in its progress from youthful
susceptibility to permanence of passion.

The two lectures on *Romeo and Juliet* are, therefore, the
meeting-place for an extraordinary variety of Coleridgean
themes, and prove how deeply Coleridge's literary judgments
were involved with his moral thought, and these again with his
personal sufferings. Here the overall preoccupation with the
spiritualization of the race and of the individual meets a personal conviction about the role that 'platonic love' can play in
this high destiny; the favourite analogy between poetry and the
moral order, both of which are distinguished by the reconciliation of passion with order, supports an evaluation of Shakespeare
as the poet *par excellence* of moral and philosophical insight,

---

[1] *Shakespearean Criticism*, ii pp. 117–18 (Lecture VIII).

rivalled only by Milton; and the whole is brought to bear on an interpretation of *Romeo and Juliet* which, beginning with the comparatively minor issue of whether Romeo should have been first shown as in love with Rosaline, makes of him a representative of the human soul in its progression towards the higher kinds of love.

4

'Not what he has done, but what is he?' – so in 1804 Coleridge summed up one vital perception of his concerning our attitudes towards other people. It has already been shown that this approach to problems of relationship (essentially a religious approach, since it meant attempting to judge men as God would judge them, from the 'inside') had an immediate personal application for Coleridge, in his attitude towards Southey; and its importance in a different context, that of the quarrel with Wordsworth in the years 1808–10, is indicated by the persistence of Coleridge's admiration for Wordsworth as a man, even when Wordsworth's actions, and apparent habits of mind, were a source of pain to him.[1] Besides its application to his personal life, however, the idea 'Not what he has done, but what is he?' contributed significantly to the development of his moral thought, and has its place in the moral reflections contained in *The Friend*. In particular, it lay behind that disagreement with Hume's idea that we love or hate a person purely 'in proportion to the pleasure or uneasiness we receive from him',[2] which characterized the moral content of Coleridge's periodical. Coleridge explained what counter-truths he hoped to present in a letter to an admirer of *The Friend*:

I...shall deem myself amply remunerated if in consequence of my exertions a Few only of those, who had formed their moral creed on Hume, Paley, and their Imitators, with or without a belief in the facts of mere historical Christianity, shall have learnt to value actions primarily as the language and natural effect of the state of the agent; if they consider what they *are* instead of *merely* what they *do*; so that the fig-tree may bring forth it's own fruit from it's own living principle,

[1] See above, pp. 41–2; and Notebook 23, fols. 7–9.
[2] *A Treatise of Human Nature*, p. 348 (Book ii, Part ii, section iii).

and not have the figs tied on to it's barren sprays by the hand of outward Prudence and Respect of Character.[1]

It is well worth remarking here that Coleridge has had recourse to an 'organic' metaphor, and, moreover, one that originates in the Sermon on the Mount (Matthew VII, 17–20). The idea he expresses is a manifestation in the realm of morality of that principle of 'organic unity' whose importance in the sphere of Romantic æsthetics has now been so well appreciated.[2] In effect Coleridge pleads for the whole man to be engaged in our relations with others, not just the reasoning faculty, and for our judgment of others to begin with the realization that the act is never a perfect representative of the agent; his argument here is of a piece with his dislike of the mechanistic, analytical view of character, 'as if a human Soul were made up like a Watch', of which he believed Wordsworth was guilty. It is also related to his growing personal preoccupation with Christian doctrine. As he wrote in a notebook entry of autumn 1808, concerning his religious creed, 'not what I understand but what I *am* must save or crush me!'[3] The severe lesson of St James, that to offend in one point of the law is to offend in all, corroborated only too clearly what Coleridge himself had perceived to be the truth.

Yet the monism which Coleridge realized was characteristic of his way of perceiving even trivial things, and which Professor McKenzie has rightly connected with his æsthetic theories,[4] had its dangers when transferred to the sphere of morals. It could lead to

uneasiness at a non-harmony, the wish not to see any thing admirable where you find, especially in the moral character, any thing low or contemptible, and the consequent wish to avoid the struggle within, this anti monadic feeling, this (what shall I say?) *knowing, feeling* a man to be *one*, yet not understanding how to think of him but as two.[5]

The case in point was the troubling inconsistency in the character of Richardson, who despite his 'vile...oozy...hypocritical' mind possessed qualities that Coleridge had to admire. 'Charity'

[1] *Letters*, iii p. 216 (no. 769: 22 June 1809).
[2] G. M. McKenzie, *Organic Unity in Coleridge*, especially pp. 62, 74; and M.H. Abrams, *The Mirror and the Lamp*, chapter VII.
[3] Notebook 13, fol. 228; Notebook 14, fol. 317.
[4] AP, p. 116; McKenzie, p. 62.   [5] N 2471.

and 'Calmness', he felt, were the remedies for this dilemma, 'an heart fixed on the good parts, tho' the *Understanding* is surveying all'; but despite difficulties, the conviction remained that the 'deep intuition of our *oneness*' must contain a positive principle, something 'noble and incentive'.[1]

To see more precisely what it is that Coleridge feels to be 'noble and incentive' in this approach to relationship, we must turn to that passage of *The Friend* in which Coleridge publicly, as it were, develops his idea. As so often with important ideas of Coleridge's, it is brought into a discussion which bears on a quite different (though, Coleridge believes, related) subject, that of 'International Morality'. After a long preamble concerning the importance of intellectual honesty, as against the mere veneration of great names, when judging opinions and arguments, Coleridge declares that 'the Principles of Morality taught in the present Work will be in direct opposition to the System of the late Dr Paley'.[2] Paley's doctrine of general consequences, which makes the sum of the good or bad consequences of a particular action the only criterion of its goodness or badness, is, Coleridge points out, purely ideal;

for it depends on, and must vary with, the notions of the Individual, who in determining the nature of an action is to make the calculation of it's general consequences: and, as in all other calculation, the result depends on that faculty of the Soul in the decrees of which men most vary from each other...But surely Morality, which is of equal importance to all men, ought to be grounded, if possible, in that part of our Nature which in all Men may and ought to be the same: in the Conscience and the common sense.[3]

Paley had attributed to God only that limited means of moral judgment which it is given to men to exercise, the judgment of consequences, the only part of the act which is overt. But the essence of morality lies in the will, in 'the inward motives and impulses'.[4] Paley has taken a man's-eye-view of morality; Coleridge insists that what ultimately matters (morality being, for him, only religion in its practical aspect[5]) is the God's-eye-view.

[1] *ib.* [2] TF, ii p. 313 (no. 23: 8 February 1810).
[3] *ib.*, ii pp. 313–14.
[4] *ib.* p. 314. [5] See below, p. 157.

Our Fellow-creatures can only judge what we *are* by what we *do*; but in the eye of our Maker what we *do* is of no worth, except as it flows from what we *are*. Though the Fig-tree should produce no visible Fruit, yet if the living Sap is in it, and if it has struggled to put forth Buds and Blossoms which have been prevented from maturing by inevitable contingencies of tempests or untimely frosts, the virtuous Sap will be accounted as Fruit.[1]

'Value actions primarily as the language and natural effect of the state of the agent':[2] this is the pith of the argument that is developed in the attack on Paleyism, and the reason for its being 'noble and incentive' in his judgment was that it represented in the human sphere the God's-eye-view by which we are finally to be judged, and against which, therefore, we must measure our own actions – not their consequences, but their motive, whether worthy or unworthy of the faith we profess. The one 'act' that matters in the eyes of God is the act of faith. The doctrine that is at the centre of the Protestant tradition, and whose importance Coleridge defended against the inadequate moral thinking of the eighteenth century, is here shown to have a corollary in the sphere of human relations, the recognition that actions are no more than a 'language', a secondary product of spiritual conditions which are themselves invisible to men.

No one, moreover, need be afraid that such a philosophy would lead to a complete internalization of all impulses towards the Good. Detractors of the doctrine of justification by faith are answered at one stroke; if a man is truly good, then there is no cause to fear that his virtue will remain barren, even though it is not his good works which justify him, but the faith from which they spring.

I can conceive no thing more groundless, than the alarm, that this Doctrine may be prejudicial to outward utility and active well-doing. To suppose that a Man should cease to be *beneficent* by becoming *benevolent*, seems to me scarcely less absurd, than to fear that a fire may prevent heat, or that a perennial fountain may prove the occasion of Drought...Faith is a *total* act of the soul: it is the *whole* state of the mind, or it is not at all! and in this consists its' power, as well as its' exclusive worth...Good Works may exist *without* saving Principles, and therefore *cannot* contain in themselves the Principle of Salvation;

---

[1] TF, ii p. 314.   [2] *Letters*, iii p. 216 (no. 769: 22 June 1809).

but saving Principles never did, never can, exist without good Works.[1]

The 'monadic' view of human nature here achieves its apotheosis in Coleridge's defence of justification by faith, the essential link being that the principle of judging the act only as an imperfect representative of the agent, the principle of 'Not what he has done, but what is he?', is finally meaningful only to a mind that has complete access to 'the inward motives and impulses' – only, therefore, to Deity, though man is permitted the lesser prerogative of judging acts in themselves, as the outward and visible signs of the inward character. 'But that which God sees, *that* alone justifies.'[2]

This concession to human methods of judgment may satisfy some critics of Protestant doctrine, but it does raise one further problem which Coleridge seems to have left unanswered (though it is treated at greater length in another section of *The Friend*).[3] It is the problem raised by Glaucon in the second book of Plato's *Republic*: that of the wholly just man who is judged to be irredeemably wicked, who earns no earthly rewards for his goodness, and who is finally imprisoned and put to death as a malefactor. Coleridge's belief that the true state of affairs would be known to an omniscient Creator, and that such a man would therefore be 'justified' in the sight of God, satisfies Glaucon's original question; but according to Coleridge's scheme the persecution of such a man, if he presents a threat to the state, appears *prima facie* defensible.

5

Matrimony was for Coleridge an important but painful subject. He was not, even in 1796, an adherent of that sect which Burke denounced, and which had called by the name of 'tyranny' what was for Burke the rightful 'guardianship and protection' exercised by the male sex.[4] As it became clearer that his own extremely unwise marriage was not viable, Coleridge realized that for himself, at any rate, there was simply no alternative to a

[1] TF, ii pp. 314–15 (no 23: 8 February 1810).   [2] *ib.*, p. 315.
[3] *ib.* i pp. 70–2 (no. 4: 7 September 1809); ii pp. 56–8.
[4] *Letters on a Regicide Peace*, p. 42.

happy marriage. Whatever might be the general truth about the relative importance of marriage to men and to women, his own character was such that he could not be his true self without it. There was for him no question of the compensations of freedom. A loving marriage was, he wrote in a letter to Southey, his only 'absolute wish', and he believed that had it not been thwarted, his true self, 'the actual part of me' as he expressed it, would have emerged, and might still if there were life after death.[1] Paradoxically, therefore, while his own marriage was undergoing a complete breakdown Coleridge retained a firm belief in the importance of the institution, both for the reason emphasized by Burke, that it was the very foundation of civilized life as understood in the West,[2] and for the more personal reason that it answered the need for growth and fulfilment of the individual mind. The female role was still the subservient one, of course, even when a partnership of minds was the keystone of the relationship. Coleridge wrote to Southey concerning Charles Danvers, a mutual friend, that he had married 'the woman of his choice, of whose mind his own had been the mould and model'.[3] The phrase may evoke thoughts of Arthur Clennam and Little Dorrit: it certainly does not put us in mind of Dorothea and Ladislaw, or of Heathcliff and Catherine. On another aspect of the subject, the indissolubility of the marriage bond, Coleridge's opinion remained outwardly the same, though he defended it in these years with resignation rather than with conviction. In a note of 1810 he quoted Richter's line, 'Ich finde alles eher auf der Erde, so gar Wahrheit und Freude, als Freundschaft' and set out to analyse the reasons for such a sad truth. If friendship, the note continues, makes such impossible demands on human frailty, the 'corollary' of Richter's perception is 'an argument in favor of the existing indissolubility of Marriage – To be compelled to make it up, or consent to be miserable and disrespected, is indeed a coarse plaister for the wounds of Love / but so it must be, while the Patients themselves are of coarse make, and unhealthy Humours. –'[4] As a possible line of attack on the radi-

---

[1] *Letters*, ii p. 1156 (no. 611: 10 November 1804). It is not certain that the letter was to Southey.
[2] *Shakespearean Criticism*, ii p. 107 (Lecture vii).
[3] *Letters*, iii pp. 70 (no. 679: 13 February 1808), 92 (no. 696: 18 April 1808).
[4] Notebook 24, fols. 118–19; and see AP, p. 235.

cals who advocated easier divorce, this is certainly lacking in
assurance; and it lacks even the melancholy strength which distinguished some of his reflections about friendship, and the in-
appropriateness of 'prudence' in such a sphere. Perhaps had the
moral lectures which Coleridge planned in 1812 actually taken
place, especially the first one, on 'the causes of domestic Happiness and Unhappiness', they might have provided a clearer
statement of Coleridge's considered opinions on marriage; but
illness and procrastination took their toll.[1]

On another subject close to Coleridge's heart it is possible to
see much more clearly what his beliefs truly were, chiefly because of an exhaustive discussion which took place between
Coleridge and Wordsworth, apparently in 1810, a few months
before their estrangement. This subject was the nature of
human love. Wordsworth seems to have argued that there was
no such thing as love *per se*, and that what we call 'love' was
merely an amalgam of esteem, friendship and *libido*, made permanent by the force of habit and association.[2] Coleridge of
course could not accept this. His dream experiences in Malta,
and the observation of his feelings towards Sara both in her presence and when she was absent, convinced him that he could and
did love without always feeling sexually attracted as well. There
was also the moral argument, and what we may call the Burkean
argument allied to it, according to which the stability of the
family was the basis of civilization. If man was to progress,
through the centuries, towards a more perfect state of consciousness and still greater moral excellence, according to the
Divine Will, and if the foundation of the great educational
process had been, and was forever to remain, the monogamous
marriage, was it not inconceivable that Providence had wanted
marriage to be based on nothing more permanent than mere
sensual gratification, on the kind of feeling in which man most
resembled the animals, and which often reduced him very nearly
to their level of aspiration? These two arguments, the argument
from a final cause and the argument from personal experience,
both figure in Coleridge's notes on the subject, though we
obviously do not know whether any of what Coleridge wrote was

---

[1] *Letters*, iii p. 366 (no. 852: 10 February 1812).
[2] *Letters*, iii p. 305 (no. 814: 12 March 1811).

actually used in the discussions, or even whether his thoughts were written down before or after he expounded them to Wordsworth.

Reciprocal and Exclusive Love the undoubted Source of Marriage, domestic Charities, [...] of Society, of all that [? serves], softens, ornaments, elevates, disanimalizes, ecelestializes the human Being – and the human Being must surely be deemed the principal tho' not the sole end of this planet, for it is manifest that he is destined to be its sole Inhabitant, by a right of *property* –

Is it then to be believed, is there any one analogy to render it credible, that the wisdom of God would leave so paramount, so wide-grasping an end to mere prudence, as it's source – which prudence can in truth be found or expected only when the domestic Charities have pre-existed – to mere calculations of the bad consequences of polygamy, or promiscuous Lust – If Marriage be as essential to the growth and preservation and progressive perfection of the *Man* as Coition to the propagation of the *Animal* – if for the latter Nature has provided a security in *Lust*, is it to be imagined that she has provided no end, no predisposing and peculiar cause and efficient of the former in our being – Impossible! – Love is as much an element as Lust – tho' it may require, as Reason does, a more general Climate of Circumstances to make it *manifest* as Love – yet even in the wildest it exists till it be destroyed – [1]

Love is not, then, an accidental compound of other features of human nature, but an 'element', and one which is comparable in some respects to Reason itself. The comparison between love and Reason was to be worked out in more detail in the Shakespeare lectures,[2] but even here its implications are quite clear. As Reason exists potentially in all men, indeed is the attribute which confirms them in their humanity, so love is always there, to be drawn up into the light when the 'Climate of Circumstances' permits. In a nation fortunate enough to enjoy political and economic stability, and a high standard of moral education, love between the sexes will be as far removed from lust as Reason is from the animal instinct for survival; both processes of refinement are part of the high destiny of the 'cultivated' nation.

And yet, it could be objected, sensuality does exist by the the side of more 'refined' feelings, and may combine with them,

[1] Notebook 18, fol. 152. (The preceding entry is dated 4 March 1810).
[2] *Shakespearean Criticism*, ii p. 114 (Lecture VIII).

and overwhelm them, even in a man whose Reason is not asleep. Coleridge's answer is really an attack upon the logic of this objection.

If φιλια ανευ παθος μετ' αρρενα και θηλυν be unsuitable to our mixt nature, does it therefore follow that το παθος της επιθυμιας constitutes την ουσιαν του ερωτος? I offer you a cup of cold Sweet-wort instead of fine Ale – and you reject it as insipid – it wants *Yeast* – well! then I offer you a goblet of *Yeast!* – Pooh, it is nauseous, beastly / –/ – and yet a small portion of that yeast combining with and yet concealing itself, among the sweet wort would have made the sparkling human Beverage? I leave to yourself the application.[1]

We may accept – to follow the logical point raised here – that love necessarily includes a leaven of sensuality (human nature being 'mixt'), without sensuality being the essence of love; but it still remains to be shown that love can exist in some form from which sensuality is absent. This is precisely what cannot be shown, of course. Argument becomes pointless; Coleridge can only answer that he has experienced love without desire, and has known what it is to feel all his highest aspirations as a moral and spiritual being centred on one person, in the 'brighten'd Face' of the vision.[2]

To the unquestioning dualist, the seventh commandment can mean nothing other than the subordination of fleshly desires to the conscience, the moral sense, or whatever name is given to the agency of Divine Power that works in the mind of man. Coleridge, in a *rifaciamento* of the Decalogue along Kantian lines which he wrote (probably) in 1808, but which never found its way into publication, endorsed this simple view; but, because he was by no means an unquestioning dualist, and held that human love was not wholly or mainly the expression of sensual desires, he could go further. He translated 'Thou shalt not commit adultery' into

τα της επιθυμιας παθη, negatively, – and positively commands their subordination to Reason, and to the moral sense, and it's allies – Hence it commands *Love*, in it's highest human sense – as superior [. . .]

---

[1] Notebook 18, fols. 173–4. 'Love without desire between man and woman. . .the passion of sexual desire. . .the essence of love'.

[2] N 2495; Notebook 18, fols. 157, 160–1.

generically to Lust, $\epsilon\rho\omega\varsigma$ $\epsilon\pi\iota\theta\upsilon\mu\iota\alpha$, and distinguished *specifically* from $\phi\iota\lambda\iota\alpha$, $\alpha\gamma\alpha\pi\eta$, $\phi\iota\lambda\alpha\nu\theta\rho\omega\pi\iota\alpha$.[1]

There emerges a fifth kind of love, which is not subordinate to Reason and the conscience but coequal with them; and since it is founded in the moral and spiritual being, and indeed implanted there by the wisdom of nature working in accordance with the will of God,[2] it may properly act as an incentive and impulse towards moral and spiritual advancement. This is the love which 'leads us, not to sink the mind in the body, but to draw up the body to the mind', as Coleridge expressed it in the seventh Shakespeare lecture; but it is a love which acts on the race, as well as on the individual, and when Coleridge pressed into use for the 1811 Lectures some of the ideas he had worked out in the discussions with Wordsworth, he did not neglect the social aspect. Man, being 'meant for society', has need of something more than mere lust in order to give permanence to the family unit and, through the family, the nation. Further, the element of love ensures his continual amelioration: 'From this union arise the paternal, filial, brotherly and sisterly relations of life; and every state is but a family magnified. All the operations of mind, in short, all that distinguishes us from brutes, originate in the more perfect state of domestic life.'[3] Love is given to man, as a being of reason, to answer this high moral end; Coleridge has in effect Christianized the Platonic ladder of love-consciousness, the transcendental picture of Eros which is given to Diotima in Plato's *Symposium,* and which may itself originate in a religious ritual, for Diotima's language, according to a modern scholar, contains many elements apparently borrowed from the Eleusinian mysteries.[4]

6

It has been said that Coleridge was not a 'simple dualist', though he believed that man had a 'mixt' nature, and certainly accepted

[1] Notebook 25, fol. 159. 'The passion of sexual desire...physical love...affection, brotherly love, benevolence.'
[2] Notebook 18, fol. 193.
[3] *Shakespearean Criticism,* ii pp. 108 (Lecture VII), 114 (Lecture VIII), 107 (Lecture VII).
[4] See F. M. Cornford, *Principium Sapientiæ,* p. 86.

the Christian view that the body's desires must be made sub-ordinate to conscience and the moral will. To understand fully Coleridge's idea of relationship, however, we must recognize that this is at best an unsatisfactory summary of his beliefs, and turn to another series of notes, written some years before the discussion with Wordsworth on the relationship between love and lust, but which bear tangentially on that discussion. Their subject is a difficult one: the limitations of the view that morality is a matter of the mind holding the body in subjection, and the necessity of striving for that perfectly integrated state in which duty is done, not from a sense of obligation, but from the sheer pleasure of doing it; or in other words the conversion of the individual, self-seeking will to what philosophers generally know as the 'holy will'.[1] This exalted aim is summarized in two strik-ing phrases which Coleridge wrote down while still at Malta (in January 1806), though the immediate reference was perhaps to the Eucharist, the 'body' being the body of Christ: '$\Sigma\omega\mu\alpha$ $\psi\upsilon\chi o\pi\lambda\alpha\sigma\tau o\nu$ $\Psi\upsilon\chi\eta$ $\sigma\omega\mu\alpha\pi\lambda\alpha\tau\tau o\upsilon\sigma\alpha.$'[2] Long before the discussion with Wordsworth, Coleridge held the view that, through the powers which had been given to him, particularly through the power of human love, man could make himself, not worthy, certainly, but less unworthy of God's love. It was with a version of this (virtually Pelagian) idea that Coleridge began the 1811 Shakespeare lectures, and it also formed the basis of those exhortations towards self-amelioration and true Principles which characterized the pages of *The Friend*. Coleridge re-peatedly made it clear in *The Friend* that he took issue both with Hobbes's pessimistic view of human nature, and with Shaftes-bury's 'pious Deism', which, though a noble conception, appeared to him to be founded on the delusion that man's will was not corrupt.[3] Coleridge held that man was indeed a fallen creature, but not irredeemable; and he consistently rejected the belief that human nature must ever consist of a lawless, naturally vicious fleshly part, 'the concupiscent, vindictive, and *narcissine* part of our nature', and a godly spiritual part, 'the pure will and ever benevolent *Reason*'. Such a belief was too negative, in Coleridge's

[1] See S. Körner, *Kant*, p. 136, and F. M. Cornford, *Principium Sapientiæ*, p. 72.
[2] N 2784. 'Body that fashions the soul: soul that shapes the body.'
[3] TF, ii p. 7 (no 1: 1 June 1809); and p. 279 (unnumbered: 11 January 1810).

eyes; it led to 'Despair and spiritual Sloth'.[1] Human nature was not meant to be a battlefield, on which eternally incompatible forces perpetually struggled for supremacy. Coleridge's idea of the moral will was far subtler; it was meant to unify human nature, to make every action of mind and body actively virtuous, drawing up the body into the spirit, not mortifying the body so that the spirit might be free. He rejected an 'absolute detachment from the flesh';[2] those who denied that any human desires which expressed themselves through the body could be actively virtuous were as wrong as those who completely denied the existence of any spiritual element in man.

I trust that if I have virtue enough to live, that I shall instruct the good to put the feelings of their own Souls into ~~their~~ a language, that shall kindle those feelings into tenfold heat and blaze – so that finally whatever is really and truly a part of our existing Nature, a universally existing part, may become an object of our love, and admiration.[3]

Where the old moral theology, distrusting all manifestations of sexual love even within wedlock, had insisted 'omnis ardentior amator propriæ uxoris adulter est', Coleridge declared that there was active virtue in the caresses of a husband just as in his abstention from adultery. This follows naturally, indeed, from the premise that human nature is, or in its more perfect state can become, a single entity; but this ideal was difficult, if not impossible, to achieve, and more difficult for Coleridge than for most other men. His own body he felt to be more of a burden to him than was just – with a revulsion that recalls Baudelaire's spasms of self-disgust he called it 'a crazy tenement . . . a ruinous Hovel', and his actions were forced upon it by the will, not by that 'spirit of Life that makes Soul and Body one'.[4] His intellect was convinced of the truth of the contrary doctrine, but there was still an aridity at heart which made him write (in the same month of his residence in Malta, April 1805) 'Let us do our *Duty*: all else is a Dream, Life and Death alike a Dream.'[5] Coleridge was, in truth, just as much aware as Blake that a morality which took Duty for the sake of Duty as its highest aim

---

[1] N 2495.
[2] From a margin note on *Tom Jones*: *Miscellaneous Criticism*, p. 304.
[3] N 2495.   [4] N 2557.   [5] N 2537.

was false to the potential nobility of human nature. Kant had argued that the worth of any action depended purely on whether or not it had been performed because it was a duty. If the agent actually had an inclination towards a certain act that was also his duty, this detracted from its moral worth, for the morally worthy act is one that is performed purely from a sense of duty, and for no other reason.[1] In a complicated notebook entry of April 1805, Coleridge set out what is, in one aspect, a confutation of this view.[2] He began with the observation which Blake enshrined in one of his 'Poems of Experience', that entitled 'My Pretty Rose Tree'. Coleridge stated the problem in this way:

Let the Lover ask his Heart whether he can endure that his Mistress should have *struggled* with a sensual impulse for another man, tho' she overcame it from a sense of Duty to him?...Love in short requires an absolute Peace and Harmony between all parts of human Nature, such as it is; and it is offended by any War, tho' the Battle should be decided in favor of the worthier. This is perhaps the final cause of the *rarity* of true Love, and the efficient and immediate cause of its Difficulty.[3]

Then, in a remarkable new turn of thought, Coleridge placed the whole question in an entirely different perspective. As in a relationship the concept of Duty is an unwelcome one, a discordant element, so in the life of the spirit Duty appears simply as part of the ladder by which the imperfect and disunited nature was enabled to ascend to a higher state of perfection. Kant's moral imperatives are seen as a pitiful human expedient, but a necessary one, given the unsuitability of unregenerate man to the pure life of the Spirit. Innocence, in the life of the spirit as in human love, is only to be attained when duty and inclination are one and the same.

Ours is a life of Probation / we are to contemplate and obey *Duty* for its own sake, and in order to do this we – in our present imperfect state of Being – must see it not merely abstracted from, but in direct opposition

---

[1] *Fundamental Principles of the Metaphysic of Morals*, in *Critique of Practical Reason*, translated by T. K. Abbott, pp. 14–15.

[2] Coleridge would almost certainly have had Kant in mind. K. Coburn and G. N. G. Orsini find the evidence for Coleridge's having read extensively in Kant by 1805 is conclusive: see N 1517n, 2151n, 2316n, and Orsini, *Coleridge and German Idealism*, p. 49.

[3] N 2556.

to the *Wish,* the *Inclination* / having perfected this the highest ~~part~~ possibility of human nature, he may then with safety harmonize *all* his Being with this – he may love. To perform Duties absolutely from the sense of Duty is the *Ideal,* which perhaps no human Being ever can arrive at, but which every human Being ought to try to draw near unto – This is – in the only wise, and verily, in a most sublime sense – to see God face to face / which alas! it seems too true that no man can do and *live,* i.e. a *human* life.[1]

This ideal re-creation of the self is the essence of religion for Coleridge – he points out, indeed, that the root meaning of the very word 'religion' is 'a binding-again' – and it must be carefully distinguished from the concept of 'enlightened self-interest' around which Paley and other moralists had built their schemes. They 'annihilated the Idea of Virtue by placing its essence in Selfishness'[2] – inevitably, for they based their ethic on a system of reward and punishment, which clearly appealed to the intrinsically selfish in man, and commended good actions to him not because they were good, but because they would be to his own advantage in the long run. Coleridge attacked the very principle of making Christianity into a 'code of ethics', and emphasized that it was not concerned with intellect, except as a means, but with the regeneration of the will.[3]

The WORD of God did not exclusively bid men avoid the *wrath* to come – *He* likewise said – Be ye *perfect,* even as your Father in Heaven is perfect. And we are assured, that unless that *Fear,* which is the *Beginning* of Wisdom, shall proceed to LOVE, there can be no Union with God: for God is Love. To the *Diseased* Christ says, Love yourselves so as to leave your *Vices;* but to the *Convalescent,* Love your Neighbour as yourselves; and God *above all.*[4]

As in many of the writings of Søren Kierkegaard, the emphasis here is on the spiritual state of the individual person, rather than on any aspect of his conduct, and on the individual person in his relationship, through Christ, with God. Like Kierkegaard Coleridge held that the ideal offered to us as the goal of religious faith was 'singleness of heart', the complete expulsion of all contradiction from the consciousness.[5] The awakening of a sense

---

[1] N 2556.　　[2] *Letters,* iii p. 153 (no. 734: 30 December 1808?).
[3] Notebook 18, fol. 198.　　[4] *Letters,* iii p. 153.
[5] TF, ii p. 56 (no. 4: 4 September 1809).

of contradiction and 'disharmony' in our nature, and of the in-
appropriateness of human feelings to their first objects – whether
this awareness arose from remorse, grief, love, or any other kind
of suffering – was the first stage in the long search for an abiding law, which ends only with the discovery that freedom, hope
and the final reconciliation of warring impulses can be enjoyed
only under the law of God.[1] Wordsworth's famous lines,

> The Child is father of the Man;
> And I could wish my days to be
> Bound each to each by natural piety[2]

were to Coleridge a poetic statement of this truth. Why can we
not enjoy in the life of the mind and the moral sense that continuity which sustains our bodily life?

If men laugh at the falsehoods that were imposed on themselves
during their childhood, it is because they are not good and wise enough
to contemplate the past in the present, and so to produce by a virtuous
and thoughtful sensibility that continuity in their self-consciousness,
which Nature has made the law of their animal Life.[3]

Clearly it is true that, as Dr Beer has put it, religion 'meant,
among other things, stability' for Coleridge,[4] not because it
offered a prescriptive code in which each of our duties could be
read off against some kind of reward – what Coleridge scornfully called the 'auditing' of our duties – but because it made us
conscious of our selves as permanent beings.[5] Kierkegaard put
it in this way: 'Each one who in truth would will one thing must
be led to will the Good.' Unlike Kierkegaard, however – and
the distinction is vital – Coleridge believed that the man of faith
desires the Good, not as an individual solely, but as a member of
the whole race of men. In Kierkegaard's view, the New Testament was a demand 'to dare as a single person to have to do with
God':[6] Coleridge by contrast emphasizes the Pauline concept of
the Christian people as a community. 'What I hope for myself'.

---

[1] *ib.* p. 7 (no. 1: 1 June 1809).   [2] *Poetical Works*, p. 62.
[3] TF, i p. 40 (no. 3: 10 August 1809; ii p. 41).
[4] *Coleridge the Visionary*, p. 17.
[5] *Letters*, iii p. 485 (no. 922: April 1814).
[6] S. Kierkegaard, *Purity of Heart*, translated by Douglas Steere, p. 58; and *The
Last Years: Journals 1853–1855*, translated by R. Gregor Smith, p. 101.

he writes, 'I hope for all men – I cannot hope Heaven for myself as myself, but for all good men in the number of which *I* may be included.'[1] The 'religation', the reconciliation of his will with duty under the new law of conscience which the man of faith strives for is not, in Coleridge's eyes, a rejection of his humanity, or a severing of the ties which bind him to other men, but the very reverse – the realization of his humanity. 'Without God Man ceases to be Man, and either soars into a Devil or sinks into a Beast.'[2] For Coleridge, such an idea involved the hope that the whole of mankind, and not just oneself as an individual, would progress towards true humanity. Indeed, as has been shown, this hope, in the form of a particular Christian view of history, was hinted at in the Shakespeare lectures,[3] and it reached its fullest expression in the additional material written for the 1818 edition of *The Friend*.

In both these works, however, Coleridge left undeveloped one important question central to the Christian hope as he expressed it, and this question figures in the notebook passages of 1808 and 1810 which we have been discussing. Paley's morality had given to God the attributes of a judge, dispensing reward and punishment according to the merits of the individual. Just as Coleridge's idea of morality was different from Paley's, so was his idea of the relationship that should exist between God and man. In the letter to Sir George Beaumont which has already been quoted here[4] Coleridge said 'Unless that *Fear*, which is the Beginning of Wisdom, shall proceed to LOVE, there shall be no union with God: for God is Love.' Fear and Love were the two poles of man's relationship to God; but was it possible to assert 'God is Love' if man first came to know God through fear? An attempt to resolve this difficulty is made in a note of 1810 (which appears to be a sketch for an essay, perhaps for an issue of *The Friend*.) Fear *is* Love – Love 'in its first specific Involucrum or state – Love in the Chrysalis'.[5] As morality, in the first instance, presented itself in the form of Duty, of a command as it were *ab extra* which is against our inclination, but in its per-

[1] *Letters*, iii p. 154 (no. 734: 30 December 1808?).
[2] Notebook 18, fol. 168.
[3] *Shakespearean Criticism*, ii, (Lectures I, VII, VIII).
[4] See above, p. 114.   [5] Notebook 18, fol. 167.

fected state is the complete unification of Duty with the moral will, so while man is in a state of guilt and bondage God can only be feared; and he is known as love only when man enjoys the true freedom of obedience to the law of universal Reason.[1]

In the coming-to-consciousness of ourselves 'as permanent beings', however, all forms of love play a part. Much private thought about the nature of consciousness, as well as first-hand experience of the apparent psychological effects of deep love for another person, lay behind Coleridge's use of the Platonic ladder of love-consciousness in the seventh Shakespeare lecture. In the long letter to Clarkson, written in October 1806, in which he set out the principles of his religious creed, Coleridge explained that he believed the soul of man belonged to a class of being 'who tho' not conscious of the whole of their continuousness, are yet both conscious of *a* continuousness, and make that the object of a reflex consciousness'.[2] The idea of reflex consciousness as such, and of the apperception of the permanent substantial self by this means, was undoubtedly introduced to Coleridge by one or other of Kant's followers, as W. Schrickx shows. Platner, for instance, asserts,

so wie ich die Theile jeder einzelnen Vorstellung auf mich beziehe, indem ich fühle, dasz ich dasselbige Subjekt bin, welches die letztern und welches die erstern in sich hatte, so bin ich mir bewuszt, dasz ich dasselbige Subjekt bin, welches die gegenwärtigen, und die vergangenen Vorstellungen meines Lebens hatte.[3]

In the transcendental idealism of Schelling, self-consciousness, or 'das Akt des Sich-denkens', is made the condition of the very existence of the 'Ich'; for Schelling, the 'Ich' can be said to exist only as long as it is thought, and is therefore dependent upon an act, that of self-consciousness. Since such knowledge transcends the subject–object relation, it becomes (in the *System des transcendentalen Idealismus*) the very starting-point of all knowledge – an argument which it will be necessary to follow in greater detail

[1] See Notebook 18, fol. 168

[2] *Letters*, ii p. 1197 (no. 634: 13 October 1806).

[3] W. Schrickx, 'Coleridge and F. H. Jacobi', *Revue Belge de Philologie et d'Histoire*, vol. xxxvi no. 3 (1958), (812–29) pp. 824–5. 'As I see the parts of every separate conception in me while I perceive that I am the same Subject which had in it the last and the first, so am I known to myself, in that I am the same Subject which has the present and the passing conceptions of my life.'

in a later chapter. For the moment it is important to remark only that Coleridge had learned from Kant's followers, from Schelling or from Platner, of the significance of 'reflex consciousness', and that he was sceptical of the possibility that the mind could spontaneously acquire this knowledge, without, that is, the influence of other minds upon it. Coleridge is not so much challenging the philosophical basis of 'reflex consciousness' as taking the argument out of the theoretical sphere and into the practical, as is apparent in a letter of 1806:

This state and growth of reflex consciousness...is not conceivable without the action of kindred souls on each other, i.e. the modification of each by each, and of each by the Whole. A male and female Tyger is neither more or less whether you suppose them only existing in their appropriate wilderness, or whether you suppose a thousand Pairs. But Man is truly altered by the co-existence of other men; his faculties cannot be developed in himself alone, and only by himself. Therefore the human race not by a bold metaphor, but in a sublime reality, approach to, and might become, one body whose Head is Christ (the Logos).[1]

With delight Coleridge traced the ramifications of this belief; it amounted to a revitalization of the theory expounded by Shaftesbury that no man could declare himself spiritually unique, for all were united by their participation in a universal Soul. It also provided a philosophical underpinning to Coleridge's emerging belief in human society as itself the great practical agent of human perfectibility, a belief probably encouraged by Joseph Priestley's affirmation (in his *Essay on the First Principles of Government*) that society, and consequently government, were the instruments chosen by Divine Providence for the perfection of man.[2] Indeed, in following up the 'tyger' comparison in Notebook $3\frac{1}{2}$, Coleridge expanded the scope of the comparison from the initial significance of the 'I–Thou' relationship, to encompass the incalculably great forces which are brought to bear on the individual mind and personality by the nation – the 'larger Hedge-girdle of the State'.[3] Can the individual self be conceived

[1] *Letters*, ii p. 1197 (no. 634: 13 October 1806).
[2] Second edition (London 1771), p. 1. Quoted by John Passmore, *The Perfectibility of Man* pp .173–4.
[3] Quoted by D. P. Calleo, *Coleridge and the Idea of the Modern State*, p. 82. Calleo's chapter 5, 'The Psychological Basis of the State', deals more fully with this subject.

at all, without the surrounding influences, not only of the primary 'I–Thou' relationships, but of the institutions which make up the State within which he is a citizen? A self *without* these influences is merely an abstraction, and in this sense the 'Homo Phænomenon' is more of a reality than the 'Homo Noumenon'.

Undoubtedly this early realization of the insubstantiality of some German conceptions of 'reflex consciousness' helped Coleridge, in his later political writings, to remember that national institutions have to be psychological realities, so to speak, before they can be effective, and that they are important precisely because they mould and to a large extent furnish the intellects of individuals.

An instructive contrast can be drawn here between Coleridge's estimate of the importance of relationship and Hazlitt's. In his *Principles of Human Action* (published in 1805), Hazlitt argued that self-love was not necessarily the dominant principle of human conduct, for the mind is influenced most by that of which it has the most vivid idea. If this is the self, then the individual concerned will act selfishly; but if, through the imagination, he acquires a vivid idea of the 'identity' of another person, he will be capable of sympathy.[1]

It will be seen that this theory, though bringing together two of the most important strains in Romantic thought, emotion or sympathy, and the power of 'imagination', is weak by comparison with Coleridge's; for Coleridge sees that the crux of the matter is not so much the presence or absence of an idea of someone else's identity in the individual's mind, however caused, but the nature of the individual's self-consciousness.

This was an aspect of the subject which evidently meant much to Coleridge personally; he had himself known the intensifying effect which love for another person could have on perception, understanding, on all the operations of the mind, and he was sure that there was a link between love in the individual, and that individual's attainment of self-consciousness, consciousness, that is, of the *permanent* self, not the self which appears in arbitrary and fleeting thoughts and judgments. These things create a 'phænomenon' of self which is no more than the shadow of the real, substantial self – this can only be known through a

[1] See W. J. Bate, *From Classic to Romantic*, pp. 176–7.

relationship with what is outside one, and the desire for this knowledge is love; love is 'Being seeking to be self-conscious'. (The passage is hard to follow, but the chief obstacle is simply the absence of punctuation).

All our Thoughts all that we abstract from our consciousness and so form the Phænomenon Self is a Shadow, its whole Substance is the dim yet powerful sense that it is but a Shadow, and ought to belong to a Substance / but this Substance can have no marks, no discriminating Characters, no hic est, ille non est / it is simply Substance – and this deepliest felt during particular phænomena with a consciousness that the phænomenon is in us but *it* not in the phænomenon, for which alone we yet value the phænomenon, constitutes the craving of True Love. Love a sense of Substance / Being seeking to be self-conscious, 1. of itself in a Symbol. 2. of the Symbol as not being itself. 3. of the Symbol as being nothing but in relation to itself – and necessitating a return to the first state, Scientia absoluta.[1]

Coleridge seems to have perceived, through the inadequacies of the terminology available to him, a possible way of answering the deepest philosophical question of them all, 'How can I be certain that I exist?' How, that is, can I penetrate the shifting phenomena of mind, my thoughts, volitions and so on, and apprehend the permanent substance of my self underneath – if such a substance does in truth exist at all? A theory of Jacobi's, that 'Personality depends on Recollection and Reflection', that is, on the mind's observation of its own representations, did not satisfy Coleridge's inquiring spirit; he commented on the assertion of Jacobi, that 'das Daseyn eines jeden endlichen Wesens ist ein successives Daseyn: seine Personalität beruht auf Gedächtnisz und Reflexion; seine eingeschränkte aber deutliche Erkenntnisz auf Begriffen, folglich auf Abstraction, und Wort-Schrift- oder andern Zeichen' as follows: ''Tis a strange assertion, that the Essence of Identity lies in recollective Consciousness – 'twere scarcely less ridiculous to affirm, that the 8 miles from Stowey to Bridgewater consist in the 8 mile stones.'[2] It was then Coleridge's view that absolute knowledge, 'scientia

[1] N 3026.
[2] W. Schrickx, 'Coleridge and F. H. Jacobi', pp. 822–3. 'The existence of any finite being is a successive existence: its Personality depends on Recollection and Reflection; its narrow but clear Understanding on Perception, therefore on Abstraction, and on spoken, written or other signs.'

absoluta', is only possible when Being encounters something that is not itself. The other is known, not internally of course, but through a symbol; and Coleridge is here interested, not in the intrinsic meaning of the symbol as such, but in its relation to that which perceives it. Indeed the truth here expressed is that the symbol has no *intrinsic* meaning. It acquires meaning, it exists as a symbol, only when it is part of the process of knowing : and it is only this process – strictly, only in that 'first state' where Being is 'conscious...of itself in a Symbol' – that the substance of the self is apprehended.

Professor McFarland, apropos of Coleridge's argument for personëity of God, the eternal I AM, has made good use of a passage from Coleridge's 'Essay on Faith' in which the problem of self-consciousness is raised.[1] The roots of the 'Essay on Faith' go back further, however, than Professor McFarland has indicated; I believe that a full analysis of Coleridge's thinking concerning self-consciousness must begin with the October1806 letter to Clarkson.[2] It is probably true, as Professor McFarland suggests, that Coleridge found in Jacobi's 'ohne Du, ist das Ich unmöglich' ('without a Thou, the I is impossible'), as well as in St John's Epistles and the writings of the Early Fathers, clarification and corroboration of his ideas on the subject; but these ideas, particularly in the form of 'his own reflection on the needs of his own nature' as McFarland calls it,[3] reached a much higher state of development before the writing of the 'Essay on Faith' (in 1825) than is apparent from Professor McFarland's presentation of them. In particular, Coleridge did not need the Kantian theory of 'apperception', to judge by the notes of these years, in quite the way that McFarland suggests.[4]

7

In no way did Coleridge's fuller understanding of the inter-human, and the delight which he evidently felt at the 'harmony'

---

[1] *Coleridge and the Pantheist Tradition*, pp. 236–42.
[2] Quoted, in part, above, p. 118.
[3] *Coleridge and the Pantheist Tradition*, p. 238; see p. 378.
[4] The 'Essay on Faith' and other relevant writings of the later period are discussed in chapter III below.

he was discovering,[1] make it easier to face the isolation which now seemed to be inescapable, an isolation only confirmed, hardly begun, by the quarrel with Wordsworth in the autumn of 1810. De Quincey's memorable description of Coleridge in these years – 'he burrowed continually deeper into scholastic subtleties and metaphysical abstraction; and...lived chiefly by candlelight'[2] – corresponds well with the picture that emerges from the notebooks, Coleridge's 'sole Confidants'.[3] In one respect, Coleridge's unhappiness is less of a mystery to us than it was to De Quincey, for Coleridge's 'confidants' reveal that opium was only one strand in the web which entrapped him, and that it was something even more addictive than opium which 'poisoned all natural pleasure at its source'. By the year 1808, the year to which De Quincey's description especially applies, Coleridge had come to feel, not only that his nature demanded external support and 'completion', but that his need, 'this innermost and holiest Instinct', had indeed 'discovered its' Object, as by a flash of lightning, or the Strike of a Horse's Shoe, on a Flint, in utter darkness – '.[4] Nothing is said in these years which corresponds to his earlier declaration, 'I am far too contented with Solitude';[5] solitary meditation, as it became more and more his necessary mode of existence, lost the romantic attraction of that 'Crowding of Thoughts'[6] which enlivened his earlier studies, and came to resemble a kind of voluntary self-incarceration, a way of mortifying the spirit in the hope that it would cease to be troubled by the call of the temporal, and attach itself more purely to the eternal. It would be misleading to suggest that Coleridge 'turned to' religion, in the common phrase, for, as has been shown, he saw all the self-questionings of the human mind, however prompted, as the manifestations of an essentially religious impulse; and he was still very far, in his own terms, from a religious solution, since the contradiction and disharmony suffered by all but the most dedicated of men continued to torment him. As he understood too well, the knowledge that a clear duty lay ahead of him only served to increase the torment, by recalling him to a consciousness of what he lacked.

[1] N3231.   [2] *Reminiscences of the English Lake Poets*, p. 54.
[3] Notebook 21½, fol. 220.   [4] Notebook 23, fol. 3.
[5] *Letters*, ii p. 1021 (no. 529: 5 December 1803).   [6] *ib.*

The very Duty must for ever keep alive feelings, the appropriate Objects of which are indeed in another world; but yet our human nature cannot avoid at times the connection of these feelings with their *original*, their first, the mistaking forms and objects – and so far therefore from removing the scar, will often and often make the wound open and bleed afresh / – but still we know that the feeling is not *objectless* – that the counterfeit has a corresponding *Genuine* – and this is the comfort. – 1808.[1]

It was clear to Coleridge that his feelings would give him no peace until they could all find their completion in the love of God. This he understood very well, and indeed it is a recurring theme in *The Friend* that our passions are disproportionate to their earthly objects, and that they must be redirected by the man of faith towards their eternal objects. Coleridge also knew, however, that to understand was not enough. 'Not what I understand but what I *am* must save or crush me.'[2] Moreover, that very self-consciousness which made it possible for Coleridge to give powerful expression to his convictions in *The Friend* and the Shakespeare lectures also made it doubly difficult for him to pray. Opium, or rather the self-disgust which his addiction to opium brought upon him, was one obstacle, draining him of the power to do what he now felt was, literally, vital to him;[3] but an equally serious obstacle was his self-knowledge. Coleridge knew that the unsleeping mind, 'consciousness /With the fierce thirst of death – and still unslaked'[4] in Byron's words, was the most terrible of all punishments. Self-doubting, preying on its own failures, 'whirled about without a center',[5] Coleridge's mind enjoyed none of the peace which Wordsworth looked for at the end of *The Prelude*. Wordsworth's belief that

> the mind of man becomes
> A thousand times more beautiful than the earth
> On which he dwells, above this Frame of things
> . . . In beauty exalted, as it is itself
> Of substance and of fabric more divine[6]

could not be an antidote for the spiritual sickness that plagued

[1] Notebook 25, fol. 163.   [2] Notebook 13, fol. 228.   [3] Notebook 13, fol. 227.
[4] *Manfred*, Act II, scene 1: *Poetical Works*, p. 395.
[5] Notebook 13, fols. 228–9; and Notebook 14, fol. 322 (dated 29 October 1810).
[6] Book XIII, lines 446–52 (1805 version).

Coleridge. He had learned that the mind of man is not, in itself, divine, but must become like God in order to behold him, as the eye is formed like the sun in order that it may perceive the sun. This is the real purpose of contemplation. In the words of the Platonist John Smith, the man of faith 'endeavours the nearest Union with the Divine Essence that may be, κέντρον κεντρῳ συνάψας, as Plotinus speaks, knitting his own centre, if he have any, unto the centre of the Divine Being'.[1] Though, therefore, he had followed what he believed to be the necessary path, from Unitarianism through Spinoza to Plato, St John and Trinitarianism, had won illumination in the understanding of 'intellectual or spiritual Christianity', and was to all outward appearances a believer, he still lacked that knowledge of the permanent being, the *forma efformans*, which was vital to the regeneration of the will, and the only part of him that could have meaning or value *sub specie æternitatis*.[2]

[1] N 2167 n.   [2] N 2444–8, N 2550.

III

1814–1834

According to the Platonic philosophy, *ens* and *unum* are the same. And consequently our minds participate so far of existence as they do of unity. But it should seem that personality is the indivisible centre of the soul or mind, which is a monad so far forth as she is a person. There-fore person is really that which exists, inasmuch as it participates of the divine unity...It seemeth that the mind, so far forth as person, is individual,...therein resembling the divine One by participation, and imparting to other things what itself participates from above.

George Berkeley*

'I am not a God afar off, I am a brother and friend;
Within your bosoms I reside, and you reside in me:
Lo! we are One, forgiving all Evil, Not seeking recompense:
Ye are my members, O ye sleepers of Beulah, land of shades!'

But the perturbed Man away turns down the valleys dark:

'Phantom of the over heated brain! shadow of immortality!
Seeking to keep my soul a victim to thy Love! which binds
Man, the enemy of man, into deceitful friendships,
Jerusalem is not! her daughters are indefinite:
By demonstration man alone can live, and not by faith.'

William Blake†

1

'It was the will of Providence', Coleridge wrote in one of the notebooks which he designated 'Fly-catchers, for impounding stray thoughts', 'that I should pursue my pilgrimage *alone*.'[1] In some ways he was far from being alone during the last quarter of his life: in April 1816 he took up residence at the house of

---

* *Siris*, paragraphs 346, 356; *Works*, edited by A. A. Luce and T. E. Jessop, vol. v, pp. 156, 160.
† *Jerusalem*, chapter i; *Poems and Prophecies*, edited by Max Plowman, p. 164.
[1] Notebook 36, fol. 217.

James Gillman in Highgate, and from then until his death was never for long away from the watchful eyes of Gillman or of Gillman's wife. It is apparent from the letter he wrote to Gillman shortly before joining his household that one of the chief reasons why he craved company was that it helped to alleviate the physical pain he suffered.[1] But when well, Coleridge appeared younger than his years, as Leigh Hunt records: 'a good-natured wizard, very fond of earth, and conscious of reposing with weight enough in his easy chair, but able to conjure his etherealities about him in the twinkling of an eye'.[2] In 1824 began the famous 'Noctes Atticæ', though as early as 1820 Coleridge seems to have gathered his friends about him occasionally for what he facetiously called, not *conversazioni*, but '*One*versazioni'.[3] A continuous procession of admirers and disciples provided him with some form of intellectual companionship – chiefly J. H. Green and Thomas Allsop, but there were many others: Charles Aders, John Anster, William Worship, Giovanni de' Prati, Emmanuel Hurwitz, Alaric Watts. His unfulfilled hopes included that of founding a 'Teutonic Club' in London, with a German library which would be open to subscribers on the plan of the Bristol Library.[4] He won public recognition, of a kind, when in 1825 he was elected Honorary Associate of the Royal Society of Literature, with emoluments of £100 a year – though this source of income disappeared when William IV came to the throne. With the help and collaboration of J. H. Green he completed, not, certainly, the *Opus Maximum* he had hoped to write, but a manuscript on Logic which remains of immense value and interest: and there must have been many who felt at his death as Hazlitt did, when he wrote 'He is the only person from whom I ever learnt anything', or, as Charles Lamb expressed it, 'I cannot think a thought, I cannot make a criticism on men or books, without an ineffectual turning and reference to him. He was the proof and touchstone of all my cogitations...Great in his writings, he was greatest in his conversation.'[5] All this is well known: it is the accepted picture of

---

[1] Lucy E. Watson, *Coleridge at Highgate*, p. 25.
[2] R. C. Bald, editor, *Literary Friendships in the Age of Wordsworth*, p. 199.
[3] *Letters*, vi p. 790 (no. 1660: 5 May 1829).
[4] *ib.* pp. 543–4 (no. 1512: 20 January 1826).
[5] *Literary Friendships in the Age of Wordsworth*, pp. 161, 273.

Coleridge as he was in later life. In the notebooks and some of the letters, however, we learn about a different side of his life, his inner loneliness and the sense of emotional desiccation which is expressed in some unpublished 'extempore' lines.

> Idly we supplicate the Powers above!
> There is no Resurrection for a Love
> That unperturb'd, unshadowed, wanes away
> In the chill'd heart by inward Self-decay.
> Poor Mimic of the Past! the Love is o'er,
> That must *resolve* to do what did itself of yore.[1]

It is not clear to which 'love' these lines refer – if to any. In 1824 such a reflection could refer to all Coleridge's past friendships collectively, including that with Wordsworth; for Coleridge still lacked a companion who besides being his intellectual equal could provide the 'heart-nursing Sympathy'[2] that he so much desired. He was even to some degree estranged from his children; it was through one of them, Hartley, that a fourth sorrow was added in 1820 to the three he had already suffered, the unhappiness of his marriage, his estrangement from Sara Hutchinson, and his quarrel with Wordsworth. Hartley Coleridge, after a probationary year as a Fellow-elect at Oriel College, Oxford, was refused a permanent Fellowship, and among the charges named against him was that of intemperance.[3] Something of the pain that this incident caused to Coleridge is perhaps present in the item of Table Talk that appears under the date 2 January 1833: 'Can anything be more dreadful than the thought that an innocent child has inherited from you a disease or a weakness, the penalty in yourself of sin or want of caution?'[4] But besides these major sorrows there were lesser ones that still plagued Coleridge: the outside world, he told de' Prati, knew of the 'well-off man', but not of 'the sick, anxious, embarrassed Man...preserved from actual privations only by obligations to Friends'.[5] Coleridge felt himself to be under obligations to many friends – particularly, of course, to the Gillmans – which nothing he could conceivably do would ever

---

[1] Notebook 28, fol. 327 (dated 24 April 1824: above these lines C has written 'n.b. composed extempore').
[2] 'Ode: Dejection', edited by E. de Selincourt, *Essays and Studies* vol. xxii (1937) (7–25), p. 23.   [3] See *Letters*, v pp. 57–78.   [4] *Table Talk*, p. 174.
[5] *Letters*, vi p. 767 (no. 1643: 14 October 1828).

repay; and this was a flaw in the closest of his friendships. Further, he never entirely lost the sense of disappointment in his male friends which had come upon him most strongly after his separation from Wordsworth; and though he admired many women, from Charlotte Brent to Mrs Charles Aders, there was never a replacement for 'Asra'. His chief comfort was his religious faith. On Christmas Day 1827, he received the Eucharist for the first time since his undergraduate days.[1] This was not a sudden decision, but the result of a long process of thought and feeling, which produced not only a changed attitude towards prayer, but also a serious attempt to find a credible and satisfying approach to the Scriptures, and to religious faith in general – one result of which was his *Confessions of an Inquiring Spirit* and his 'Essay on Faith', both of 1825. That there was a connection between Coleridge's disappointment in friendship and his development in religious faith is suggested by a letter of 1818 – 'To feel the full force of the Christian religion, it is perhaps necessary, for many tempers, that they should first be made to feel, experimentally, the hollowness of human friendship, the presumptuous emptiness of human hopes.'[2] Like many another parent before him and since, Coleridge hoped that the mistakes of the father would be redeemed by the rectitude of the children. One of his major anxieties was therefore the reports he heard that Derwent, while an undergraduate at St John's College, Cambridge, had professed scepticism on many religious questions; and further, that he hoped to earn a living after coming down from the university by writing for journals in London. This plan was to Coleridge almost as pernicious as Derwent's atheism. He was far more concerned that his son should have a sound basis of religious faith than that he should achieve literary distinction, and when he found that Derwent had renounced his infidel creed his relief was great, indeed, but qualified; for he wrote to Edward Coleridge of Derwent, 'If I could keep the Press, and Critical Essays out of his head, I trust, he will be a comfort to me on the whole.'[3]

[1] See Notebook 36, fol. 203.
[2] *Letters*, iv p. 893 (no. 1159: 6 December 1818); see also v p. 334 (no. 1376: 18 February 1824) and *Miscellaneous Criticism*, p. 250.
[3] *Letters*, vi p. 565 (no. 1521: 8 February 1826).

Coleridge had good personal reasons for warning his son away from 'the Press, and Critical Essays', and for keeping his own relations with that many-headed monster as distant as possible. After the *Edinburgh Review* had dismissed his *Statesman's Manual* as incomprehensible, and rebuked him for having 'lost himself in the depths of philosophy',[1] the sobriquet of 'German metaphysician' followed Coleridge to Highgate and hampered his every attempt at publication. Publishers looked askance at every proposal of Coleridge's that smelt of metaphysics. Yet as we know from Coleridge's own comments on his *Opus Maximum*, it was on 'metaphysics' that Coleridge felt himself compelled to spend the greater part of his labour in the last twenty years of his life. It is not part of my purpose to explore the question how much of Coleridge's metaphysics *was* German, and how much his own; but some examination of certain features of his philosophy is necessary if we are to understand Coleridge's later conception of human relationship; and, even more to the point, many of Coleridge's ideas about relationship are themselves expressed in metaphysical terms. It may be observed, too, that it is precisely in his conception of human relationship that Coleridge most differs from Kant. Kant did not accept that love lay under the control of the will; it was outside the sphere of rational self-government, and could form no part of a system of moral philosophy.[2] In a contribution to Southey's *Omniana*, and in his 1811 Shakespeare lectures, Coleridge had taken the exactly opposite position, describing love as 'an act of the will'.[3] He did not abandon this belief. Indeed, he developed it, in part of the *Opus Maximum*, by conceiving of love as analogous to that first, disastrous choice in man's moral history, the choice of disobedience to God's will (though love is of course seen as a choice on the right side).

What Kant affirms of man in the state of Adam, an ineffable act of

[1] Anonymous review in *Edinburgh Review*, vol. xxvii (December 1816) (444–59), p. 451.
[2] 'Preface to the Metaphysical Elements of Ethics', section 11, part C. *Critique of Practical Reason*, p. 312. See R. Wellek, *Immanuel Kant in England*, p. 89.
[3] *Shakespearean Criticism*, ii p. 163.

Will choosing evil, and which is underneath or within consciousness, though incarnate in the conscience, inasmuch as *it must be conceived* as taking place in the *Homo Noumenon* not the *Homo Phænomenon* – something like this I conceive of Love, in that higher sense of the word which Petrarch understood.[1]

Redeemed from what Coleridge regarded as the immoral trivialities with which it was associated in the works of Laurence Sterne, Henry Mackenzie and other men of feeling, love could appear as what it was, an act of moral, indeed of religious, significance, since it proceeded not from the ephemeral appetencies and emotions of which we are all constantly aware – the 'homo phænomenon' – but from the unknown but essential self that is the ground of moral choice, the 'homo noumenon'. Nor is this belief inconsistent with the seeking after self-knowledge that Coleridge advocated in *Aids to Reflection*. The desire for external correspondences, of which love is one manifestation, is not antagonistic to self-discipline, but its justification; for without self-discipline man does not realize his true nature in obedience to a higher will, and so remains incapable of any response to the divine presence in others. It is only the unregenerate man who is isolated. When the selfish will has been lost, what Coleridge knew as 'the misery of self' is overcome. J. H. Muirhead saw the importance of Coleridge's disagreement with Kant over the moral significance of love:

It was the growing conviction of his later years that individuality, in the only sense in which it was of moral and religious significance, consisted, not in the narrowing down of life to an exclusive point, but in the expansion of it towards the inclusion of the Whole – Man in God, doubtless, but also God in Man.[2]

Though accepting, then, that Coleridge may have been 'unable to hold to Kant's actual starting-point',[3] and that he possibly lessened his stature as a philosopher by betraying the critical philosophy, I begin this section with the above quotation from the *Opus Maximum*, and Muirhead's comment on it, since to evaluate Coleridge's stature as a philosopher forms no part of my intention.

[1] Printed in J. H. Muirhead, *Coleridge as Philosopher*, p. 158.
[2] J. H. Muirhead, *Coleridge as Philosopher*, p. 159.
[3] R. Wellek, *Immanuel Kant in England*, p. 109.

It is evident even from this one quotation that Coleridge could not rest satisfied with a philosophy in which the proof of the existence of God – and therefore, by an inevitable if illogical association of ideas, God himself – was as remote as it was in Kant's system. De Quincey, one of the few who penetrated behind the popular conception of Coleridge and caught glimpses of his private self, wrote of how Coleridge in 1807 regretted his early assertion that prayer was a manifest impertinence, and told him that he now believed prayer to be 'the very highest energy of which the human heart was capable'.[1] The austere view of prayer outlined by Schleiermacher, who held that prayer was a useful instrument of self-discipline, but no more, was strongly repudiated by Coleridge. He told his nephew Edward Coleridge that petitionary prayers could rationally be considered as 'appointed means to rightly desired ends', just as actions could.[2] But not until the time of the publication of *Aids to Reflection* did Coleridge arrive at a firm conviction of the *efficacy* of prayer, for he told Daniel Stuart in a letter of April 1826 that such a belief had recently become a firm part of his faith. The 'more cheerful sense of *freedom*' which it gave him also rested on faith in a personal God, if indeed the two beliefs can be said to be separate.[3] In what is now known (following Muirhead's classification) as 'MS "C" ', Coleridge described prayer as 'the mediator or rather the effort to connect the misery of the self with the blessedness of God',[4] a connection that would have been inconceivable for the strict rationalist or follower of Kant; but Coleridge was not interested in the inconsistency of prayer with a rationalistic conception of God, but in the possibility that prayer opened up of satisfying his craving for a closer approach to the Deity. Coleridge had an acute sense of the 'incompleteness' of the godless man, a condition held by St Thomas Aquinas to be inevitable once humanity forsakes its relationship to God.[5] Whether Coleridge's belief in the efficacy of prayer grew out of his faith in a personal God is a question on which we can scarcely even speculate: but we do know that Coleridge's sense of need

---

[1] *Reminiscences of the English Lake Poets*, p. 18; see Wellek, p. 94.
[2] *Letters*, vi p. 555 (no. 1521: 8 February 1826).
[3] *Letters*, vi p. 577 (no. 1527: 18 April 1826).
[4] J. H. Muirhead, *Coleridge as Philosopher*, p. 219.
[5] John Passmore, *The Perfectibility of Man*, p. 71.

for a religious faith had taken this form ten or more years before
he avowed a change in his attitude to prayer. The following note
is placed by E. H. Coleridge between 1814 and 1818: 'To Christ
from Bernard – Nec mihi tua sufficiunt sine te, nec tibi placeant
mea sine me. – N.b. This single Epigram – worth shall I say?
O far rather – a sufficient antidote to – a Waggon load of Paleyian
Moral and Political Philosophies.'[1] The attraction of traditional
metaphysics was precisely that it permitted such a *rapprochement*
with the Divine Nature, Man in God and God in Man; if God
possessed such attributes as will, intelligence and personality
which were reflected, albeit imperfectly, in man, there were
grounds for hope that by developing these qualities in accordance
with his belief a man may make himself a little less unworthy of
the relationship. In the philosophers who followed Newton,
Coleridge saw 'an increasing unwillingness to contemplate the
Supreme Being in his personal attributes'. They had mistaken
the 'laws' by which the Newtonian universe was governed for
God himself, and so made it impossible to conceive of God as a
'moral Creator and Governor'. A God who announces his
presence by increasing gravitational attraction inversely as the
square of the distance cannot *at the same time* be a God to whom
we address our prayers.

When...the genius of Kepler, expanded and organized in the soul of
Newton...had expelled the Cartesian *vortices*; then the necessity of an
active power, of positive forces present in the material universe,
forced itself on the conviction. For as a law without a lawgiver is a mere
abstraction; so a law without an agent to realise it, a constitution
without an abiding executive, is, in fact, not a law but an idea...the
Deity itself was declared to be the real agent, the actual gravitating
power! The law and the lawgiver were identified.[2]

Blake also understood this, and caricatured the Newtonian world
as a cruel machine, 'wheel without wheel, with cogs tyrannic
/Moving by compulsion each other',[3] and though Coleridge
could write of God as 'the Synthesis of all conceivable antitheses',
he preferred the 'moral definition', as he called it, 'God is love'.
In a passage commenting on one of Donne's sermons, but which

[1] Notebook 23, fol. 68; see AP, p. 273.
[2] *Aids to Reflection*, pp. 319–20.
[3] *Jerusalem*, chapter 1; *Poems and Prophecies*, p. 177.

nevertheless seems to have the Kantian ethic particularly in view, he wrote:

the best moral Definition is – God is L O V E – and this is (to *us*), the high prerogative of the *moral* that all it's dictates immediately reveal the truths of intelligence, whereas the strictly Intellectual only by more distant and cold deductions carries us towards the moral. For what is Love? Union with the desire of union. God therefore is the Cohesion and the oneness of all Things – and dark and dim is that system of Ethics, which does [not] take 'oneness' as the *root* of all Virtue![1]

Confusion is liable to arise when Coleridge combines this kind of un-Kantian declaration with concepts that are evidently borrowed from Kant, if not always used in a properly Kantian fashion. In the 'Essay on Faith', for instance, which (as René Wellek points out) relies heavily on Kantian concepts, Coleridge asserts that ignorance of the categorical imperative 'constitutes either the non-personality of the ignorant, or the guilt', yet almost in the same breath he announces his subject as faith, defined as 'fidelity to our own being, so far as such being is not and cannot become an object of the senses'.[2] It was one of the central maxims of the critical philosophy that a thing-in-itself, the *Ding an sich*, could not be known, nor be the subject of rational thought. For Coleridge, then, to announce as his subject faith, defined as it is here defined, was to lay claim to an entirely different sphere of speculation from that delimited by Kant. Yet it was necessary to do so: belief in God's presence, not of course in appearances, but in Being itself, the *noumenon*, was a real possibility to Coleridge, to whom it meant 'never to be friendless, never to be unintelligible!'[3] Long before writing the 'Essay on Faith', Coleridge criticized the Newtonian philosophers for emptying the idea of divine omnipresence of all significance;[4] now his treatment of what he felt to be the *sine qua non* of religion had to begin, understandably enough, with a rejection of the limitations placed upon discourse by Kantian rationalism.

Schelling had already attempted to supply a defence of one important condition of the man–God relationship, namely, human

[1] R. F. Brinkley, editor, *Coleridge on the Seventeenth Century*, p. 201.
[2] *Literary Remains*, iv p. 425.   [3] AP, p. 127.   [4] BL, ii p. 59 n.

freedom. Freedom was in any case (as will be shown in a discussion of 'apperception' and 'self-consciousness') a vital condition of Schelling's philosophy (and moreover one body of opinion appeared to hold that human freedom was incompatible with the very notion of a philosophical system, whatever its basis). In his *Philosophische Untersuchungen Ueber das Wesen der menschlichen Freiheit* (1809), Schelling set out to show initially that belief in the immanence of our world in God is by no means incompatible with belief in human freedom: a concern which Coleridge certainly shared. (See A. O. Lovejoy's essay, 'Coleridge and Kant's Two Worlds', where Lovejoy speaks of Coleridge's 'engrossing concern to establish the freedom of the will'.)[1]

In the process, Schelling showed no mercy to his predecessors; Fichte's defence of freedom, in which freedom is ascribed to the individual wills of men, was asserted to have collapsed into 'contradictions and inadmissible statements' ('sie aber unmittelbar in Widersprüche und Unstatthaftigkeiten geriet'),[2] while Jacobi's attempt to oppose the dry abstractions of French atheistic rationalism by reasserting the importance of human feeling – the heart against the head – is treated with equal contempt. Schelling's tone of high theocentric *Erhebung*, very different from the careful steps of Kant, and if only for that reason promising a closer approach to Deity than the critical philosophy permitted, is established almost at the outset by a quotation from Sextus Empiricus, relating to Empedocles: 'Der Philosoph eine... göttliche Erkenntniß behaupte, weil er allein, den Verstand rein und unverdunkelt von Bosheit erhaltend, mit dem Gott in sich den Gott außer sich begreife.'[3] The assumption that Pantheism and freedom are incompatible is based on a misconception of the Pantheist's picture of the relationship which God bears to his Creation, Schelling argues, and to elucidate this relationship he avails himself of an analysis of the law of Identity (an analysis which is itself based, as Professor McFarland points out, on

---

[1] *Essays in the History of Ideas*, p. 255.

[2] *F. W. J. von Schellings Sämmtliche Werke* (1856–1860) [hereafter referred to as *Schelling*], vii p. 338.

[3] *Schelling* vii 337. 'The Philosopher lays claim to divine insight because he alone receiving understanding pure and unobscured by Evil, embraces the God without, together with the God within.'

Fichte).[1] In other words, Schelling will retain the Pantheistic
doctrine of the immanence of Creation in the Creator, while yet
arguing that the highest product of Creation, Man, though
dependent on God, is not manipulated or determined by him.
We can be sure that the notion of Freedom furnished by this
argument will be very different from human freedom as represented by traditional Christianity. Evidently enjoying his paradox,
Schelling argues that though the sense of fatalism or determin-
ism is often bound up with Pantheism in men's thinking, this
merely indicates how lively the sense of freedom is, for if there
were no sense of freedom in man, no one would feel the need to
describe Pantheism as deterministic. But the very notion of
Omnipotence is contradictory to Freedom: 'Absolute Causalität
in Einem Wesen läßt allen andern nur unbedingte Passivität
übrig.'[2] Furthermore this must mean that the finite being is
furnished from the start with certain thoughts, aspirations and
actions, and no other. In a sentence which perhaps is intended to
recall Kant's 'Denn sind Erscheinungen Dinge an sich selbst, so
ist Freiheit nicht zu retten', Schelling asks, 'Gibt es gegen diese
Argumentation einen andern Ausweg, als den Menschen mit
seiner Freiheit, da sie im Gegensatz der Allmacht undenkbar
ist, in das göttliche Wesen selbst zu retten, zu sagen, daß der
Mensch nicht außer Gott, sondern in Gott sey, und daß seine
Thätigkeit selbst mit zum Leben Gottes gehöre?'[3]

Schelling then commences his attack on the notion that Pan-
theists profess a completely deterministic identification of God
with created things. Nowhere can a more thorough-going *division* of Things from God be found than in the classic exponent of
Pantheism, Spinoza (a statement which is surely aimed at jerking
the reader out of the last of his prejudices): but even Spinoza has
not escaped such a misinterpretation.

Der Grund solcher Mißdeutungen, welche auch andre Systeme in

[1] *Coleridge and the Pantheist Tradition*, p. 148.
[2] *Schelling*, vii 339. 'Absolute causality in One Being leaves all others only unconditional passivity.'
[3] *Schelling*, vii 339. 'Is there any other way out of this argument than to save man and
human freedom by drawing them into the Divine Being itself, since it is unthink-
able that they should be in contradiction to Omnipotence; to say that man exists,
not outside God, but within him, and that his power of action is itself part of the
life of God?'

reichem Maß erfahren haben, liegt in dem allgemeinen Mißver-
ständniß des Gesetzes der Identität oder des Sinns der Copula im
Urtheil. Ist es gleich einem Kinde begreiflich zu machen, daß in
keinem möglichen Satz, der der angenommenen Erklärung zufolge
die Identität des Subjekts mit dem Prädicat aussagt, eine Einerleiheit
oder auch nur ein unvermittelter Zusammenhang dieser beiden ausge-
sagt werde – indem z.B. der Satz: dieser Körper ist blau, nicht den
Sinn hat, der Körper sey in dem und durch das, worin und wodurch er
Körper ist, auch blau, sondern nur den, dasselbe, was dieser Körper
ist, sey, obgleich nicht in dem nämlichen Betracht, auch blau: so ist
doch diese Voraussetzung, welche eine völlige Unwissenheit über
das Wesen der Copula anzeigt, in Bezug auf die höhere Anwendung
des Identitätsgesetzes zu unsrer Zeit beständig gemacht worden.[1]

In a statement of identity, that is to say, what is asserted is not
that the subject and the predicate are in all respects co-extensive,
but that (as the older, more profound logic has it) predicate is
dependent upon subject: predicate is *consequens*, subject *antece-
dens*. If the Absolute be represented as 'A', and one of its consequences as 'A/a', the relationship between A and A/a is not one
of uniformity, but of dependence: A/a can still be a particular,
proper Substance, even though dependent upon A.[2]

It is thus no contradiction to say that the finite being is
dependent upon the idea of the Eternal, and at the same time
possesses his own power of self-determination; an organic indi-
viduum is dependent as regards Becoming (*das Werden*), but
not as regards Being (*das Sein*), just as the eye is dependent
upon the body for its existence, and yet possesses a separate life,
to the extent that it can move, and fall ill, independently of the
rest of the body. (Compare a passage in *Ideen zur einer Philosophie der Natur* where it is pointed out that the fact of evolution

[1] *Schelling*, vii 341. 'The basis of such misunderstandings [of Spinozism], which
other systems have also suffered in prodigious numbers, lies in the universal
misunderstanding of the law of Identity, or of the meaning of the copula in a
judgment. Even to a child it should be quite comprehensible that in no possible
axiom which declares the identity of Subject with Object (as a consequence of the
hypothetical explanation) is a uniformity, or even only an un-mediated coherence
of the two, established – for example, the axiom "this body is blue" does not have
the sense, "this body, in that and by virtue of the fact that it is a body, is blue",
but only the sense, "that which this body is, is also blue, though not in the same
conception"; yet this assumption, which betrays a complete ignorance concerning
the essence of the copula, has repeatedly been made in our age, in respect of the
higher application of the law of Identity.'
[2] *Schelling*, vii p. 342, 344–5.

does not prevent the evolved being from having a particular, independent nature.)[1] 'Abhängigkeit hebt Selbständigkeit, hebt sogar Freiheit nicht auf.'[2]

Schelling goes so far as to state that God can be revealed only in a being similar to him, a being who acts in freedom from God, though owing his very existence to God's power of self-revelation – another paradox which one suspects Schelling rather relished.[3] Nevertheless, as Professor McFarland shows, the freedom which Schelling can build upon such a basis – in spite of his insistence that he rejects Spinoza's mechanistic treatment of created things as 'mere' Things – is unsatisfactory; it is only a formal freedom, answering to a formal, Spinozistic and essentially impersonal conception of Deity.[4] (To be wholly fair to Schelling, however, one must look at this deduction of freedom in the context of the *System des transcendentalen Idealismus*, where Spinozism is treated as the philosophy of physical science – a *Naturphilosophie* – demanding to be complemented by Transcendental Idealism, which takes as its starting-point not Being, not an 'I am', but the necessary limit imposed on knowledge by self-consciousness.)[5] To wish to make God an object of knowledge, as Coleridge did, has been represented as a victory of emotion over mind:[6] a charge which may or may not have weight. But it is important to understand, at the same time, that Coleridge was quite positive about his conception of religious faith. In accusing Schelling and Fichte – as, in the end, Coleridge did – of 'gross materialism',[7] he was articulating not the emotional reaction of the religious enthusiast, but the clear perception that religion, if it be anything at all, must germinate in the relationship of a person to a person. To refer again to 'MS "C"':

To be Religion it must be the reference of an intelligent responsible Will Finite to an Absolute Will, and the reference must refer as a Will and a Life, i.e. a Person to a living I am. We may feel *from* and about a thing, an event, a quality, we can feel toward a Person only. The

[1] *ib*. ii p. 172
[2] *ib*. vii p. 346. 'Dependence does not invalidate Independence, nor indeed Freedom.'
[3] *ib*. vii p. 346.   [4] *Coleridge and the Pantheist Tradition*, p. 152.
[5] *Schelling*, iii p. 356.
[6] See G. M. McKenzie, *Organic Unity in Coleridge*, p. 12.
[7] In a margin annotation to *Ueber das Wesen der menschlichen Freiheit*: see BL, i p. 248, note 9.

personal in me is the ground and condition of Religion, and the Personal alone is the Object.[1]

An important part of the labour of Coleridge's last ten years went into his efforts to elucidate the theology of the Hebrews according to this principle, and to establish in particular the points in which the priests of Israel differed from the early philosophers of Greece. Had they understood their own theology aright, Coleridge maintained, the Hebrews would have looked, not for a Messiah who was to be a new David, but for one who was 'the Word incarnate in the Son of Man...together with this personëity assuming personal individuality in Jesus, born of Woman'.[2] Rightly or wrongly, Coleridge believed it must be possible to demonstrate that Hebrew theology had a logic of its own; that, given a God whose name was not 'the boundless' or 'the All', but 'I Am', there must of necessity be a Son, who would redeem the erring children of God. In the *Philosophical Lectures*, Coleridge made clear his sense of the vital difference between the theologies of Israel and of Greece. The Greeks, by making their imagination the judge of all things, had arrived at an impersonal conception of Deity. For them, just as the power that enabled a man to think and move was a 'soul', and partook of the divine, so the power that animated the All was divine. For the Greeks, in other words, the word 'God' was predicative.[3] Some writers represented this as the equivalent of the Christian belief that 'all things exist in God', but for Coleridge it was nothing of the kind. He contrasted it with the Hebrews' concern for conduct, justice and moral values: they 'attended more to their moral feeling', and as a nation they were 'bred up by inspiration in a child-like form, in obedience and in the exercise of the will'.[4] To the Greeks it was given to see how far unaided human reason could progress in exploring the beginning of all things, the ἀρχή; and this they came to identify with the divine, τὸ θεῖον. To the Hebrews, even before the time of Moses (according to Moses' own declaration), it was revealed that God was One, and (in Coleridge's phrase) 'a moral Creator and Governor'. But Coleridge did not see himself as abandoning

[1] J. H. Muirhead, *Coleridge as Philosopher*, p. 36.   [2] Notebook 26, fol. 70.
[3] See Werner Jaeger, *The Theology of the Early Greek Philosophers*, p. 173
[4] *Philosophical Lectures*, edited by Kathleen Coburn, pp. 92, 112 (Lecture 11).

Reason for Revelation; for him they were but two aspects of one thing. He reminded J. H. Green in March 1832 that he had always during their association worked on the principle that Revelation was but *'objective Reason'*, and that far from deriving authority from the Old Testament, he must give it authority on the basis of Reason.[1] He was not afraid of suggesting, in his attempts at scriptural hermeneutics, how Hebrew thinkers might have progressed from animistic conceptions to that of an intelligent Deity:

The Hebrew Sages began to look more deeply into the idea of the divine Ether, or Deus in diffuso – / and must have detected the gross ill*ud* pro ill*um* into which <they had been seduced by> the ambiguous generalness of a term, or half-thought, fluctuating between proper and improper, <Representative and Thing>. They must have seen, that if this Aura divina was <a partible Continuum, it must be a Thing; and if> a *Thing*, it could not be God, or the principle of Mind. <vice versa, > if it were God or Mind, it could not be a partible universum at *all*. They must have seen, that tho' *Mind* was no adequate or commensurate Expression of God, yet still less could God be conceived without *Mind*: and Distincity [sic] is as essential an Attribute of Mind as Unity. Now this Distincity in the Unity by a most happy Analogy they named the Word, Logos – and the instant Consequence was the εν αρχη ην ο Λογος/.[2]

The first words of St John's Gospel are then the logical summit of the old Hebrew theology, not a wholly new and revolutionary dispensation: they are a Revelation that is Reason in a different guise. Coleridge goes on to argue that the creation of a Son was the only possible act by which the emergence of 'Alterity' out of 'Essence' could be established, for only in the begetting of a Son could the supreme Being create something not himself which yet was part of himself.

Coleridge elaborated these views in his Royal Society of Literature lecture of 1825, which draws heavily on Schelling (particularly on his *Ueber die Gottheiten von Samothrace*, 1815). In this lecture, he suggested that the *Prometheus Bound* of Æschylus embodies in poetic form certain philosophical truths, known to the priests of the Orphic mysteries, but which the doctrines of the State religion had ousted, with a consequent

[1] *Letters*, vi p. 895 (no. 1736: 29 March 1832).   [2] Notebook 37, fols. 280–1.

demoralization of the people. The play retold 'the sublime mythus περι γενέσεως τοῦ Νοῦ ἐν ἀνθρωποις',[1] the story of the birth of Mind in men, which the philosophers, in their attempt to establish the origin of all things, had made their primary subject. The fire that Prometheus brought was symbolic of the *Νοῦς*, and since, according to the Orphic philosophy, mind was that part of man which was closest to the Divine, it was represented as being a gift from Heaven; brought by a god older than Zeus, but yet akin to him, 'to mark the pre-existence, in order of Thought, of the Nous, as spiritual, both to the objects of sense, and to their products'.[2] Man is by this gift set apart from the rest of creation: he does not stop at merely being, like a plant, nor at moving and perceiving, like an animal, but has the power of realizing in himself the Idea which is the law of his being. That is, he can live not just for his own material self-preservation but for the enlargement of Mind in himself, and the reconciliation of his earthly nature with what is divine in him. In him, Nature becomes self-aware[3] – a proposition which undoubtedly has more of Schelling in it than of Coleridge, for it was the salient characteristic of Schellingian idealism that consciousness was treated as the consummation, even the final cause, of Nature.

For Coleridge, however, the importance of this interpretation of Æschylus' play as a celebration of Mind, or, in Schellingian terms, of Consciousness, was that it showed the gulf between the philosophy of Greece and the revealed religion of Israel not to be altogether impassable. It was bridged, indeed, at the time of Christ's incarnation, when, as Coleridge saw it, the Hebrews learned to interpret their scriptures more 'spiritually', and the Greeks learned the reality of what alone is real.[4] In a sense, *Aids to Reflection*, though focusing on revealed religion, is an attempt to revitalize the view of man implied in the *Prometheus* lecture; that is, of man as a creature who has the power of realizing in himself the Idea which is the law of his being. A passage from Bishop Leighton, which Coleridge selected to print in *Aids to Reflection*, shows that the framework within which Greek beliefs (of the Orphic or pre-Socratic period) and Hebrew doctrines might be reconciled, lay already to hand.

[1] *Transactions of the Royal Society of Literature*, ii (1834) (384–404), p. 389.
[2] *ib.* [3] *ib.* ii p. 403. [4] *Phil. Lects.*, p. 112 (Lecture ii).

God hath suited every creature He hath made with a convenient good to which it tends, and in the obtainment of which it rests and is satisfied. Natural bodies all have their own natural place, whither, if not hindered, they move incessantly till they be in it. ...Sensitive creatures are carried to seek a sensitive good, as agreeable to their rank in being, and, attaining that, aim no further. Now in this is the excellency of man, that he is made capable of a communion with his Maker, and, because capable of it, is unsatisfied without it: the soul, being cut out (so to speak) to that largeness, cannot be filled with less.[1]

Part of the reward for realizing this 'largeness' is the overcoming of that 'misery of the self' of which Coleridge had spoken in one section of the *Opus Maximum*. The Hobbesian system of materialism, and, no less, the 'splendid but delusory tenets' of the 'pious Deists', condemned the individual to isolation: the first, because it rested on the belief that 'motives act on the will, as bodies act on bodies', so that anything not consonant with our own immediate self-interest is supposed to be out of our power; the second, because the Deists ignored the fact of the corruption of the will, the fault which it was essential to overcome before the individual could escape from his selfishness.[2] Hobbes, and Shaftesbury too for all his optimism, depicted a being who was truly alone in the world, whose crimes and occasional generosities were alike meaningless, whose every act referred to nothing beyond itself. To Coleridge both crime and generosity had meaning, for one was an example of the unregenerate will at work, the other an example of men's wish to act by a higher law, or by the will of God in man: by their conscience, in short.[3] Coleridge saw that systems which left out God, or in which God was either remote, as for the Deists, or ubiquitous, as for Schelling, rendered the concept of a conscience meaningless. Schelling, to be sure, had voiced the same criticism of Spinoza that Coleridge had made against Hobbes; that he treated the Will as a Thing, not as a power.

Der Fehler [Spinozas] Systems liegt keineswegs darin, daß er die Dinge in Gott setzt, sondern darin, daß es Dinge sind – in dem abstrakten Begriff der Weltwesen, ja der unendlichen Substanz selber, die ihm eben auch ein Ding ist. Daher sind seine Argumente gegen die

---

[1] *Aids*, pp. 92–3 (Aphorism XLVII).   [2] *ib.* pp. 102–3.
[3] On the 'particular' and 'universal' applications of every fact, see SM, p. 36, and below, p. 254.

Freiheit ganz deterministisch, auf keine Weise pantheistisch. Er behandelt auch den Willen als eine Sache, und beweist dann sehr natürlich, daß er in jedem Fall des Wirkens durch eine andere Sache bestimmt seyn müsse, die wieder durch eine andere bestimmt ist u. s. f. ins Unendliche. Daher die Leblosigkeit seines Systems, die Gemüthlosigkeit der Form, die Dürftigkeit der Begriffe und Ausdrücke, das unerbittlich Herbe der Bestimmungen, das sich mit der abstrakten Betrachtungsweise vortefflich verträgt; daher auch ganz folgerichtig seine mechanische Naturansicht.[1]

But Schelling's own answer to the inadequacies of this mechanistic view provided, as we have seen, not 'the reference of an intelligent responsible Will Finite to an Absolute Will', but what amounted to no more than a redefinition of human Freedom as a mere formal reflection of the creative process – a guarantee of human participation in the coming-to-consciousness of Nature, not the genuine power of moral choice for which Coleridge was searching. It was essential to any definition of being a person, in Coleridge's view, that moral choices could be made – that one could will the Good, independently of *Kraft*, Nature, and other merely impersonal powers. If a personal God could not be found in Reason, or rather in the rationalistic systems of Spinoza and the Deists, one must look to Revelation.

Since we know we are not angels, if we heartily desire the happiness of someone other than ourselves it must be because some power teaches us that it is better to take another man's interests to heart than our own, and likewise that, our will being free, it is possible for us to will another man's good rather than our own. The Deists and Spinozists could not easily account for such a power, their God being apersonal. Unaided reason can of itself arrive at the conclusion, or the hypothesis, that the

---

1 *Schelling*, vii 349. 'The error of [Spinoza's] system does not stem from the fact that he places Things within God, but from the fact that it is *Things* – from the abstract notion of the Universe, indeed of infinite Substance itself – which is also a "Thing" to him. Hence his arguments against Freedom are wholly deterministic, in no way Pantheistic. He treats Will also as a Thing, and then quite naturally proves that in each instance of its operation, it must be expressed through another object, which in turn is expressed through another object, and so on to infinity. Hence the lifelessness of his system, the soullessness of its form, the meagreness of ideas and expressions, the inexorable brusqueness of statements, which is excellently suited to the abstract mode of viewing things; hence also – very properly – follows his mechanistic view of Nature.'

existence of the world is not an accident, and must have a First Cause: this is no more than the Greeks succeeded in discovering. It is only by the Hebraic acknowledgment of conscience and free will as, not self-interest in disguise, but of the essence of Revelation, that we can understand God's possession of personality: by this acceptance of conscience, Coleridge asserts, 'the hypothesis of a one ground and principle of the universe... is ... raised into the idea of the living God, the supreme object of our faith, love, fear, and adoration.'[1]

Coleridge's argument has some affinity with Kant's, in the *Critique of Practical Reason*, except that instead of holding that the argument from conscience completes and 'raises' our idea of God, as Coleridge does, Kant dismisses the ontological argument as relying on reason in a field where reason is not competent to operate. Kant replaces it by the argument that it is morally necessary to believe in God (though we can know nothing about him), because if there exists no God who is outside nature and yet is its cause, the 'highest good', which is the goal of all morality, cannot possibly be achieved.[2] Though not necessarily believing that this argument reduces God to the level of a useful fiction (which it does not), Coleridge would still have wished for a metaphysic that left more room for exploration of the personal nature of God – not for 'emotional' reasons, but because only a personal God could complete the logic of man's moral nature as Coleridge saw it. Though he adopted a notably Kantian defence of the doctrine of free will, he did not allow such arguments to undermine his belief that man is (as Leighton put it) 'made capable of a communion with his Maker'; which creates problems for the student of Coleridge who is not prepared to accept such a breadth of concern. Indeed Coleridge went so far as to suggest (though only as a 'hint') that God may be conceived of in two distinct ways: one way, as τὸ θεῖον, he was infinite; the other way, as ὁ θεός, personal.[3] The theme of personality was too important to Coleridge to be neglected. To him, 'being a person' meant not something incidental to morality which must be cultivated by the individual for his own self-improvement, but a realization of all one's powers of sympathy

---

[1] *Aids*, p. 122.   [2] See S. Körner, *Kant*, p. 167.
[3] *Letters*, iv p. 850 (no. 1126: April 1818).

COLERIDGE AND THE IDEA OF LOVE

and unselfishness. J. H. Muirhead thus summarizes part of
Coleridge's 'MS "B" ':

> In reality personality becomes more perfect in proportion as a man
> rises above the negations and privations by which the finite is differen-
> tiated from the Absolute, the human will from the divine, man from
> God... [it is] a circumference continually expanding through sympathy
> and understanding, rather than... an exclusive centre of self-feeling.[1]

Here we are close to the crux of Coleridge's later thinking about
human relationship, where several trains of thought interlock.
They may be summarized as: the argument for belief in a personal God, whose interest in human conduct is vouched for by
the presence in us of a conscience, and a 'largeness' of soul; the
moral duty of keeping alive the distinction between 'person' and
'thing', and never on any provocation treating a person otherwise than as such; and the belief that consciousness, self-
consciousness and conscience all stem in the first place from
loving and being loved. The germ of all these is in the 'few loose
Hints' Coleridge offered a friend in a letter of April 1818.[2]
Personality, he first suggests, necessarily supposes 'a *ground*
distinct from the Person, id, *per* quod sonat A'. It is not what
distinguishes us from others, but what makes us prize their
interests above our own – the universal law or the categorical
imperative speaking through the individual and so enabling him
to renounce his individuality, or rather his isolation. But where
does consciousness begin? In awareness of another, or what we
may call 'an I–Thou relationship', Coleridge suggests. (I have
here translated his rather dusty scholastic Latin). 'To be conscious', he writes, 'is to be aware both of myself and of another
at the same time – therefore, selfconsciousness is to be aware of
myself *as if I were another*. The *Me* in the objective case is
clearly distinct from the *Ego*.'[3] As elsewhere, Coleridge has
mingled philosophical statement with psychological speculation,
and we need to distinguish the one from the other if Coleridge's
thought is to be clear. To the philosopher of ethics, Coleridge

[1] J.H. Muirhead, *Coleridge as Philosopher*, pp. 228–9.
[2] So dated, conjecturally, by Professor Griggs.
[3] *Letters*, iv p. 849 (no. 1126; April 1818.) For a fuller treatment of Coleridge's
idea of self-consciousness and his use of the Kantian concept of 'apperception', see
below, pp. 169–94.

states that the idea of person and personality has meaning only when we postulate a universal moral law, through obedience to which individuals cease to act selfishly, and so put the good of mankind at large above their own. To treat another as a person became virtually synonymous, for Coleridge, with just behaviour: he used the expression as the current coinage of his practical morality. His advice to James Gillman, son of his host at Highgate, when the boy was about to embark upon his career, was never to treat another man as anything less than a person, whatever the circumstances: 'the more he forgets himself, the more do you remember *him*'.[1] In more formal terms the doctrine is set out in *Aids to Reflection*, where Coleridge states that 'the ground-work of personal being is a capacity of acknowledging the moral law'.[2]

To the psychologist, and to those who desire a somewhat less theoretical basis for their moral views, Coleridge suggests that in time, though not in logical sequence, morality and even religious belief take their origin from personal relationships, and in the first instance from the mother–child relationship (a view which modern psychologists would agree to be fraught with meaning, though for them it would perhaps in most cases disprove rather than substantiate Coleridge's belief in a personal God). 'MS "B"' contains a chapter entitled *The Origin of the Idea of God*, from which Muirhead quotes the following passage:

Why have men a faith in God? There is but one answer. The man and the man alone has a Father and a Mother. The first dawnings of [the infant's] humanity will break forth in the eye that connects the mother's face with the warmth of the mother's bosom...Ere yet a conscious self exists the love begins, and the first love is love to an other.[3]

Born with no sense of his own separate existence, but aware that another being exists who seems to be there solely in order to care for him, the infant acquires from the first the desire of giving and receiving love to a seemingly omnipotent and ever-caring parent; here Coleridge saw 'reason,' as he put it, 'mutely prophesying of its own advent'. Later, the infant becomes aware of the separate existence of his mother, and then of his own, and from this consciousness of another and consciousness of self

[1] *ib.* vi p. 929 (no. 1761: 9 November 1832).
[2] *Aids*, p. 219. [3] *Coleridge as Philosopher*, p. 252.

grows, if Coleridge is right, the conscience, or awareness of the moral law. As with any other Idea, perfection in obedience to the law cannot be attained in a single human lifespan, only approximated to. But Coleridge was so far a believer in humanity as to cherish the memory of a few people who, he believed, had come close to such perfection. Moral perfection was in his eyes far superior to any intellectual accomplishment,[1] and he recognized that it was not in his nature to love except where he was convinced that there was moral perfection – a characteristic that left him exceedingly vulnerable to disappointments, it may be added. The links between Coleridge's morbid self-distrust, his admiration of the moral strength of others, and – by an amazing leap of the imagination – his belief in a personal God, are all shown in an extraordinary passage, contained in one of his letters to his young friend and admirer, Thomas Allsop, which though in prose exhibits as few other passages do, even in Coleridge's writings, how the poet's eye 'doth glance from heaven to earth, from earth to heaven'.

My eloquence was most commonly excited by the desire of running away and hiding myself from my personal and inward feelings, and not for the expression of them...I fled in a circle still overtaken by the Feelings, from which I was evermore fleeing, with my back turned toward them – but above all, my growing deepening conviction of transcendency of the moral to the intellectual, and the inexpressible comfort and inward Strength which I experience myself to derive as often as I contemplate Truth realized into Being by a human Will – so that as I cannot love without esteem, neither can I esteem with loving. Hence I *love* but few – but those I love as my soul – for I feel that without them I should – not indeed cease to be kind, and effluent; but – by little and little become a soul-less fixed Star, receiving no rays nor influences into my being, a solitude, which I so tremble at that I cannot attribute it even to the Divine Nature. – [2]

3

John Keats describes in a letter of December 1817 a conversation he had with Dilke, whom he characterizes as 'a Godwin per-

[1] See *Shakespearean Criticism*, ii pp. 239–40.
[2] *Letters*, v pp. 239–40 (no. 1309: 29 June 1822).

fectibility man'. Such believers in 'perfectibility' set themselves a wrong and impossible goal, Keats argues, including Coleridge in this condemnation. They react to the existence of evil by an 'irritable reaching after fact and reason', whereas a really great poet such as Shakespeare confronts the evil in human life, and incorporates it into the beauty which he creates: he does not yearn for a remote and blessed state in which 'the burthen of the mystery' is 'lightened', and the presence of evil no longer disturbs his peace.[1] There is room for a world of comment upon this opinion of Keats's, and on the differences it implies between the Coleridgean outlook and his own; but it makes one thing immediately clear. The poet Keats felt it his duty to serve Truth in the sense that he was not entitled to misrepresent, in any essential way, the condition of men in this life; everything, misery and pain as well as joy and beauty, was potentially a subject for his pen. The poet Coleridge felt he must serve Truth too, but in a quite different sense. As I have above suggested (p. 141) crimes and acts of generosity had meaning to him not because they merely happened, but because they pointed to something beyond themselves. He could not view men's acts and lives without either a sense of admiration or one of disgust; to him, men could sometimes succeed, but generally failed, in translating themselves out of the sublunary sphere into a state of reconciliation with the Divine Will. The moral, as he told Allsop, counted for far more with him than the intellectual, though he felt that the intellectual should be subordinated to the moral, rather than opposed to it.[2] In this respect Coleridge is closer to Blake than he is to Keats or Wordsworth. Henry Crabb Robinson tells how he lent Blake a copy of Wordsworth's poems, and on receiving the volumes back – after Blake's death – found in the flyleaf this comment pencilled: 'I see in Wordsworth the natural man rising up against the spiritual man continually; and then he is no poet, but a heathen philosopher, at enmity with all true poetry or inspiration.' Against Wordsworth's lines 'And I could wish my days to be /Bound each to each by natural piety', Blake had written: 'There is no such thing as natural piety, because the natural man

[1] See Keats' *Letters*, edited by M. B. Forman (4th edition) pp. 234 (no. 94: October 1818), 71 (no. 32: 22 December 1817).
[2] See *Shakespearean Criticism*, ii pp. 239–40.

is at enmity with God.'[1] Like Blake, Coleridge believed that there was a divide between the 'natural' and the 'spiritual' in man, though to him the conflict resolved itself in a different way; the difference being crystallized, perhaps, in Coleridge's assurance in *Biographia Literaria* that we can love our neighbours as ourselves, only if we love God above both.[2] And the difference between Coleridge's beliefs and Wordsworth's is no longer merely one of emphasis. After Coleridge's separation from Wordsworth in 1810, there seems to have been a divergence of views between them, as well as an emotional estrangement. Coleridge forgot, or renounced, the admiration he had felt for *The Prelude* on first hearing it read, and expressed so finely in the poem 'To William Wordsworth'. In 1807, he would not have said, with Blake, that 'the eloquent descriptions of Nature in W.'s poems were conclusive proof of atheism, for whoever believes in Nature. . .disbelieves in God. For Nature is the work of the Devil.'[3] But in 1820 he was much closer to Blake's point of view, wishing to contradistinguish love of God from love of the natural world, as well as from love of 'the natural man'; he attacked as 'unhealthful' and 'contagious' Wordsworth's 'misty, rather than mystic, Confusion of God with the World and the accompanying Nature-worship'.[4] Like Blake, Coleridge now held that Wordsworth praised the wrong things; the energies that should go towards love of men, and (a prerequisite of that) love of God, he would direct mistakenly towards 'Nature'. Men were called upon, not to build upon a universal given ground, but to attain an ideal, and it was in that ideal that man's 'nature' really resided. The phrase 'natural humanity' used by Sir Walter Scott in *Old Mortality*, meant no more to Coleridge than the phrase 'round square',[5] and man could not reach his 'natural' state until the first corruption of his will had been overcome. So much is stated in an MS note of 1827:

It is eminently distinctive of Man, that his State of Nature is necessarily *ideal*, and instead of being the antecedent ground and condition of

[1] R. C. Bald, editor, *Literary Friendships in the Age of Wordsworth*, p. 265.
[2] BL, ii p. 210.
[3] Henry Crabb Robinson, *Blake, Coleridge, Wordsworth, Lamb &c.*, p. 23.
[4] *Letters*, v p. 95 (no. 1245: 8 August 1820).
[5] *Miscellaneous Criticism*, p. 326.

<the> developement of his characteristic form and faculties must <be> proposed as the *consequent* of such developement. In the inferior world, the natural State <is required> to the adequate realization of the Animal – here, it is the Creature's aim and proper business to realize his Natural State.[1]

Nature to Coleridge was but 'a term or name for Hades, the Chaos',[2] and the man who remained in the 'state of nature', in this sense, was truly isolated, related neither to God nor, *a fortiori*, to man. Coleridge's horror of the implications of such an isolation, already evident in the letter to Allsop quoted above (p. 146), became if anything more marked as he grew older. In 1828 – a time when no task mattered to him as much as the completion of what he had begun to call 'the Greenoesteesian Philosophy', and the close study of the Scriptures which accompanied that work – he wrote again of 'the misery of self':

My Soul. *My*? Yes! as long as Sin reigns, so long must this *"my"* have a tremendous force, a substantial Meaning. Every Sin and thought of Sin sink us back in upon the swampy rotten ground of our *division* from God, make us participant and accomplices of the Hades, the only conceivable contrary of God.[3]

In this sense, Selfhood had all the terrors of death, conceived as Claudio describes it in his despairing plea to Isabella:[4] an infinity of pain, solitude and restlessness – an unforgettable vision, that represented to Coleridge 'the fearful dream of ever surviving Self-being'. Against this, to represent the Christian vision, he put St Paul's assurance to the Christian community in Rome, 'None of us liveth to himself, and no man dieth to himself.'[5] It was the peculiar attraction of Christianity to Coleridge that it promised not merely immortality – which, if viewed by the light of mere natural theology, was the terrifying 'imperishable death' imagined by Claudio – but the resurrection of one's full personality, which, as we have seen, meant not 'individuality', but that by which a man overcomes selfhood, and loves other men as he loves himself. Coleridge's treatment of the Gospels in his *Philosophical Lectures* centres on just this point; it is unfortunate that the transcript is incomplete, so that all the points

---

[1] Notebook 34, fol. 101.   [2] Notebook 43, fol. 248.
[3] Notebook 38, fol. 347.   [4] *Measure for Measure*, Act III scene 1, lines 119–33.
[5] Romans XIV, 7; Notebook 39, fol. 38.

COLERIDGE AND THE IDEA OF LOVE

of Coleridge's argument cannot be followed, but the main outline is clear.

Having discussed the prevalence in Eastern religions of the belief that the souls of men were 'immortal', and went round in an endless cycle of death and rebirth, Coleridge turns to Christian belief: 'it is in the Christian religion only, and I mention this particularly because from the manner in which natural theology in the last century was said to be the theology of human nature...' – Coleridge must then have spoken of the way that Christianity saw human nature as an ideal, a second birth, not as a *datum*, and perhaps also of Kant's definition of the term 'person' by reference to the concept of 'conscience', for the transcript resumes – 'immortality is only immortality for us as far as it carries on our consciousness, and with our consciousness our conscience; that is truly the resurrection of our body, of our personal identity and with it all by which and for which we are to be responsible.'[1] It was not only in his exposition of Christianity, however, that Coleridge had in mind the horror of selfhood which is our main theme. It is clear from this and previous quotations that religious belief was to Coleridge the only path that led out of self into true human concern and a sense of responsibility towards others, those great *desiderata* which in the atomistic philosophy of Hobbes and the utilitarians had no place. It is also true, however, that all philosophy, not only post-Christian philosophy, afforded examples to Coleridge of this problem of isolation, and sometimes of attempts to overcome it. In contrast to our preconceived ideas about the Romantic outlook as one in which the solitary, Faust-like thinker defies all attempts by man or God to alleviate his solitude, Coleridge's view is that the greater the mind, the less it is in isolation. In the *Philosophical Lectures* he presented to his audience a picture of true genius that owes a great deal to the concluding stanzas of the 'Ode: Dejection'. Do not, he says, trust the genius of an envious man, 'for all genius exists in a participation of a common spirit'.

In joy individuality is lost and it therefore is liveliest in youth, not from any principle in organization but simply from this that the hardships of life, that the circumstances that have forced a man in upon his little

---

[1] *Phil. Lects.*, p. 224 (Lecture VI).

unthinking contemptible self, have lessened his power of existing universally; it is that only which brings about those passions. To have a genius is to live in the universal.[1]

A thinker to whom the duties of men towards each other meant less than the selfhood which divided them was pernicious, not only to himself, but to whole nations, and a good part of Coleridge's first five lectures was devoted to contrasting the spirit of the sceptical philosophers with that of the Pythagoreans and other idealists who sought to ground moral and philosophical systems on a different and higher principle. For we know from other sources that Coleridge held the prevailing philosophical climate to be important not merely to the intellectual but to the moral state of society – a thing of far greater importance. The scepticism of Leucippus and Zeno corrupted that 'upon which the state of society must always depend, namely the tone of mind'. In contrast to their misuse of the faculty of Reason, Coleridge admired Pythagoras for his realization that virtue could be learned only by the practice of virtue, not from any *a priori* theory; that as the practice of virtue depended upon the will, it could not be said to be influenced by any prior act (for this act would of course depend upon the will itself, in turn, so that the result would be an endless progression); and that moral education must therefore begin with revelation – with principles 'delivered from the Gods'. The legendary loyalty and friendship shown by the disciples of Pythagoras towards each other, and their magnanimity towards others, proved the value of Pythagoras's first principle, that of 'deducing the true character of man as he ought to be, not, in the first instance, from the intellect but from a higher principle, and then employing the intellect as constantly educing this and bringing it into more perfection.'[2] This sentence could well stand as a motto to *Aids to Reflection*, for it summarizes perfectly the premise on which that work is based. It is doubtful whether *Aids* was the *result* of Coleridge's admiration for Pythagoras in any simple sense: in an earlier lecture in the 1818 series Coleridge praised Pythagoras for attempting to improve his nation's morals by addressing moral discourses to each of the classes in succession, beginning with the

[1] *ib*. p. 179 (Lecture v).　　[2] *ib*. p. 119 (Lecture iii).

highest, which is what Coleridge himself had done, of course, in his two *Lay Sermons*.[1] It is more likely that Coleridge found in Pythagoras an instance of a philosopher whose aims seemed somewhat similar to his own, and that his account of Pythagoras therefore naturally reflects this sense of identification. It may be that Coleridge drew some inspiration from a knowledge of Pythagoras's methods.[2] Other philosophers too, however, have suggested that virtue can never be produced out of intellect alone: Berkeley, to take one instance, used this argument against the Deists, charging them with undermining morality by weakening religious faith, for virtue, to most men, is a meaningless fiction unless there exists a God to approve it. The man who can love and practise virtue for its own sake is a rare phenomenon.[3] Berkeley also has an elegant statement of the view of 'human nature' as an ideal, so often put forward by Coleridge:

EUPHRANOR The nature of anything is peculiarly that which doth distinguish it from other things, not what it hath in common with them. Do you allow this to be true?

LYSICLES I do.

EUPHRANOR And is not reason that which makes the principal difference between man and other animals?

LYSICLES It is.

EUPHRANOR Reason, therefore, being the principal part of our nature, whatever is most reasonable should seem most natural to man. Must we not therefore think rational pleasures more agreeable to humankind than those of sense?[4]

In *Aids to Reflection* Coleridge assumes that the reader is aware of the existence of a 'largeness' such as Leighton speaks of, a spiritual part of humanity which is more than can be attributed to 'the life of nature and the mechanism of organization'.[5] Coleridge explains that the Will is this spiritual part, and that it is only by the submission of the Will to the 'Supreme

[1] *Phil. Lects.*, pp. 101–2 (Lecture II).
[2] Plato mentions Pythagoras by name only once, and Aristotle never, but Aristotle often speaks in a vague manner of the 'Pythagoreans'. Iamblichus wrote a life of Pythagoras of which C may have known. See J. Burnet, *Early Greek Philosophy*, pp. 85–6.
[3] See T. E. Jessop's introduction to *Alciphron*, Berkeley's *Works*, edited by A.A. Luce and T. E. Jessop, vol III, p.6.
[4] *ib.*, p. 86 (Dialogue 2, section 14).   [5] *Aids*, p. 99.

Reason' that humanity is improved.[1] Much of the debate that took place in the eighteenth century in England about the nature of Christian belief had been grounded on the assumption that it must be possible either to prove or to disprove the Gospels, and so compel men to believe, or not to believe, by sheer weight of argument. Coleridge rejected this kind of controversy utterly: 'the Christian', he wrote, 'asserts what he can neither prove, nor account for, nor himself comprehend.'[2] Yet there are three 'ultimate facts' which demand a response, Conscience, Will and Evil. These need no proof. What is offered to the believer is summarized in the quotation from St Augustine which Coleridge gives in his preface and again in the body of the work: 'Sic accipite, ut mereamini intelligere.' René Wellek argues that Coleridge is here in an *impasse* from which he extricates himself only by changing his point of view. Had he not done so, he would have had to use the word 'Reason' in two different senses, as meaning sometimes that power in the individual man which convinces him of sin, and sometimes — as in the phrase 'the supreme Reason' — the Nous. This would be a form of 'Neoplatonic Pantheism', Wellek believes; which of course would have been unacceptable to Coleridge.[3] Wellek's criticism is correct, I would suggest, only if we begin with 'Greek' assumptions about the nature of the divine — that it must be everywhere if it is anywhere, and therefore that if John and Mark both become Christian it is because they have each perceived the existence of part of the divine in themselves. Viewed in this light, Coleridge's argument does demand two kinds of Reason: one which resides in each man's mind, and one — the Nous — which has universal existence. If however we begin with Hebraic assumptions about the Divine, there is, I believe, no inconsistency. We may now say that John and Mark, like all men, have a Will; that is to say, it is, and always has been, in their power to make moral choices according to their own desires, or according to a higher law. So far they have chosen according to their own desires or selfish natures. They were 'fallen' creatures (for as Coleridge later explains, the Fall is not a calamity of nature, nor

[1] J. H. Green restated this idea in his *Spiritual Philosophy*, i pp. 180–2; see below, pp. 170–2.   [2] *Aids*, p. 101.
[3] R. Wellek, *Immanuel Kant in England*, p. 128.

a hereditary defect passed down from Adam, but the first truth of all human conduct). But precisely because they knew they were choosing selfish ends, they became aware that the Will could assert itself in another way – this, I take it, is the meaning that Coleridge gives the word 'conscience' in *Aids to Reflection*. 'Conscience' may be a divine gift, but it is not strictly true to say that it is part of the divine, τὸ θεῖον; for Hebrew or at least Mosaic thought, as Coleridge saw it, began with ὁ θεός, a personal God, not with the attribute of divinity. John and Mark, by separate acts of the Will, then each committed himself to a higher law than that of the self; they willed only the Will of God, and since God is a person, they could will the same as he without taking part of the divine mind into themselves (except by a kind of metaphor: so, if you and I both love music we may say that we are of one mind, though your love for music is in no sense a result of mine). But human intelligence, or the Understanding, is by itself inadequate to the redemption of the corrupt Will; men must first acknowledge the divine Will, and act by it, and then they will 'understand' its dispensation. Virtue is learned by the practice of virtue.[1] This was the essence of Coleridge's new message, which became the starting-point for what Leslie Stephen called 'that metaphysical theology which attempted to revive the ancient religion by spiritualising it after a new fashion'.[2] Its 'spirituality' consisted not in an artificial removal of man from his present state of existence, but in the presentation of a different and less neutral view of that state (we remember Coleridge's insistence that the concern of the Christian church must be, not 'the next world', but *another world that now is*').[3] The corollary of the doctrine of free will is that of original sin – another fragment of 'the ancient religion' which Coleridge made new. Sin cannot, he argues, originate in nature, for nothing in nature has an origin, except in God: and God can do only good. It must originate outside nature; therefore in the spiritual; 'But the spiritual in man is the will'; therefore sin originates in the will of man. It is 'original' in this sense only – a self-

---

[1] *Aids*, pp. 104, 162–77.

[2] *History of English Thought in the Eighteenth Century*, i p. 393.

[3] A phrase first used in a letter to Edward Coleridge (*Letters*, vi p. 596 (no. 1537: 27 July 1826)) which was printed as an appendix to *On the Constitution of Church and State* – see CCS pp. 132–6 and below p. 253.

originating corruption – not a calamity of nature, or a hereditary defect.[1] Coleridge adds an interesting twist to his argument by further suggesting that, since the corrupt will subjects itself to nature, and so losing its freedom becomes merely part of 'the mechanism of cause and effect', the corruption of the will is an abandonment of personality. Man becomes less than a person at the point where his spiritual part admits into it any part of nature: this is 'a fall of man, inasmuch as his will is the condition of his personality'.[2] But this was no mere trick of dialectic to Coleridge: the antagonism between what we may now call the 'personal' and the self-will was a real one to him, and frequently figures in his MS reflections upon prayer and religious discipline. A note of 1826 on prayer ends with this reflection: 'Self-contempl, or a Sinking back into the potential, a willingness to evanescence of the Personal in us, is virtual Suicide – it is truly a self-centering – we will not the Will of God. – It is likewise presumption: for hereby we will to be lower than Reason.'[3] Preoccupation with the self, according to Coleridge's metaphysic, was not a mere negative sin, a sin of omission; it was a crime against what 'human nature' can and must be. Selfishness repeats the Fall: it 'tends to destroy the division between our person and our corrupt nature – to restore and reproduce the identity or indistinction of the "I" and the Nature. We *become* Evil and burrow in the Ground which God hath cursed.'[4] The heart of Coleridge's concern in *Aids to Reflection* is, then, not personal salvation, but that 'ever-expanding circumference' which J. H. Muirhead felt defined Coleridge's idea of personality; not self-centred piety, but a rediscovery of human love; not self-consciousness, but relationship.

4

Some of the ramifications of Coleridge's new and more 'metaphysical' way of thinking about relationship, and in particular the emphasis on religious belief as the key to 'another world that now is', are evident in the views he expressed on marriage and

---

[1] *Aids*, pp. 207, 222.   [2] *ib*. p. 219.
[3] Notebook 26, fols 53–4.   [4] Notebook 46, fol. 148.

love in the years 1814–34. An 'Essay on Marriage', written, it would seem, in 1821, possibly as a letter to the sister of a friend (Allsop),[1] combines the solemn affirmation of the greater moral demands made upon a married woman's character, and her greater capacity for either sorrow or happiness, with some pragmatic advice on such points as the foolishness of marrying a weak and sickly man, who may die, and leave his widow with unhealthy children to bring up. Coleridge's admiration for the 'German' ideal of equality in marriage, expressed in *The Watchman*, has given place to a not incompatible but certainly differing point of view: that marriage implies a greater change for a woman than for a man, since it 'fills the *whole* sphere of a Woman's Moral and personal Being'. Marriage is spoken of, not as an institution which may serve a social need or the high purpose of the 'cultivation' of the race, but as a moral and spiritual state which makes its own demands upon the individual.

Even those Duties (if any such there be) which it may seem to leave behind, it does but *transfer*. Say rather, it re-imposes and re-consecrates them under yet dearer names; (tho' names more dear than those of Daughter and Sister it is not easy to imagine) – at all events with obligations additionally binding on her Conscience, because undertaken by an act of her own free will.[2]

The insistence on the seriousness and the moral importance of such a step as marriage is to be expected in a letter addressed to a young protégée; and Coleridge does not envisage the submission of the woman to the man, but merely says that the change in the woman's life and duties will be much more far-reaching than that in the man's. Yet this is a double standard of a kind, though one not totally incompatible with the point made in the third issue of *The Watchman*. Indeed in some sense it substantiated it, for Coleridge appears to argue that a married woman is a more considerable person, by the mere fact of being married, than a single woman. Naturally, he does not pretend that happiness is attainable only in the married state, but he does say that 'a Woman in a single state may be happy, and may be miserable.

1 See *Letters*, v pp. 152–8 (no. 1268: ? June, 1821). T. J. Wise printed a version of this letter in 1919, under the title 'Essay on Marriage' (British Museum, C 57 e 54 and Ashley 2877).
2 *Letters*, v pp. 152–3.

But *most* happy, *most* miserable – these are epithets which, with rare exceptions, belong exclusively to a Wife.'[1]

What is perhaps rather more interesting, however, is the importance Coleridge attaches to the fact that marriage is an act of the free will, and not a state into which we are born with its loyalties and obligations awaiting us. While not inconsistent with respect for filial duties, Coleridge's reference to 'obligations additionally binding... because undertaken by an act of her own free will' reveals how far he had now moved towards the formulation of an essentially Protestant morality. Duties are imposed on us, not solely by the Will of God in giving us a certain place in society and a certain structure of familial relationships (as Burke argues in *An Appeal from the New to the Old Whigs*),[2] but by our own options; and – an important rider – these latter are in some sense more significant. Coleridge is not of course defending a sectarian attitude towards marriage. His definition of 'religion', when he comes to deal with the matter of choosing a marriage partner, is wide. Religion, he writes, is 'Morality in reference to all that is *permanent* and *imperishable*, God and our Souls, for instance: and Morality is Religion in it's application to Individuals, Circumstances, the various Relations and Spheres in which we *happen* to be placed.'[3] Like Carlyle's statement that 'a man's religion is the chief fact with regard to him... the thing a man does practically believe',[4] these definitions of Coleridge's transfer the emphasis from creeds and formal avowals of belief to the practice of the individual, and what the individual is in himself. Naturally this movement affects many other human institutions besides that of marriage: it is indeed a major element in Romantic thought: but here Coleridge is concerned only to give some very practical advice. It really amounts to an injunction to choose wisely, for he warns his young reader to beware of the irreligious, self-centred man, who lives by the false 'maxim', 'Each for himself, and God for us all', as she would of the physically weak man: a man's 'religion', in this sense, is at least as much an element of what he really is as his

---

[1] *Letters*, v p. 153.
[2] See A. Cobban, editor, *The Debate on the French Revolution* p. 253.
[3] *Letters*, v p. 155.
[4] *On Heroes, Hero-Worship and the Heroic in History*, pp. 8–9 (Lecture I).

physical constitution. The Letter ends with a further apo-
strophe to duty and faith: 'Woe to the Man who is incapable of
feeling that the greatest possible good he can do for himself or
for others, is to *do his duty* and to leave the consequences to
God.'[1]

Far from regarding the love of another person as an obstacle
to the love of God, Coleridge held that 'there is a religion in all
deep love',[2] and there is much evidence that to him there was no
antithesis between love human and love divine, such as was
often assumed by writers on religion, and in particular by the
early Church Fathers. He found a 'leaven of Manichæism' in the
writings of the Fathers when marriage and human love was their
subject.[3] In an episode in Henry Brooke's novel *The Fool of
Quality*, the heroine laments the fact that her love for a man has
'stood between' her and God. Coleridge commented on this,

The Crown and Base, the Pinnacle and Foundation of a regenerate and
truly Christian State of Mind, as long as our Souls are within the
fleshly Coil, is to love God in all that we love, to love that only therefore in which we can at the same time love God – and thus gradually,
in the growth towards our final perfection, more and more to love all
things in God.[4]

So far from being incompatible with Christianity, as it was to
Kierkegaard, to Coleridge love of a human being was capable of
being refined and intensified by the influence of religious belief.
Yet not all love was capable of such transformation, or not
everything that men call love. All the passions whose end is the
mere use of another person for pleasure cannot be consistent with
the love of God, because they involve still 'the misery of the
self'. Coleridge does not, therefore, incorporate all breathing
human passion into the range of religious experience, or into the
ever-expanding circumference that is his image of personality.
The height of the Christian state of mind is 'to love that only in
which we can at the same time love God', and this means that
any form of self-seeking is rejected. But that there are more
subtle temptations, and more difficult to fight, than sexual attraction, Coleridge well knew. The pain that a lover suffers through

[1] *Letters*, v p. 158.   [2] *ib.* p. 180 (no. 1279: 20 October 1821).
[3] Notebook 35, fols. 165–6.   [4] Notebook 47, fol. 176.

knowing that his love is, like all other things, transitory, and his
longing to possess the beloved so completely that the transitori-
ness no longer matters, Coleridge recognized to be an essentially
selfish impulse. Not trusting the future, yet dissatisfied by the
present, the lover is driven to

press the Beloved Object closer to himself, as if to inclose it in his own
Life, and to <confound> it with his Being, thus sacrificing in order to
secure it! this excitement of the selfish Greed comes Grasping with
restlessness and turbid feelings / Lake, Vale, and Forest, Mountain and
the Glory of the Light are eclipsed – [1]

Coleridge's feeling is not that such a desire is intrinsically evil,
or even that passion is intrinsically evil (for he thought it a
necessary, if small, ingredient of love between the sexes); but
that by itself it is bad, as tending to entrap men in the sub-
personal, selfish part of their being. 'Human nature' may find
nothing abhorrent in various sexual practices – polygamy or
even community of women – but humanity, or the 'Reason and
Religion that constitute [man's] moral and spiritual nature',
forbids them.[2] In all human emotion, given that human nature
in Coleridge's special meaning is an ideal, there is bound to be a
conflict, because of the distance between what are called in
Green's *Spiritual Philosophy* the 'two states or spiritual conditions' of the soul: one (adopting the Pauline terms), the
πνευμάτικος, the other the ψυχικός, which in actual living agency
combines with the corporeal.[3] Coleridge could not accept Pope's
idea that love was a refined and purified kind of lust: so
far did he disagree with this that he in fact saw love as the
'antidote' to lust, as so fundamentally different that it could not
even be treated as its opposite pole (for this would mean that
they were inseparable, like the two poles of a magnet). Having
allowed love between the sexes a part, even an important part,
in the growth of 'personality', Coleridge found he must assume
that lovers are aware of the selfish as well as of the selfless part
of their love, and accept the selfish only as an unfortunate result
of what he calls 'the temporary Contradiction, Man'.

[1] Notebook 26, fols 5–6.
[2] R. F. Brinkley, editor, *Coleridge on the Seventeenth Century*, p. 214.
[3] *Spiritual Philosophy*, i p. 289.

The inner view, the intellectual Beholding of the two unequal Co-ingredients of a *Godly* exclusive attachment is then only attained when the *duplicity*, = the double or twofold nature, of the temporary Contradiction, Man, is known, seen, and understood. Then it will at once appear that Lust and Love are in their essences as contrary as God and Hades, as the self-seeking Emptiness, as the eliciting Light and the dark consuming Fire, as the <divine> and the bestial, in short as the φρονημα σαρκος, = the Mind of the Flesh, and the πνευμα θεου, 'the mind that was in Christ Jesus:' – and yet, on the other hand, having the same Analogy and Correspondence to each Man, as the Soul to the Body – even as we say, the Eagle is the King of Birds, and a great King the Eagle of Men. – For every lower Nature repeats the attributes of the immediate higher in its' own form.[1]

In some of his earlier writings, Coleridge had been, though no less aware of a contradiction between love and lust as such, less inclined to subject love to such a strict test as is here implied.[2] But between the early high valuation of love, and the more ambivalent reflections of his last years, when the 'spiritual philosophy' was in preparation, came the dark years of 1813 and 1814, and the search for a basis of religious faith, one result of which was Coleridge's conviction – deduced, he told a correspondent, from St Paul and St John – that Christianity was incompatible with 'whatever betrays or fosters the mind of flesh.'[3]

Though troubled by what he felt to be the ambivalent nature of love between the sexes, however, Coleridge had no doubts about the value of other kinds of love. Psychotherapists have in this century written at length on the importance for every infant's future development of the care and attention bestowed on him by his parents. Erik Erikson points out that philosophers speak of a 'female principle', but never of 'the fact that man is born and reared by women': and Anthony Storr, a psychotherapist with long experience of treating adult patients, believes that 'the development of the individual and the development of his relationships proceed *pari passu*; and the one cannot take place without the other'. This *pari passu* development must continue, Storr finds, into adulthood, if the mental health of the individual is to be unimpaired; both 'objective love' in childhood

1 Notebook 48, fols. 229–30.
2 For instance, see Notebook 23, fol. 63.
3 *Letters*, iv p. 697 (no. 1038: ? 1816).

and, in maturity, 'adult loving and being loved' are vital to human fulfilment.[1] Coleridge knew how vital parental care was; in particular, he knew that love without possessiveness – what Storr calls 'objective love' – was essential to the healthy growth of a child's personality. Speaking in a lecture about the education of children, he told his audience: 'Love is first to be instilled, and out of love is obedience to be educed' – before any appeal to intellect is made; then only can 'the ends of a moral being' be put before the child.[2] A margin note in a copy of the *Life of Bishop Sandford* is extant, in which Coleridge points to the 'moral interest' of the Bishop's fatherly qualities:

The father recognises in his daughters the representations, and (as it were) the renewed types of their mother, and repeats towards them, delicately modified by the difference of the relation, the tender reverence, the inward gentle awe inseparable from all true love that is at once pure and deep. From the father the same tone and feeling, only again modified by the different relation, will pass to the brothers; and thus the parental home be a rehearsal of the finest duties of the continuous affections of the conjugal state.

Reverence of *womanhood* is the ground of all manly virtues, and a main condition of all female excellence.[3]

The final sentence expresses a favourite opinion of Coleridge's, which he put to use in his lectures of 1818 on Shakespeare and other poets. T. M. Raysor says that Coleridge may have borrowed from Schlegel the attribution of the Germans' 'higher moral character' to their showing greater respect towards their womenfolk than did the Romans: but Coleridge had made a similar point in issue III of *The Watchman* – and the connection was originally pointed out by Tacitus.[4] Perhaps this is another case of Coleridge discovering in another author insights half-formed already in his own mind, and from this discovery gaining fresh confidence in what he had previously only guessed at. Certainly Coleridge continued to be interested in the connection between Christianity and reverence of womanhood, long after he

[1] Erik Erikson, *Childhood and Society*, p. 393; Anthony Storr, *The Integrity of the Personality*, pp. 45, 178.
[2] *Miscellaneous Criticism*, p. 194; see also H. C. Robinson, *Blake, Coleridge, Wordsworth, Lamb &c.*, pp. 105–6.
[3] Lucy E. Watson, *Coleridge at Highgate*, p. 153.
[4] *Miscellaneous Criticism*, pp. 8–9; *The Watchman*, p. 89 (no. iii).

had ceased to give lectures: it was (he told Charles Stutfield in 1831) the peculiar character of Christianity that it raised the qualities already possessed by women to a far higher power.[1] In the *Confessions of an Inquiring Spirit* he reminds us that Deborah, in her condemnation of her people's cowardice, spoke not as a prophet but as *'a mother in Israel'*,[2] and this observation has an extraordinary parallel in a criticism of what Coleridge saw as the excessive 'Parthenolatry' or 'Mariolatry' practised by the Roman Catholic Church. Far from truly expressing the 'affections and aspirations' which the Virgin Mary felt for her divine child, the 'Romish Deification' of Mary abolished its real meaning by endowing it with an aura of holiness. Mary, like Deborah, was a mother in Israel, and to Coleridge the fullest meaning of her love for her child was to be found in the realization that she shared every human mother's feeling – indeed she shared in the 'storgè', or parental love, that is shown in increasing intensity through the entire scale of animal life, to its highest form, its 'irradiation by the Reason and Conscience in the human Mother'.[3] The power of Mary's love was not an exceptional gift from heaven; it was the special quality – holy indeed, but not supernatural – of human motherhood.

5

In spite of a great admiration for Kant's powers, Coleridge firmly repudiated the suggestion that he had adopted his philosophy.

Of the three schemes of Philosophy, Kant's, Fichte's and Schelling's . . . I should find it difficult to select the one from which I *differed* the most – tho' perfectly easy to determine which of the three *Men* I hold in highest honor. And Immanuel Kant I assuredly do value most highly; not, however, as a Metaphysician but as a Logician, who has completed and systematized what Lord Bacon had boldly designed and loosely sketched out in the miscellany of Aphorisms, his Novum Organum.[4]

Coleridge's careful distinction between Kant's achievement in

[1] *Letters*, vi p. 869 (no. 1714: 21 August 1831).
[2] *Confessions of an Inquiring Spirit*, edited by H. St J. Hart, p. 53; see also *Shakespearean Criticism*, ii p. 102.   [3] Notebook 26, fol. 69.
[4] *Letters*, v p. 421 (no. 1438: 8 April 1825).

logic, and his use of the logic in delimiting metaphysical speculation, which Coleridge regarded as illegitimate, is worth bearing in mind when we come to consider Coleridge's attitude
towards Kant as a moralist. Coleridge repeatedly reminds us that
he considers philosophy to be a specialism, not something to be
turned to as a Bible of conduct for Everyman. Writing to J.
Gooden in 1820, he told him 'in [Kant] is contained all that can
be *learnt*', and said that he agreed with Kant's principle of
establishing the existence of God, or free will and immortality
on 'Postulates authorized and substantiated solely by the *Moral
Being*'. The ground of their disagreement – whether the Ideas
are regulative, as for Aristotle and Kant, or constitutive, as for
Pythagoras and Plato – was not something that need concern
Gooden or anyone else other than 'the Philosopher by Profession'.[1] But Coleridge himself could not keep the two spheres,
those of philosophy with its logical basis, and morality with its
religious basis, as strictly separate as he here advised his friend
to do. The difference between an idea that is constitutive and one
that is regulative is not one of (as we might say) merely
technical interest. For Kant, moral freedom was an attribute of
the noumenal, unknowable self: a regulative not a constitutive
idea. Had it been applicable to the empirical self, and amenable
to the Understanding, it would have clashed with the category of
causality (one of the categories by which we judge of Relation).
It can only be 'saved', as Kant puts it, by being treated as a
regulative idea. Kant's extrication of moral freedom – which for
Schiller and Coleridge was the most significant of his successes –
depended on the refutation of the theory that things-in-them-
selves could be known. 'Denn sind Erscheinungen Dinge an sich
selbst, so ist Freiheit nicht zu retten.'[2] But as A. O. Lovejoy has
shown, Coleridge's conception of moral freedom, as expressed
in chapters V–VIII of *Biographia Literaria*, is unKantian, since
it treats moral freedom as a property of the empirical or
phænomenal self, not merely of the noumenal self;[3] and indeed,

[1] *ib.* p. 14 (no. 1223: 14 January 1820). See G. N. G. Orsini, *Coleridge and German Idealism*, pp. 248, 255.
[2] See *Critique of Pure Reason*, p. 466; R. D. Miller, *Schiller and the Ideal of Freedom*, p. 1. 'If appearances are things in themselves, freedom cannot be salvaged.'
[3] A. O. Lovejoy, 'Coleridge and Kant's Two Worlds', *Essays in the History of Ideas*, (254–76), p. 265.

Coleridge deduces the categorical imperative from the knowledge of moral freedom, not vice versa as in Kant.[1] The issue of whether moral freedom is a constitutive or a regulative idea is thus for him no mere academic question, but one vital to the coherence of his method as expounded in *Aids to Reflection*.

For the great majority of Englishmen, Kant's mind was either unintelligible or – as De Quincey found it – 'essentially destructive'. De Quincey contrasted Kant's qualities of penetration and logical precision, suited to the task of exposing the fallacies of older systems, and Coleridge's essentially creative instinct: '[Kant] had no instincts of creation or restoration within his Apollyon mind; for he had no love, no faith, no self-distrust, no humility, no childlike docility; all which qualities belonged essentially to Coleridge's mind, and waited only for manhood and sorrow to bring them forward.'[2] This is, as J. H. Stirling pointed out,[3] an extremely partisan view, though it may be said in De Quincey's defence that his account was meant to be impressionistic rather than analytical. It does at least show us how great was the English prejudice against Kant – a prejudice which, as René Wellek shows, was not really overcome until the 1830s. It is understandable if Coleridge sometimes represented Kant as being more on his side than he actually was, and confused what he so carefully advised his friends to distinguish. This tendency to sacrifice logicality for the sake of creation is most pronounced in Coleridge's criticism of Kant's moral doctrines.

Kant's argument that both the imitation of a supreme example, and the love of perfection in virtue for its own sake, are insufficient grounds for a rational morality, and that we should admire moral acts more, the less they are in accord with 'subjective impulses', is well known. Reason does not determine the will; the will is free to obey or to disobey its dictates. Kant's position is that we know even when we transgress that there is a moral law; but we have made an exception in our own favour on this occasion, and we do not really will that the maxim of our act should be the law of all rational beings, indeed we cannot will this. The imperatives are 'formulæ to express the relation of

[1] G. N. G. Orsini, *Coleridge and German Idealism*, p. 158.
[2] *Reminiscences of the English Lake Poets*, p. 17.
[3] 'De Quincey and Coleridge upon Kant', *Jerrold, Tennyson and Macaulay, &c.*, p. 180.

objective laws of all volition to the subjective imperfection of. . .
e.g. the human will'.[1] An imperative that raises an ideal such as
perfection in virtue, or the imitation of an example, to the status
of an objective law is in Kant's terms a hypothetical imperative,
because it presupposes that something else is willed besides the
act itself: but Kant means to build the practical Reason upon
what is in itself necessary, and so he rejects the hypothetical
imperative in favour of the categorical imperative, which he
finds to be unique, namely 'Act only on that maxim whereby
thou canst at the same time will that it should become a universal
law.'[2] In passing, a curious irony may be noted here: while the
ideas of God and immortality reached in the *Critique of Pure
Reason* are regulative, that is, may not be known as they in themselves are, the dictates of Pure Reason in the domain of ethics
are constitutive – they may be so known, even though (as before
shown) the idea of moral freedom itself pertains to the noumenal, unknowable self. As Professor Orsini points out, following Ewing, a theory of ethics which only stated what our duty
seems to be, not what it is, would be useless.[3]

The hypothetical imperatives are rejected, then, because they
involve the prior orientation of the will towards something other
than the reasonableness of the act (though Kant does not deny
that this 'something' may be itself objective), and of course subjective impulses are ruled out, because it is manifestly impossible
rationally to will that the maxim of every act prompted by subjective impulses should become a universal law. It follows that
the man who performs his duty when it is contrary to his subjective impulses is more worthy of admiration than he who does his
duty in accordance with such impulses.[4] This has become known
as Kant's 'stoic principle', perhaps a misleading term, but it was
under this title that Coleridge attacked it, in a letter to J. H.
Green, as 'false, unnatural, and even immoral'.

I reject Kant's *stoic* principle, as false, unnatural, and even immoral,
where in his Critik der Practischen Vernun [f]t he treats the affections

---

[1] *Critique of Practical Reason*, translated by T. K. Abbott, pp. 25, 31, 43–4. (Section
II of 'Fundamental Principles of the Metaphysic of Morals.')
[2] 'Fundamental Principles of the Metaphysic of Morals', section II; *Critique of
Practical Reason*, pp. 31, 38.
[3] Orsini, *Coleridge and German Idealism*, pp. 149–50.
[4] *Critique of Practical Reason*, p. 43.

as indifferent (ἀδιάφορα) in ethics, and would persuade us that a man who disliking, and without any feeling of Love for, Virtue yet *acted* virtuously, because and only because it was his *Duty*, is more worthy of our esteem, than the man whose *affections* were aidant to, and congruous with, his Conscience. For it would imply little less than that things not the Objects of the moral Will or under it's controul were yet indispensable to it's due practical direction. In other words, it would subvert his own System.[1]

It is immediately obvious of course that Coleridge found Kant's system emotionally distasteful, and this was undoubtedly one reason for his rejection of it. But what is more important is this criticism of a fundamental inconsistency in Kant's system, and the hidden premise that gives rise to the criticism. For there is a hidden premise in Coleridge's phrase about the man who, disliking Virtue, yet acts virtuously: it is that a man cannot act virtuously without at the same time showing affection. Coleridge's belief that the two go together was apparently so deep-rooted that he actually assumed that Kant held the professing of affection, where none existed, to be more estimable than the virtuous act done out of genuine affection. Yet Kant had already argued that affections were not under the power of the will. He was therefore, Coleridge believed, asking us to accept that the will could empower a man to exhibit these subjective impulses, which were not, according to his own argument, under its control, solely in order to obey an imperative that had nothing to do with any subjective impulse. On these grounds, Coleridge argued that Kant had 'subverted' his own system. The argument may be represented schematically thus:

1 *Kant's premise*: the will has no control over the affections.

2 *Coleridge's premise*: the man who acts virtuously towards another, by that act shows affection.

3 *Kant's deduction*: the man who acts virtuously because it is his duty is more admirable than the man who does so out of affection.

4 *Coleridge's interpretation*: Kant asks us to admire the man who out of a sense of duty pretends to feelings he does not have.

The unstated premise here attributed to Coleridge will, I

[1] *Letters*, iv pp. 728–9 (no. 1089: 13 December 1817).

believe, be found to make sense of the criticism of Kant contained in the letter of December 1817, which otherwise makes little sense. Of course Coleridge's criticism is open to the charge of confusing psychology with ethics, but Kant had arguably invited this kind of criticism by the polemical expression of a 'stoic principle' when his system would perhaps have suffered no substantial loss without it. Coleridge, for his part, had never been willing to leave the affections outside the sphere of ethical discussion; as René Wellek rightly states, 'Coleridge could not see why our emotional nature should be excluded from the elements of ethics'.[1] In suggesting merely that Coleridge favoured a 'religious anodyne' to Kant's severity, in contrast to Schiller's 'æsthetic anodyne', Wellek leaves aside most of the links between religious belief, moral conduct and 'our emotional nature', of which Coleridge had always been aware, even before 'manhood and sorrow', in De Quincey's phrase, brought them out. For in his political lectures of 1795, Coleridge was already insisting that right principles were in themselves not enough, but they must irradiate the affections, which in turn must be cultivated by the light of the understanding.[2]

Coleridge's thought is in some respects not 'Platonic', but pre-Platonic, or rather pre-Socratic. Like Pythagoras and Plato themselves, Coleridge combines the aims and ideals of an older way of thought with the discipline of a new rationalism, and so produces results that are, as theirs often were, apparently inconsistent. F. M. Cornford has pointed out the importance of that moment in one of Plato's Dialogues, the *Euthyphro*, when Socrates' interlocutor is made to concede that the gods must love what is righteous because it is righteous. This admission shifts the emphasis of religious teaching away from doing the will of God, purely because it is his will, to doing what reason or conscience bids us do.[3] As we have seen, Coleridge's trend (except for a short period in 1805, when he raised the concept of moral duty above that of self-originating love),[4] is towards the former doctrine, in so far as he asks the aspiring Christian (in *Aids to*

[1] René Wellek, *Immanuel Kant in England*, p. 88.
[2] *Lectures 1795*, pp. 33, 49 ('Conciones ad Populum', Introductory Address).
[3] F. M. Cornford, *Principium Sapientiæ*, p. 139.
[4] N 2556. See Orsini, *Coleridge and German Idealism*, pp. 154–5.

Reflection) to believe first, and learn afterwards;[1] and like Berkeley in *Alciphron* he rejected the view that the beauty of virtue was in itself a sufficient inducement to the pursuit of virtue. Certain of Kant's criticisms of this view, the chief defender of which in the eighteenth century was Shaftesbury, held a strong attraction for Coleridge, since Kant was able to demonstrate that morality as well as faith in God, free will and immortality, was (as Coleridge told Gooden) 'acquiesced in, indeed, nay, confirmed by the Reason and Understanding'.[2] But Coleridge still rated much higher the view of virtue which Plato outlined in the *Republic*, and which Cornford summarizes as 'a harmony of all desires, secured by the reorientation of desire itself'. This stands in strong contrast to the Aristotelian picture of the temperate man, whose irrational desires are still at war with the restraints imposed by reason, and who can never, therefore, achieve the 'harmony' which for Plato characterized true virtue, and which enabled desire or Eros to be directed towards the highest good, instead of towards more physical pleasure. In another dialogue, the *Phædrus*, Plato showed that the proper end of Eros was the *summum bonum*.[3] I do not suggest that Coleridge derived the doctrines expounded in *Aids to Reflection* solely from Plato, but that Coleridge's theory of human nature, and its relationship to the Good, is in many important points similar to Plato's, and particularly in those dialogues where the influence of the pre-Socratic thinkers on Plato is most evident. In *Aids*, Coleridge specifically rejected the view that virtue contains its own inducements, as tending dangerously towards an egotistical pride in the possession of virtue: indeed he argued that the very word 'virtue' was inconsistent with Christian humility, and should be left to 'the modern Pagans'. But he found already existing in humanity the possibility of an ascending scale of concern, an ever-expanding love, analogous to the Platonic conception of an Eros turned away from selfish pleasures towards its proper goal: he did not find it a part of Christian duty to 'take angel's wings to overfly my own human nature'. In this conception he found the only real possibility of conquering selfhood: not by Kant's 'stoic principle', basing

[1] See above, pp. 151–5.　　[2] *Letters*, v p. 14 (no. 1223: 14 January 1820).
[3] Cornford, *Principium Sapientiæ* pp. 70–2.

morality on the demands of an intractable logic, nor by a 'eudæmonism' resting on the basis of an equally remote system of reward and punishment.[1] A long manuscript note of 1827 expressed his conviction that the purification of the already-existing human love from selfishness was the only ground of morality. It also affirmed his resolution to illustrate this in a future work – which was, needless to say, never written.

In the first heat of the Kantéan School it was normal with the high-flying Moralists to inveigh against the Christian Morality as an impure eudæmonism grounded on each Individual's hopes and fears of the lot to be bestowed or inflicted on him after death – and therefore essentially selfish. Every awakened Christian knows the practical falsehood of this charge – , knows, that one of the earliest symptoms and results of a <convinced> state, and an <actual> reception of the Word into the Will and affections is the urgent and tender interest, <the awakened> Believer begins to feel for the <future> welfare of those around him; which <cannot stop there, their spiritual> Health and Sickness being too closely and too extensively connected with the whole State and Condition of the Individual, in the present Life, their conduct, habits, tempers, opinions, feelings and outward circumstances. Many a Father can say, that it was since he had become a serious Christian that he first knew what it was to be verily and indeed concerned for a Son – what the *wrestling* of Love was – Nevertheless, it would be a most serviceable labor to <prove> the reality and necessity of such a result, <as soon as the life of> faith <begins> to pulsate, and a man had in good earnest enter <ed> into the Christian Warfare, both from the Nature of the Causes at work and from the constitution of the human Mind – to shew the whole process, and to exhibit it's operation in all the various incidents, relations and ties of the Social State; man, we, us, are the Christian Pronouns – me, and my being for the greater part reserved for moments and occasions of contrition, and self-abasement.[2]

6

In Browning's early dramatic monologue, 'Pauline', the distracted poet who is the suppositious author of the piece 'strips his mind bare', and asserts the following:

> I am made up of an intensest life,
> Of a most clear idea of consciousness

[1] *Aids*, pp. 143, 145 (Aphorism V).   [2] Notebook 36, fols. 190–1.

Of self, distinct from all its qualities,
From all affections, passions, feelings, powers;
And thus far it exists, if tracked, in all.[1]

This assertion is a clear taking of sides. By such a statement Browning's *persona*, if not Browning himself, firmly rejects the sceptical view of David Hume that consciousness of personal identity is merely a convenient fiction, and that man has knowledge only of a succession of impressions, and ranges himself with the Romantic adherents of 'Idealism'. An idea of self, Hume had argued, 'must be some one impression, that gives rise to every real idea', for we cannot be conscious of anything, according to Hume's philosophy, except through an impression. Now believers in an 'abiding self' hold that it is something to which all passions and sensations relate; but it is contrary to all our experience to pretend that all passions and sensations have one impression in common.

If any impression gives rise to the idea of self, that impression must continue invariably the same, thro' the whole course of our lives; since self is suppos'd to exist after that manner. But there is no impression constant and invariable. Pain and pleasure, grief and joy, passions and sensations succeed each other, and never all exist at the same time. It cannot, therefore, be from any of these impressions, or from any other, that the idea of self is deriv'd; and consequently there is no such idea.[2]

One version of the opposing idealist point of view was put forward by Coleridge's pupil, Joseph Henry Green, in his posthumously published *Spiritual Philosophy*. Green stated that this question of self-consciousness, or the mind's knowledge of its own unity, was an essential problem for any true philosopher to answer.

One of the greatest difficulties, in the way of a true philosophy and of a well-grounded system of Realism, is and has been the position, maintained by Hume and Kant, that we have no proper Self-consciousness or Knowledge of a Self, and that what we call Self-consciousness is the cognizance only of the mental presentations of that which we may infer indeed to be a one mind, but of which we have no knowledge beyond its manifestations in the consciousness – its appearances or phænomena

[1] *Poetical Works*, p. 4.
[2] David Hume, *A Treatise of Human Nature*, edited by L. A. Selby-Bigge, pp. 251–2 (Book I, Part iv, section vi).

...Thus all reality of a mind or self, a substance or spirit, is at once destroyed, and the *soi-disant* philosopher is left to deal only with thoughts, with a representative shadow or image of the thinker himself, or of a mind which according to this view is beyond the limits of knowledge.[1]

There is much evidence in Coleridge's later notebooks and letters to show that a large proportion of the discussions which Coleridge had with Green during the Highgate years were devoted to the problem of self-consciousness. Nevertheless it is not possible to say with any degree of certainty that the solution propounded by Green in the *Spiritual Philosophy* is Coleridge's own. On the evidence of the notebooks, Coleridge continued to revise his thoughts on self-consciousness until at least 1830, and there is no reason to suppose that he would not have continued revising them, had it been in his power to do so. Of course Green's statement of the problem, and his attempted solution, have a distinctly Coleridgean character, but that is not the same as saying that Coleridge would have given his sanction to them. Green's solution deliberately overpasses the limits set by Kant to the explorations of Reason, and ventures into the realm of the transcendent. For him the Will is not (as it was for Kant) 'a necessary *postulate* of moral faith', but a fact of human con-sciousness. In the act of self-consciousness, Green argues, 'I must be...distinctly conscious that it is I, who am the Subject, I must know that it is I, thinking, willing, feeling.' What is there in the subjective relation without which these mental acts are impossible? 'The Will', is Green's answer, 'if by "Will" we mean as we cannot but do, a self-determinant agency and the only source of originative power.' ('Will' is here used as a virtual synonym for 'Spirit'.) Green does not accept, therefore, the Kantian emphasis on thoughts as mere representations – whether these representations are 'internal' or 'external' in origin. Those sceptics who 'contemplate the inward world of thought as they do outward objects' cannot but exclude the spiritual. Kant was wrong to confine human knowledge to the knowledge of phænomena; in inner consciousness, Green asserts, we have direct knowledge of a noumenon, and contemplate the

[1] J. H. Green, *Spiritual Philosophy*, i pp. 172–3.

identity of Being and Knowing in the subject's awareness of itself.[1]

Kant is not as much on the side of the sceptics as Green implies, however, and in order to understand Coleridge's own thinking on the subject of self-consciousness we must give some attention to the doctrine which Kant sought to substitute for the theory of personal identity so much distrusted by Hume: the doctrine of the transcendental unity of apperception. Hume's attack is averted from the start by two relatively simple steps. Firstly, Time, in the *Critique of Pure Reason*, does not exist in itself, but is merely the form under which all *inner* representations are perceived, as space is the form under which representations of 'external' objects are perceived.[2] Secondly, Kant realizes that if the mind is to be aware of itself, it must be affected by itself in some way; that is, there must be a representation of the mind of which the mind can be inwardly sensible. But in this case what is inwardly sensed is not the mind as it is, but the mind as it appears to itself. Kant discounts the possibility of the mind's being self-active, and is therefore constrained to class this form of consciousness, or 'empirical apperception', with other forms of empirical perception, in that it is a perception of appearance only, not of the thing-in-itself.

Everything that is represented through a sense is so far always appearance, and consequently we must either refuse to admit that there is an inner sense, or we must recognize that the subject, which is the object of the sense, can be represented through it only as appearance, not as that subject would judge of itself if its intuition were self-activity only, that is, were intellectual.[3]

Empirical apperception, therefore, gives us only appearances, and these not only differ from the thing-in-itself, but also are subject to change, so that no constant representation of the 'I' is possible. Some form of apperception must be constant, however, otherwise knowledge would be impossible, for we should have no means of connecting representations with one another and thereby arriving at knowledge. We should experience merely a chaos of unrelated impressions, without succession, without unity, without any possibility of being combined to-

[1] *Spiritual Philosophy*, i pp. 180, 185–6.   [2] *Critique of Pure Reason*, p. 76.
[3] *Critique of Pure Reason*, p. 88.

gether in order to form concepts; we should live perpetually in the inconsequential world of the dream. Knowledge of any kind has, as Kant puts it, a transcendental condition. This condition or ground he names 'transcendental apperception'.

There can be in us no modes of knowledge, no connection or unity of one mode of knowledge with another, without that unity of consciousness which precedes all data of intuitions, and by relation to which representation of objects is alone possible. This pure original unchangeable consciousness I shall name *transcendental apperception*. That it deserves this name is clear from the fact that even the purest objective unity, namely, that of the *a priori* concepts (space and time), is only possible through relation of the intuitions to such unity of consciousness.[1]

The consciousness here described has certain similarities to Coleridge's primary and secondary imaginations, as they are defined in chapter XIV of *Biographia Literaria*, especially since Kant accepts that one implication of his doctrine is that the unity of nature itself – which is, after all, none other than the unity of the representations of the natural world in man's mind – depends on the transcendental unity of apperception. 'The order and regularity in the appearances, which we entitle *nature*, we ourselves introduce. We could never find them in appearances, had not we ourselves, or the nature of our mind, originally set them there.'[2] Transcendental apperception is thus of supreme importance to Kant's epistemological preparation for his critique of Reason; but it should be emphasized that it is not equivalent to the self-consciousness spoken of by the idealists. It is Kant's way of showing that knowledge is possible, given that the thing-in-itself cannot be known. As Kant shows, if the object is, strictly speaking, no more than an inward representation, connections between objects, under the forms of space and time, necessitate a unity of possible consciousness. 'To assert in this manner, that all these appearances, and consequently all objects with which we can occupy ourselves, are one and all in me, that is, are determinations of my identical self, is only another way of saying that there must be a complete unity of them in one and the same apperception.'[3] None of this, however,

[1] *Critique of Pure Reason*, p. 136. [2] *ib*. pp. 140, 147.
[3] *ib*. p. 149; see pp. 209–10 and (for the 1787 revision) pp. 152–4.

justifies us in asserting that the mind can be conscious of its own existence in time as a thing-in-itself, independent, that is, of the perception of 'external' objects. In a section entitled 'Refutation of Idealism' (added to the *Critique* in the edition of 1787) Kant denied that the element of permanence on which all determination of time must be founded exists as an intuition in the mind. Time-determinations can be associated only with 'actual things which I perceive outside me' – even if their externality is an illusion, as is the case with dreams or hallucinations – and therefore, 'the consciousness of my existence is at the same time an immediate consciousness of the existence of other things outside me'; or, as it was later expressed, 'inner experience in general is possible only through outer experience in general'.[1] Thus Kant avoided the trap of solipsism, and the equally treacherous position, from his point of view, of empirical idealism. In place of Descartes' 'Cogito, ergo sum', Kant has 'the mere apperception *"I think"*, by which even transcendental concepts are made possible; what we assert in them is "I think substance, cause", etc.'[2] Körner summarizes Kant's theory of self-consciousness in this way: 'The introspected or empirical self is knowable and known; the self of pure apperception is thinkable but cannot possibly be known.'[3]

As G. N. G. Orsini points out, what Kant wholly ignores in the construction of the categories is the fact that we do not only perceive inert material objects, but the actions of other men and women; there is in the *Critique of Pure Reason* no hint of the greater complexity of perceptions which involve the presence of another person. The concept of the person is introduced in the *Critique of Practical Reason*, and that of the living organism in the *Critique of Judgment*: but nowhere does Kant suggest that what we might call an I–Thou relationship could affect our consciousness of personal identity, though he does suggest (in the *Metaphysical Elements of Ethics*) that a man's conscience deals with him as if it were the representation of another person; the conscience is the Homo Noumenon speaking to the Homo Sensibilis.[4]

[1] *Critique of Pure Reason*, pp. 245, 247.   [2] *ib.* pp. 329–30.   [3] *Kant*, p. 67.
[4] G. N. G. Orsini, *Coleridge and German Idealism*, pp. 115–22; *Critique of Practical Reason*, p. 322.

In the work of Schelling, the question whether there can be, in Browning's phrase, 'a most clear idea of consciousness /Of self', or only the momentary impressions which are the only furnishings of the mind according to David Hume, assumes an even greater importance, not only for the science of epistemology but, indirectly, for moral philosophy as well. Although it is obviously impossible to discuss at this juncture every significant aspect of Schellingian idealism, and its divergences from Kant, it will be necessary to observe a few of the most important elements of Schelling's idea of the Self, or the 'Ich', before posing the (for us) more material question of the extent of Coleridge's agreement with Kant and his most important disciple. In the process, however, there will also be reason to notice the attraction that this aspect of Schelling's philosophy may have had for Coleridge, and some of the ways in which it seemed to hold out the promise of an antidote to the aridities of Kantian logic.

Schelling misses no opportunity of reminding readers of the *System des transcendentalen Idealismus* that it is a work on epistemology, not on ontology: an attempt to explain how experience and knowledge are possible, not how anything can be proved to exist.[1] As is by now well enough known, a translation of the first few pages of the *System* was incorporated by Coleridge into *Biographia Literaria* (i pp. 174–8), and (with some other passages transmogrified from the *System* and other writings of Schelling) served as a rather disappointing statement of Coleridge's philosophical standpoint. Incomplete as the argument is in this patchwork form, however, the fulcrum about which it turns is evident enough. Knowledge can be attained in either of two ways, by proceeding from the objective, or by proceeding from the subjective.[2] The problem of natural philosophy is – assuming the existence of an unconscious nature, to which we cannot (to begin with) impute any intelligence whatsoever – to show how intelligence may emerge from such an unconscious nature. 'The highest perfection of natural philosophy would consist in the perfect spiritualization of all the laws of nature into laws of intuition and intellect.'[3] (This was the aim of the

[1] See *Schelling*, iii pp. 330–2, 356, 357–8.
[2] See T. McFarland, *Coleridge and the Pantheist Tradition*, pp. 148, 151–2.
[3] BL, i p. 175.

Schellingian *Naturphilosophie*.) The other means of knowing (which, it should perhaps be emphasized, is not concerned with a totally different realm of knowledge, but with a different approach to what is ultimately, in Schelling's view, a single body of laws, governing both 'subjective' and 'objective' worlds) – the other means of knowing begins with the subjective, and on the basis of that alone, must show how Man can translate the deductive laws of Intelligence into perceptions of, and a practical relationship to, the objective world. Only when this means of knowing has been firmly established on a philosophical basis can the Transcendental Philosophy be said to be complete; but this does not mean that it is finally fused with the *Naturphilosophie*. On the contrary, the two 'ways of knowing' must ever be kept strictly separate from one another.[1]

It is possible to view the first part of the *System* as an advance on two philosophical fronts. One has the aim of proving that nothing can be claimed to be 'known' at all, until a highest principle of knowledge is established, which principle must be above and beyond the object – subject relation: an Absolute knowledge, needing no corroboration from without. The other aims to show that only one thing fulfils this requirement: namely, Self-consciousness. So that, with Schelling, Self-consciousness, knowledge of the 'I', the mind's awareness of its own essential unity, or (in Kantian terms) 'pure apperception' – the existence of which was for Kant, we remember, outside the domain of rational proof – becomes the very keystone of Transcendental Idealism.

Here again Schelling reminds us that we are not immediately concerned with *Being*, but with *Knowing*:

Die Transcendental-Philosophie hat zu erklären, wie das Wissen überhaupt möglich sey, vorausgesetzt, daß das Subjektive in demselben als das Herrschende oder Erste angenommen werde.

Es ist also nicht ein einzelner Theil, noch ein besonderer Gegenstand des Wissens, sondern das *Wissen selbst*, und das *Wissen überhaupt*, was sie sich zum Objekt macht.

Nun reducirt sich aber alles Wissen auf gewisse ursprüngliche Ueberzeugungen, oder ursprüngliche Vorurtheile; diese einzelnen Ueberzeugungen muß die Transcendental-Philosophie auf Eine

[1] *Schelling*, iii p. 331.

ursprüngliche Ueberzeugung zurückführen; diese Eine, aus welcher alle anderen abgeleitet werden, wird ausgedrückt im *ersten Princip dieser Philosophie*, und die Aufgabe ein solches zu finden heißt nichts anderes, als das absolut-Gewisse zu finden, durch welches alle andere Gewißheit vermittelt ist.[1]

By 'knowledge', Schelling proceeds, two things are commonly understood; first, that experience is possible, or in other words that the representations in our minds correspond to a world of things independent ('unabhängig') of us, and second, that these representations, arising in us by free action and not by Necessity (a reminder of Schelling's divergence from eighteenth-century models of perception), can be transmitted to the real world, and so attain 'objective' reality.[2] The former is the problem of theoretical philosophy, the latter, of practical philosophy. On the face of it the two demands are incompatible, for according to the first, the representation is merely the servant of the objective world, yet according to the second the Ideal must be supreme over the 'real'. We must obviously transcend the division between theoretical and practical, and reach the point where a pre-established harmony between real and ideal is evident; and in order for such a harmony to exist, it must be the case that the power which produces the objective world is, in its origin, the same power which is manifested in the operations of the Will in Man.

At this point we may exclaim that we have landed in a Pantheistic trap: the attempt to reconcile truth in our perceptions of the outer world with freedom in our means of altering and affecting that world has resulted in a simple identification of the will of the Divine, or of the world-spirit, with human Will. Schelling insists, however, on the compatibility of freedom of

---

[1] *Schelling*, iii 346. 'It is the task of the Transcendental Philosophy to show how the act of knowing is possible at all, presupposing that the Subjective is taken to be the dominant or first element in it.

'It is thus not a single *part*, nor a particularly specific *area*, of knowing, but *the act of knowing* in itself, and knowing *in general*, that it takes for its subject.

'All acts of knowing, however, are reducible to certain fundamental convictions, or basic prejudices: Transcendental Philosophy must trace these separate convictions back to the One fundamental conviction: this One, from which all others are derived, is expressed in the *first principle of this Philosophy*, and the problem of finding this principle is none other than that of finding Absolute Certainty, through which all other certainty is mediated.'

[2] *Schelling*, iii p. 347.

Will with the purposefulness, or teleological character, of Nature (see *Ueber das Wesen der menschlichen Freiheit*). More important here, however, is his treatment of the phenomenon of consciousness. It has been assumed, we remember, that the productions of Nature are the result of *unconscious* activity, and that the power of action *with consciousness* is given only to the intelligence of Man. The Transcendental Philosophy must therefore show, by reasonings confined to the realm of the subjective, that within Intelligence there exists at the same time both unconscious and conscious activity. The 'pre-ordained' harmony necessary for the solution of the apparent conflict between practical and theoretical philosophy will then be shown to exist within Mind itself. The key passage is as follows:

Nun ist es allerdings eine *produktive* Thätigkeit, welche im Wollen sich äußert; alles freie Handeln ist produktiv, nur *mit Bewußtseyn* produktiv. Setzt man nun, da beide Thätigkeiten doch nur im Princip Eine seyn sollen, daß dieselbe Thätigkeit, welche im freien Handeln *mit Bewußtseyn* produktiv ist, im Produciren der Welt *ohne Bewußtseyn* produktiv sey, so ist jene vorausbestimmte Harmonie wirklich, und der Widerspruch gelöst.

Setzt man, dieß alles verhalte sich wirklich so, so wird jene ursprüngliche Identität der im Produciren der Welt geschäftigen Thätigkeit mit der, welche im Wollen sich äußert, in den Produkten der ersten sich darstellen, und diese Produkte werden erscheinen müssen als Produkte einer zugleich *bewußten und bewußtlosen* Thätigkeit.[1]

In Mind, that is to say, the unconscious activity of Nature is for the first time found together with the conscious exercise of Will, a conjunction which represents the first element of all knowledge. Schelling now proceeds to show that this Absolute Knowledge, the vital starting-point of epistemology, exists only in Self-

---

[1] *Schelling*, iii 348–9. 'Now it is certainly a productive activity that manifests itself in the act of willing; all free action is productive, only productive *with consciousness*. If one posits, since both activities should be one only in principle, that this activity which in free action is productive *with consciousness* is, in the production of the world, productive *without consciousness*, then this pre-ordained harmony is real, and the contradiction solved.
'If one posits that all this really obtains, then that fundamental identity at work in the production of the world, along with that which expresses itself in the Will, will manifest itself in the products of the former, and these products must appear as the products of an activity at one and the same time conscious and unconscious'.

consciousness, or in what he terms 'Das Akt des Sich-denkens'. Here there occurs another divergence from Kant which is too important to pass over completely; whereas Kant, in his discussion of apperception, discounts the possibility of the mind's being self-active,[1] Schelling positively proclaims it, though admittedly warning that it is an activity which the philosopher can only appeal to, not compel. In a passage used by Coleridge in *Biographia Literaria* (i, 171–2), Schelling contrasts the 'inner sense' of the philosophizing man with the lines of the geometer. Whereas a mathematical theorem can be wholly demonstrated by such lines, because what interests the mathematician is the construction which the lines illustrate, with Transcendental Philosophy the subject of enquiry is the process of construction itself – the inner sense. The sole condition of entry into an understanding of Transcendental Philosophy is 'that one should be at once the observed (produced) and the observer' ('daß man immer zugleich das Angeschaute (Producirende) und das Anschauende sey').[2]

Now, if it is true that the mind can become an object for itself, can view its own productions, what is there which is clearly the starting-point of its knowledge? – which is quite beyond the subject–object relationship? Schelling is asking a question quite foreign to Lockean philosophy; the question 'what is there *in knowledge itself* which establishes the possibility of knowledge in the first place?' Locke's discussion of the 'way of ideas' is based upon his assumption that it is superfluous to look for any principles of knowledge within mind itself, even the simplest propositions of logic, if it can be shown how the mind might have learned such principles by reflecting on the perceptions aroused in it by exterior sensation.[3] In Schelling's view, for knowledge to be possible at all (remembering that he stipulates 'all knowledge rests on the coincidence of an object with a subject')[4] there must be a point where mind contains both object and subject in one; where knowledge may be said to begin, and beyond which the mind cannot pass. This point is Self-consciousness. 'Dieses *erste Wissen* ist für uns nun ohne Zweifel das Wissen von uns

[1] *Critique of Pure Reason*, p. 88.   [2] *Schelling*, iii p. 351.
[3] See *An Essay Concerning Human Understanding*, edited by A. S. Pringle-Pattison, pp. 17–18 (Book I, chapter ii, paras. 1–10).
[4] BL, i p. 174; *Schelling*, iii p. 339.

selbst, oder das Selbstbewußtseyn. Wenn der Idealist dieses Wissen zum Princip der Philosophie macht, so ist dieß der Beschränktheit seiner ganzen Aufgabe gemäß, die außer dem Subjektiven des Wissens nichts zum Objekt hat.'[1]

As G. N. G. Orsini points out, the Ten Theses Coleridge set out in *Biographia Literaria* are based on passages in the *System des transcendentalen Idealismus* which deal with this first principle of knowledge. A form of the apperception theory deriving from Schelling, and based on what is summed up by Professor McFarland as 'a polarity that has arisen in the individual consciousness itself'[2] is the definition of 'selfhood' in Thesis VI. This thesis – transmogrified, as Orsini shows, from the *System des transcendentalen Idealismus* – asserts that the 'truth self-grounded' and 'unconditional' which is the necessary basis of all knowledge 'manifests itself in the SUM or I AM; which I shall hereafter indiscriminately express by the words spirit, self, and self-consciousness. In this, and in this alone, object and subject, being and knowing are identical, each involving, and supposing the other.'[3] In the process of recasting Schelling, however, Coleridge shifts the focus of his attention away from epistemology and towards ontology; his footnote to Thesis VI, by one of the amazing leaps of thought which both inspire and baffle the student of Coleridge, turns Schelling's limiting concept of 'das Akt des Sich-denkens' into a proof of the dependence of human existence and self-affirmation on divine existence and self-affirmation – in other words, self-consciousness becomes (in the famous phrase) 'a repetition in the finite mind of the eternal act of creation in the infinite I AM'.[4] Schelling's treatment of the idea is rather less soaring; he means to use Self-consciousness only as the basis of our subjective knowledge, and points out that we have been searching for a limit to our knowledge, not a passport to the infinite –

Das Selbstbewußtseyn ist der lichte Punkt im ganzen System des Wissens, der aber nur vorwärts, nicht rückwärts leuchtet. – Selbst

---

[1] *Schelling*, iii p. 355. 'This primary knowledge, without doubt, is for us the knowledge of ourselves, or Self-consciousness. If the Idealist makes this knowledge into a principle of philosophy, this is in accord with the limitation of his whole area of concern, which has no other focus besides the Subjectives of knowing.'
[2] *Coleridge and the Pantheist Tradition*, p. 239.   [3] BL, i p. 183.   [4] BL, i p. 202.

zugegeben, daß dieses Selbstbewußtseyn nur die Modification eines von ihm unabhängigen Seyns wäre, was freilich keine Philosophie begreiflich machen kann, so ist es für mich jetzt keine Art des Seyns, sondern eine *Art des Wissens,* und *nur in dieser Qualität betrachte ich es hier.* Durch die Beschränktheit meiner Aufgabe, die mich ins Unendliche zurück in den Umkreis des Wissens einschließt, wird es mir ein Selbständiges und zum absolute Princip – nicht alles Seyns, sondern *alles Wissens,* da *alles* Wissen (nicht nur das meinige) davon ausgehen muß. – Daß das Wissen überhaupt, daß insbesondere dieses *erste Wissen* abhängig sey von einer von ihm unabhängigen Existenz, hat noch kein Dogmatiker bewiesen.[1]

Nevertheless we may observe at this point two consequences, for Schelling's own philosophy, of the argument we have been following. First, it makes knowledge, or rather the consciousness which stems from self-consciousness, the final cause of the existence of the natural world. In Reason and Will the natural world reaches its consummation, its pre-ordained end. (Schelling's *Ideen zur einer Philosophie der Natur* demonstrates how natural forces – light, electricity and so forth – work in the dimensions of space towards the formation of a reasoning, free-acting, conscious being, with power over Nature itself.)[2] This choice of consciousness in itself as the salient characteristic, not only of Man, but of the whole natural world as it reaches its consummation in Man, is perhaps the most important single feature of Schelling's philosophy, and one which had an immeasurable influence on German philosophy in the remainder of the nineteenth century.[3] The second important consequence of the argument relating to self-consciousness is the raising of the notion of Freedom from its significant but still dependent

[1] *Schelling,* iii p. 357. 'Self-consciousness is the luminous point in the whole system of knowledge, which however illuminates only forwards, not backwards. Even if it were conceded that this Self-consciousness were only the modification of a being independent of it, which to be sure no philosophy can make comprehensible, yet it is for me now not a manner of being, but a manner of knowing, and here I view it *only* under this aspect. Through the limitation of my task, which confines me, to all infinity, within the circle of my knowledge, it becomes a self-evident and universal principle, not of all being, but of *all knowledge,* from which *all* knowledge (not only my own) must proceed. No dogmatic philosopher has yet proved that knowledge – in particular this *primary knowledge* – is at all dependent upon an Existence which is independent of that knowledge.'
[2] *Schelling,* ii pp. 74, 177.
[3] But see T. McFarland, *Coleridge and the Pantheist Tradition,* p. 154.

position in Kant's 'Practical Reason' to a position where it is vital to the very notion of knowledge, to the idea of the Self, to physical science and to the fundamental propositions of logic.

To understand this it is essential to recall that Schelling is not building the Transcendental Philosophy on the 'Ich', the Self, as such, but on consciousness of the Self. We do indeed appear to have moved far away from Kantian concerns, but the presence of Kant is still felt, in so far as Schelling does not attempt to argue that the 'Ich' is itself an unconditioned Absolute, but shows that it is, in a sense, dependent on thought for its very existence. (In this regard, Coleridge's Ten Theses are misleading.) But in appealing to this mode of thought – to 'das Akt des Sich-denkens' – Schelling must concede that it can be initiated only by a free act, and is not a result of something which we cannot help knowing, for the whole train of his argument is aimed at the discovery of something that is simultaneously thinker and thought, object and subject. If the mind cannot freely embark on the process of self-representation ('intellektuelle Anschauung'), the Transcendental Philosophy itself is null and void. And elsewhere, Schelling shows that even the basic proposition of most logical systems, 'A = A', depends on the discovery of some point where, as Schelling puts it, 'the Identical and the Synthetic are one'; namely, on Self-consciousness.[1] All this depends on the act of making objective what is, in all other knowledge, subjective:

Der Begriff des Ich kommt durch den Akt des Selbstbewußtseyns zu stande, außer diesem Akt ist also das Ich nichts, seine ganze Realität beruht nur auf diesem Akt, und *es ist selbst nichts als dieser Akt.* Das Ich kann also nur vorgestellt werden als Akt überhaupt, und es ist sonst nichts. –

. . . Was höchstes Princip des Wissens ist, kann seinen Erkenntniß-grund nicht wieder in etwas Höherem haben. Es muß also auch für uns sein principium essendi und cognoscendi Eins seyn und in Eins zusammenfallen.

Eben deßwegen kann dieses Unbedingte nicht in irgend einem *Ding* gesucht werden; denn was Objekt ist, ist auch ursprünglich Objekt des Wissens, anstatt daß das, was *Princip* alles Wissens ist, gar nicht

---

[1] *Schelling*, iii p. 363.

ursprünglich, oder an sich, sondern nur *durch einen besonderen Akt* der Freiheit Objekt des Wissens werden kann.[1]

What is postulated, is a particular relationship between the products of mind and the process of conceiving them; the relationship of identity. As long as this relationship is latent (verborgen) in the mind, the 'Ich' can have none but a negative ground; but when by a free act we make the subjective, thinking part an object to itself, the 'Ich' is created. Schelling here repeats Kant's distinction between 'pure' and 'empirical' apperception, in a passage which has many echoes in the notebook speculations of Coleridge on the nature of the individual consciousness.

– Was das erste betrifft, so ist zu bemerken, daß wir das Selbstbewußtseyn als Akt wohl unterscheiden vom bloß empirischen Bewußtseyn; was wir insgemein Bewußtseyn nennen, ist etwas nur an Vorstellungen von Objekten Fortlaufendes, was die Identität im Wechsel der Vorstellungen unterhält, also bloß empirischer Art, indem ich dadurch freilich meiner selbst, aber nur als des Vorstellenden bewußt bin. – Der Akt aber, von welchem hier die Rede ist, ist ein solcher, wodurch ich meiner nicht mit dieser oder jeder Bestimmung, sondern *ursprünglich* bewußt werde, und dieses Bewußtseyn heißt im Gegensatz gegen jenes, *reines* Bewußtseyn, oder Selbstbewußtseyn κατ' ἐξοχήν.[2]

The versions of apperception outlined by Kant and Schelling, and the different roles assigned to apperception in their philo-

[1] *ib.* iii pp. 366, 368. 'The notion of the "I" comes into existence through the act of Self-consciousness, thus without this act the "I" is as nothing, its whole reality rests only on this act, and *it is even none other than this act*. The "I" can thus be imagined only as an act, and it is nothing apart from this.
'. . . The highest principle of knowledge cannot have its source of knowledge in anything higher. It must thus be a single *principium essendi* and *cognoscendi* for us, and cohere in a Unity.
'For this reason, such an ultimate cannot be sought in any *thing*; for what is objective, is also a fundamental subject of knowledge; whereas that which is a principle of all knowledge is not at all fundamental, nor exists in itself, but can become the subject of knowledge only through a particular act of Freedom.'

[2] *Schelling*, iii pp. 366–7. 'As regards [the act of Self-consciousness], be it noted that we clearly distinguish Self-consciousness, as act, from purely empirical consciousness; what we commonly call consciousness is something operating only in perceptions of objects, which maintains its identity through the changes in those perceptions, that is to say, is purely empirical in character, in that I remain conscious of myself, certainly, but only as a perceiver. But the act of which I speak here is the act whereby I become conscious of myself, not with this or that determination, but fundamentally conscious of myself, and this consciousness, in contrast to the other, is called *pure* consciousness, or *Self-consciousness*.'

sophies, have been outlined here not as the prolegomena to an analysis of the entire *corpus* of Coleridge's later metaphysics, showing how much of it was 'German', how much arguably his own – a task far beyond the scope of this book – but only in order to clarify one or two of the ways in which Coleridge, after the high point of his 'Schellingism' in the *Biographia Literaria*, attempted to point out the drawbacks of both Transcendental Idealism and Kant's doctrine of apperception.

Orsini says that Coleridge either did not fully understand, or having understood distrusted, the concept of 'apperception', and he quotes a comment which Coleridge wrote in the margin of a copy of Fichte's *Anweisung zum seeligen Leben* (1806): 'O woeful Love whose first act and offspring is self! "I", and this is not a present "I am", but a poor reflection thereof. In his better [? days], *I* taught a better dogma – viz., the generalization of the thou in all finite minds.'[1] Coleridge's dislike of Fichtean solipsism is well enough known–see the parody *ΕΓΩΕΝΚΑΙΠΑΝ*.[2] His work on an alternative to the Kantian concept of self-consciousness – one involving a link between consciousness, self-consciousness and the consciousness of the other-than-self – is not so widely recognized, in spite of the notice given to it by Muirhead. Muirhead finds that Coleridge was dissatisfied with Kant's moral philosophy for two main reasons, firstly, 'the treatment of [the categorical imperative] as merely a mode of our *volitional* consciousness, instead of as the foundation of all consciousness', and secondly 'the attempt to isolate it from other elements and interests of human nature, coupled with the refusal to admit it as the basis of a speculative argument'.[3] The important note of 1807 in which Coleridge points to '*Conscience*' as the foundation of his belief in '*continuous* <and ever continuable> *Consciousness*' bears out, I believe, Muirhead's thesis, though it may be susceptible of a different interpretation – the interpretation given it by Orsini, who treats it as a declaration of assent to Kant's argument for immortality based upon ethical reasons.[4]

From what reasons do I believe a *continuous* <and ever continuable> *Consciousness*? From Conscience! Not for myself but for my conscience

---

[1] *Coleridge and German Idealism*, pp. 186–7, 190.   [2] PW, ii p. 981.
[3] *Coleridge as Philosopher*, p. 107.   [4] *Coleridge and German Idealism*, p. 155.

—i.e. my affections and duties toward others, I should have no Self—for Self is Definition; but all Boundary implies Neighbourhood—and is knowable only by Neighbourhood, or Relations...

Seven years ago, but oh! in what happier times – then only deluding, not deluded and believing the echo of my own voice in an empty vault to be the substantial voice of its indwelling Spirit – I wrote thus –

> O ye Hopes! that stir within me!
> Health comes with you from above!
> God is *with* me! God is *in* me!
> I *cannot* die: for Life is Love!

And now, that I am alone, and utterly hopeless for myself – yet still *I love* – and more strongly than ever feel that Conscience, or the Duty of Love, is the Proof of continuing, as it is the Cause and Condition of existing, Consciousness.[1]

But Coleridge's interest in the implications of the 'I–Thou' relationship – later more fully developed in the work which we know as the 'Essay on Faith' – does not suffice to prove that he abandoned, after 1807, the Kantian doctrine of apperception. Coleridge studied Schelling's *System des transcendentalen Idealismus* in 1813, and a manuscript translation of part of the *System*, with Coleridge's own interpolations, is extant. The sections translated include passages on self-consciousness as conceived by Schelling out of Kant; but (as Orsini shows) Schelling's reliance on an idealistic absolute rather than the personal Godhead of Christian faith left Coleridge unsatisfied. McKenzie proffers the slightly different explanation that Schelling's conception of the ultimate ground of reality was merely too 'vague' for Coleridge. 'In Schelling the absolute was a mere selfless identity or total indifference, prior to and behind self-consciousness, which was neither subject nor object, but the mere negation of both.'[2] Whichever explanation is closer to the truth, it is clear that German idealism belied Coleridge's conviction that the sense of self must depend on something other than an isolated act of introspection. We have already seen, in the letter of 13th October 1806 to Thomas Clarkson, how early Coleridge became interested in the possibility that human relationship played an important part in the creation of self-consciousness.[3]

[1] N 3231.
[2] *Coleridge and German Idealism*, p. 212; *Organic Unity in Coleridge*, p. 26.
[3] Above, p. 118.

COLERIDGE AND THE IDEA OF LOVE

Schelling chose to develop that interpretation of the *Critique of Pure Reason* which suggests that the self or ego exists outside time and space in its noumenal aspect, as well as within time and space in its empirical aspect – the 'two worlds' distinguished by A. O. Lovejoy; and this path led to the following very unKantian claim: (Coleridge's translation): 'the pure self-consciousness is an Act, which lies *out of* all Time, [yea], it is that which constitutes Time; [while] the empirical Consciousness is that which is self-generated *in* Time and in the succession of representations.'[1] In one way, however, the establishment of the noumenal self was of abiding interest to Coleridge. Kant of course insisted that we cannot know the noumenal self, except as a mere possibility (it is, in Körner's phrase, only *thinkable*); but he did make it the basis of moral freedom, the extrication of which was, according to Lovejoy, the most important result of Coleridge's study of Kant.[2] Coleridge appears always to have allowed Kant (of whose superiority to his disciples he was, in the end, quite certain)[3] a key place in the realm of philosophical logic; but he did not find the *Critique* convincing as a model of human development, because it ignored the fact that human development is a matter of the inter-human rather than of the involution of the mind upon itself. Thus, in his *Opus Maximum*, Coleridge in speaking of human self-consciousness begins by putting forward a broadly Kantian statement of the distinction between the empirical self and the noumenal self, but then moves into the sphere of speculative psychology and leaves Kantian limits behind. A simple early statement of the idea that self-consciousness may originate in the consciousness of the other-than-self occurs in Notebook 23:

Time and Self are in a certain sense one and the same thing: since only by meeting with, so as to be resisted by, *another* does the soul become a *self*. What is Self-consciousness, but to know myself at the same moment that I know another, and vice other versa an other by means of and at the moment of knowing my Self. Self and other are as necessarily interdependent as Right and Left, or North and South.[4]

This is little more than an exploration – along the lines of

---

[1] Quoted by G. N. G. Orsini, p. 211.   [2] See above p. 163.
[3] See J. I. Lindsay, 'Coleridge Marginalia in Jacobi's *Werke*', *Modern Language Notes*, vol. L (1935) (216–44), pp. 241–4.   [4] Notebook 23, fol. 56.

N 3231, quoted above[1] – of the Kantian doctrine of apperception, except that instead of the coinstantaneous perception of an
outside object Coleridge appears to be thinking of the perception
of another *person* as that which enables the mind to become self-
conscious. In the *Opus Maximum*, however, Coleridge uses
Kant's concept of the transcendental unity of apperception to
refute those moralists who base their ideals of conduct upon 'enlightened self-interest', or upon self-love in any form. Love of
our own selves cannot precede just behaviour towards others,
because our very sensations and impressions depend upon a
unified consciousness – which is, as we have seen, all that Kant
means by the term 'self'. If therefore a man 'loves himself', he
must have in view not the substantial, noumenal self, but the
empirical self which is amenable to the inner sense. He is a slave,
that is to say, to the last strong impression which he has received – he is driven by a congeries of evanescent passions, and
in truth has no 'self' at all.

The doctors of Self-love are misled by the wrong or equivocal use of
words. We love ourselves they say: now this is impossible for a
finite being in the absolute meaning of the term Self for if by the 'Self'
we mean the principle of individuation the band or copula, which gives
a real unity to all the complex products functions and faculties of an
animal – a real unity, I say, in contradistinction from the mere semb-
lance or total impression produced by an aggregate on the mind of the
beholder and even from that combination of parts which originates and
has its whole end and object in an internal agent, a unity different in
short from that of a heap of corn or from a steam engine or other
machine – it is manifest that the Self in this sense must be anterior to
all our sensations etc. and to all the objects, toward which they may
be directed.[2]

The noumenal self cannot however be known directly – Coleridge here remains true to Kant, unlike his pupil J. H. Green – so
it must have a representation or reflection of itself (Coleridge
evidently has in mind the passage from Kant's *Critique* which
rejects the possibility of the self-activity of the thinking sub-

---

[1] See above, pp. 184–5.
[2] Quoted by Elinor S. Shaffer in 'Iago's Malignity Motivated: Coleridge's
Unpublished "Opus Magnum" ', *Shakespeare Quarterly* vol. xix no. 3 (Summer
1968) (195–203), p. 197.

ject).[1] What then serves as a 'representation' of the noumenal self? In infancy, Coleridge suggests (here moving away from Kantian ground) it is the mother or nurse of the child.

Nothing can become an object of consciousness but by reflection, not even the things of perception. Now the Self is ever pre-supposed and like all other supersensual subjects can be made known to the Mind only by a representative: And again what that representative shall be is by no means unalterably fixed in human nature by nature itself; but on the contrary varies with the growth bodily, moral and intellectual of each individual... in the earlier periods of infancy, the mother or the nurse is the Self of the child.[2]

After the period of innocence is over, however, the feelings that attach to this surrogate self become 'estranged' from their former object and attach to the image of the body, or to other outward objects: 'the self borrows from the objects a sort of unnatural outwardness'. They may even, especially when the conscious mind is inactive or only partly active, attach to our image of other people: 'who has not experienced in dreams the attachment of our personal identity to forms the most remote from our own [?]' The one thing to which self-consciousness cannot attach is the real or noumenal self; 'self-love' therefore can mean only the immediate self-seeking of the individual, who fulfils his desires without intermediate reflection, as a beast rushes to its food; 'self-love' is tantamount to an 'abandonment to its animal life'.[3]

In an interesting and, as Mrs Shaffer's article shows, highly original digression, Coleridge applies this theory to the character of Iago, who is, he suggests, an instance of a man who has annihilated his selfhood by identifying it with the stream of sense impressions – some of which may be of quite trivial objects, such as Desdemona's handkerchief – so that his self thereby acquires what Coleridge calls 'unnatural outwardness'. For a picture of the healthy development of the sense of self, however, we must turn to the 'Essay on Faith', written in 1825.

Up to the early 1820s, as Orsini points out, Coleridge's

[1] Quoted above, p. 172.
[2] Elinor S. Shaffer, 'Iago's Malignity Motivated', p. 197.
[3] *ib.* p. 198. The quotations on this and the preceding page are from MSS III and II of the *Opus Maximum* (designated MS 'B' by Muirhead), fols. 48–51, 77.

writings on apperception remain broadly within the Kantian fold; the 'Essay on Faith', however, though beginning with a clear reference to Kant in that it makes the categorical imperative the criterion of responsible humanity, puts on his doctrine the emphasis we have seen in the note of 1807.

Knowing that consciousness of this fact [that is, of the existence of a categorical imperative] is the root of all other consciousness, and the only practical contradistinction of man from the brutes, we name it the conscience; by the natural absence or presumed presence of which, the law, both divine and human, determines whether X Y Z be a thing or a person.[1]

This follows quite closely Kant's argument that only if a rational being obeys universal morality can he be an end in himself (and hence a person).[2] But Coleridge takes Kant's argument a step further: it is because conscience, or the consciousness of a universal moral law, involves the perception of a relationship to something other than the self, that the self becomes aware of its own existence. 'Self is Definition', the 1807 note phrases it, 'but all Boundary...is knowable only by Neighbourhood, or Relations.'

Conscience, in this simplest form, must be supposed in order to consciousness, that is, to human consciousness. Brutes may be, and are conscious, but those beings only, who have an I, *scire possunt hoc vel illud una cum seipsis*; that is, *conscire vel scire aliquid mecum*, or to know a thing in relation to myself, and in the act of knowing myself as acted upon by that something.

Now the third person could never have been distinguished from the first but by means of the second. There can be no He without a previous Thou. Much less could an I exist for us, except as it exists during the suspension of the will, as in dreams; and the nature of brutes may be best understood, by conceiving them as somnambulists. This is a deep meditation, though the position is capable of the strictest proof, – namely, that there can be no I without a Thou, and that a Thou is only possible by an equation in which I is taken as equal to Thou, and yet not the same...the equation of Thou with I, by means of a free act, negativing the sameness in order to establish the equality, is the true definition of conscience. But as without a Thou there can be no You, so

---

[1] *Literary Remains*, edited by H.N. Coleridge, iv p. 426.
[2] 'Fundamental Principles of the Metaphysic of Morals', section ii. *Critique of Practical Reason, &c.*, pp. 53–5, 58–9.

COLERIDGE AND THE IDEA OF LOVE

without a You no They, These or Those; and as all these conjointly form the materials and subjects of consciousness, and the conditions of experience, it is evident that the conscience is the root of all consciousness, – *a fortiori*, the precondition of all experience, – and that the conscience cannot have been in its first revelation deduced from experience.[1]

The suggestion that the mind can be so immediately aware of the existence of a selfhood is quite contrary to Kant's argument (with regard to the doctrine of transcendental apperception) that the unity of the self is never more than a conceivable possibility, which is nevertheless a necessary precondition of experience; and this is one of the reasons why René Wellek has said that the 'Essay on Faith' 'expands a point of view diametrically opposed to Kant's own aims in terms which are still Kantian in origin'.[2] The assertion that conscience is the origin of consciousness, as Wellek points out, is reminiscent of Fichte, or of Schelling in his earlier work (of which the *System des Transcendentalen Idealismus*, published in 1800, is presumably an example);[3] but the use of the 'Thou' as a boundary to the 'I' seems to be distinctively Coleridgean, though there is something approaching a parallel thought in Jacobi's 'ohne Du, ist das Ich unmöglich', according to Professor McFarland.[4] Coleridge has, in the 'Essay on Faith', done what Kant did not do for himself, that is, establish *a priori* the possibility of recognizing other human beings as themselves possessed of conscience and selfhood. The 'Thou' and the 'I' are set out in terms of thesis and antithesis: not two unrelated entities, but two correlatives, or 'correspondent opposites', each of which necessitates the other. By this 'polarity that has arisen in the individual consciousness itself' Coleridge establishes not the Kantian apperception, but the forms under which relationship itself is recognized, and out of which experience ('These' and 'Those') also takes its origin.[5] The basis of Coleridge's theory is firmly Kantian although, as in the *Opus Maximum*, Coleridge seems to reject Kant's proof of the existence of free will from the existence of a necessary moral law, and reverses the order of things, basing the

[1] *Lit. Rems*, iv pp. 428–30.
[2] *Immanuel Kant in England*, p. 133.   [3] *ib.* p. 128.
[4] *Coleridge and the Pantheist Tradition*, pp. 237–8. 'Without a Thou, the I is impossible.'   [5] *Lit. Rems.*, iv p. 429.

190

moral law on the existence of free will. Will is, in the 'Essay on Faith', that by which the selfhood discriminates itself from the Thou: it is likely, therefore, that the Will would have been deduced before the categorical imperative, had Coleridge systematized his thinking on this point. Green's *Spiritual Philosophy*, in so far as it can be taken as a guide to Coleridge's later thinking, supports this theory, since it speaks of the Will as being 'revealed' in human self-consciousness;[1] and a later passage of the 'Essay on Faith' gives the following picture of the logic of human Will:

Prothesis

Reason and Absolute Will

(coinhering in God alone)

Thesis	*Antithesis*
Reason, or the super-individual (*minus* Will)	Individual Will (*plus* Will)

Synthesis

Will subordinated to

Reason[2]

The Synthesis, or the subordination of the individual Will to the common Reason, is an image of the Prothesis, the unity, in God, of Reason with Absolute Will; and so it is 'the required proper character of man'. The argument that the individual Will must be subjugated by the Reason because this is the only way in which man can resemble his Maker, like other arguments in the 'Essay on Faith', is not so much unKantian as a pursuing of Kantian concepts beyond the limits which Kant himself imposed.

It is on this foundation, however, that Coleridge proceeds to expound his idea of the final cause of human relationships. He argues that emotions and affections, as long as they are disciplined by the Reason, are the 'ladder' by which humanity mounts to the love of God – a version of the well-known simile in Plato's *Symposium*. 'Unlike a million of tigers', the argument runs, 'a million of men is very different from a million times one man.'[3] There arise between men affections, emotions, passions; and as the Reason is no less 'super-individual' when it exists in the second or third person than when it exists in the first, these energies, if subject, as they should be, to Reason, have as their

[1] i p. 2. [2] *Lit. Rems.*, iv pp. 430–1. [3] *ib.* p. 434.

ultimate goal not the selfhood, nor even that larger selfhood which is the sum of human individualities, but reconciliation with God.

Now the reason has been shown to be super-individual, generally, and therefore not less so when the form of an individualization subsists in the *alter*, than when it is confined to the *idem*; not less when the emotions have their conscious or believed object in another, than when their subject is the individual personal self. For though these emotions, affections, attachments, and the like, are the prepared ladder by which the lower nature is taken up into, and made to partake of, the highest room, – as we are taught to give a feeling of reality to the higher *per medium commune* with the lower, and thus gradually to see the reality of the higher (namely, the objects of reason) and finally to know that the latter are indeed and pre-eminently real, as if you love your earthly parents whom you see, by these means you will learn to love your Heavenly Father who is invisible; – yet this holds good only so far as the reason is the president, and its objects the ultimate aim.[1]

It will be clearly seen that this argument depends for its force on the previous proof that the 'I' and the 'Thou' cannot exist independently of each other, but are 'correspondent opposites': hence it is no mere repetition of the beliefs that we have already noted as expressed in *The Friend* and elsewhere, but a new and more philosophical attempt at establishing a connection between human and divine love.

The later notebooks, as I have said, show that Coleridge continued to wrestle with the problem of defining human selfhood as he and Green worked on what was jokingly referred to as 'the Chloro-esteesian Philosophy'. The tendency of all the notes on this subject is yet further away from Kant and apperception, towards an almost mystic belief in a divine element in man, influenced strongly by the close study which Coleridge undertook in the last years of his life of the Gospels, particularly of St John's Gospel. In one note, dated Christmas Day 1829, Coleridge shrinks from claiming either the 'Light of the Spirit' or the 'dark Life of the Flesh' to be the real 'I', and ends, 'In vain would a solution be sought except in the Great all-pregnant Postulate of the Προπρωτον – The Will, *causa sui, even a man* – Aweful confirmation of my Assertion that we cannot believe aught of God

---

[1] *Lit. Rems.*, iv p. 435.

but what we find in ourselves.'[1] But one possible way out of the dilemma is to accept this duality from the outset, and argue that man has two kinds of consciousness of self, one somewhat like the 'empirical apperception' of Kant's *Critique,* and enjoyed in common with the higher forms of animal life, the other more like Kant's 'transcendental apperception', but with the very un-Kantian characteristic that it is recognized as having a divine source, and represents the Logos as it is manifest in human life. 'In him was life; and the life was the light of men.' In this way Coleridge believed he might avoid what had become a worrying confusion in the logical 'subject–object' approach to the problem, the lack of any distinction between the mind as a whole – which must include all thoughts and representations – and the substantial personality 'I'. 'Have I not in my former disquisitions,' he wrote, 'fallen into some error, from ... <identifying> the definitions of Mind and der *Ichheit* ?'[2] If the duality, or 'duplicity' of man's nature is accepted, and if the Logos is held to be thinkable (νοητός was Plato's term) by man, the way is open for a theory which gives the empirical 'I' its due place, while not excluding the substantial, or noumenal, and ultimately heavenward-tending 'I'. The most connected statement of this idea is in a note dating probably from November or December 1827.

Thro' every new Opening I am enabled to see more and more clearly the momentous Advantage, which the Commencing with the ὑπερουσιω Προπρωτῳ, και τῳ Ειμι, και τῳ Οντως Οντι (= τῳ Λογῳ, τῳ φωτι νοητῳ και νοερῳ;) και συν τη ζωη; affords to my System –

Thus in reference to the deep and difficult problem, proposed in p. 94 of No. III, it enables me to presume the *Objective* in order to the finite *Subject*, without involving the consequences, into which it led Spinoza, while it saves me from the unreality of the Objective in Schelling's Scheme, and from the incapacity of explaining and thence the temptation to omit, the Subject's recognition of itself as a *Subject* – in other words the distinction between the I (= das Ich, die *Ichheit*) and Mind. I now see that the I is Life in the form of Mind – and look forward to the establishment of a twofold I – the accidental or phantom I, and the substantial personal I – the first being the transformation of the Self-finding of Animal Life in its' first dim participation of Mind – and this empirical I is doubtless possessed by the higher Order at least

---

[1] Notebook 41, fol. 145.   [2] Notebook 35, fol. 169 (this is 'p. 94 of No. III').

of the Animals, by the Dog, the Elephant etc – of the substantial I I only
anticipate the solution in the immanent Life in the communicative
Logos – εν αυτῳ ην η ζωη – and which being communicated is the
Light of Man, the Spirit which subsists subjectively by its' Unity with,
and correlation to, the Holy Spirit objectively.[1]

The proof to which Coleridge 'looks forward' is never fully
given, however, and it is impossible to evaluate the theory here
outlined in the absence of any fuller statement of it. Coleridge's
idea of the way in which selfhood might be deduced from *a priori*
principles never stabilized, but the course of his explorations
shows an adventurous and subtle intellect at work. They are
naturally tentative; the rise of the Vienna school of psychoanalysis, and the systematic study of interpersonal relationships, were
still far in the future; but his writings on the subject are still of
interest in a century which has fed on the concepts of Sigmund
Freud. For although, as one historian has put it, Freud was one
of the first systematic thinkers to see the human environment as
'basically an interpersonal one, because personality with its
physiological roots arises in the course of living and relating
oneself to others', Freud's view of man is dominated by the
Hobbesian and Darwinian models of human society, and it has
been left to later analysts (Karen Horney is one example) to
study the more positive aspects of relationship in the development of the individual psyche.[2]

[1] Notebook 36, fols. 172–3. 'The super-substantial First of all things, and the I AM,
and the being of Being (= the Logos, knowable and conceivable by man;) and
with the life that creates life.'
[2] See J. A. C. Brown, *Freud and the Post-Freudians*, pp. 11, 13, 134.

IV

The Social State

There is scarce truth enough alive to make societies secure; but security
enough to make fellowships accurst. Much upon this riddle runs the
wisdom of the world.   Shakespeare*

Animé par la chaleur de la lutte, poussé au delà des limites naturelles
de son opinion, par les opinions et les excès de ses adversaires,
chacun perd de vue l'objet même de ses poursuites, et tient un langage
qui répond mal à ses vrais sentiments et à ses instincts secrets.

De là l'étrange confusion dont nous sommes forcés d'être les
témoins.

Je cherche en vain dans mes souvenirs, je ne trouve rien qui
mérite d'exciter plus de douleur et plus de pitié que ce qui se passe
sous nos yeux, il semble qu'on ait brisé de nos jours le lien naturel qui
unit les opinions aux goûts et les actes aux croyances; la sympathie qui
s'est fait remarquer de tout temps entre les sentiments et les idées des
hommes paraît détruite, et l'on dirait que toutes les lois de l'analogie
morale sont abolies.

Alexis De Tocqueville†

1

The French Revolution differed from all previous political up-
heavals in Europe not only because of its scale, or its eventual
effect on Europe's economic and political structure – though
these were incalculably great – nor because of its toll in terms of
warfare and bloodshed. It was also the first embodiment of a
wholly new vision of the relationships between men. Through
its development of the principle of 'popular sovereignty',[1] it
brought about changes, not only in what are usually thought of
as the political relationships, but also in the social and personal

* *Measure for Measure*, Act III, scene 2, line 216.
† *De la Démocratie en Amérique*, (13th edition), vol. I, p. 12.
[1] See A. Goodwin, *The French Revolution*, p. 161.

relationships, reminding men that not even these are politically neutral, and that the kinds of relationship men may enjoy in their villages and their homes depend as much on political and economic factors as do the rates of their wages and the rent of their land. The revolutionist adds the cry of 'fraternité!' to the two maxims of Rousseau; men must be enabled to see in a new light, not only their political rights, but their neighbours and countrymen, if society is to be recast, and no man excluded from the dispensation of social justice. France became, for the more imaginative of the younger men in England, the embodiment of a moral as well as a political ideal, and many of them must have

> laid this faith to heart,
> That, if France prosper'd, good Men would not long
> Pay fruitless worship to humanity.[1]

It was more difficult for an older generation, however, to realize at once how deep an effect the Revolution was to have on 'private' relationships as well as on 'public' life; it still needed an exceptional imagination, like that of Blake, to perceive the indissoluble connection between the two, and see the Revolution as a liberation of man's moral and spiritual capacities, and not merely as a political change.

> Enitharmon laugh'd in her sleep to see (O woman's triumph)
> Every house a den, every man bound, the shadows are fill'd
> With spectres, and the windows wove over with curses of iron;
> Over the doors 'Thou shalt not', and over the chimneys 'Fear' is written;
> With bands of iron round their necks, fasten'd into the walls
> The citizens; in leaden gyves the inhabitants of suburbs
> Walk heavy; soft and bent are the bones of villagers.[2]

Edmund Burke – who was also, of course, gifted with a high degree of imagination – sensed the magnitude of the changes, not merely political, that were taking place in France, and this perception animates all his writings on the Revolution. He saw it as 'a revolution not in human affairs, but in man himself'[3] – a

---

[1] Wordsworth, *The Prelude* (1805), edited by E. de Selincourt, p. 183 (Book x, lines 222–4).
[2] *Europe*, lines 131–7; *Poems and Prophecies*, p. 75.
[3] *Thoughts on the Prospect of a Regicide Peace, in a series of Letters* (1796), p. 2.

revolution that Burke of course deplored, whereas his old ally
Tom Paine, now a bitter opponent, exulted in the prospect of
total change: 'It is an age of Revolutions, in which everything
may be looked for.'[1] The new philosophy really did throw all in
doubt, and drove most sensitive men back to a reappraisal of
every aspect of life, the personal as well as the social and the
political. No man was more deeply stirred by the Revolution
than Coleridge, of whom M. Cestre has written 'Il resta consciemment et délibérément fidèle à l'idéal proclamé par les
hommes de 1789. Il ne s'en inspira pas seulement pour entre-
tenir en lui-même la sympathie humaine et l'enthousiasme
moral: il en fit le guide de sa pensée.'[2]

Coleridge's political works – including the lectures he gave in
Bristol in 1795 as well as the seminal *Constitution of Church and
State* – attempt to answer, but to answer in a constructive way,
without losing sight of the ideals of 1789, the challenge of
'Jacobinism', a kind of revolutionary talk which most Englishmen felt was subversive of everything they most valued in their
country's institutions. The governments of the day, of course,
brought in repressive legislation,[3] but Coleridge knew that
laws could not cure the disaffection in which Jacobinism took
root, and indeed might well exacerbate it. Something more truly
radical was needed. First must come constructive development,
the moral, intellectual and economic growth which would enable
the full capacities of the community and the individual to be
realized, without severing them from the historical sources of
human progress. In this sense, M. Cestre's judgment is surely
right; what the Ancien Régime had denied to the great mass of
the people of France, and what 'les hommes de 1789' had tried
to achieve in the space of a few weeks, Coleridge believed to be
attainable only through long years of moral and spiritual matura-
tion. Every stage in the evolutionary process of Nature includes in itself all the preceding stages; in the same way, man

---

[1] *The Rights of Man* (1792), i p. 82.
[2] *La Revolution française et les poètes anglais*, p. 474.
[3] For example: Habeas Corpus suspended in 1794, 1795, 1798–1801, 1817–18.
Seditious Meetings Acts, 1795, 1817. Treasonable Practices Act, 1795. Prohibition of anonymous newspapers, 1798. Combination Acts, 1799, 1800. Prohibition
of the federation of political associations, 1799. See E. Halévy, *A History of the
English People in the Nineteenth Century*, vols i and ii; i pp. 154, 157, 160, ii pp.
24–5.

evolves only through a living contact with his past, for the principles that must govern his future growth have already been established through his history. Social disintegration does not restore any hypothetical 'natural rights', such as those postulated by Rousseau, but leaves man stripped of the only thing that had given him moral stature, his place in a living and growing community towards which he recognizes a responsibility, and which confers on him, in return, his rights and privileges.

2

Few politicians, in fact, did regard the kind of 'freedom' that would be won by equality of political rights as anything more than a dream – idle or idealistic, according to whether it was viewed from the right or from the left. Even Charles James Fox had declared that he 'did not affect a democracy',[1] because he held it to be impracticable, and preferred to keep the constitution as it stood, if it was the only viable alternative to universal suffrage;[2] Burke too, though conceding that there were such things as natural rights, believed that their 'abstract perfection' was their 'practical defect', and that a society based on them would be self-destructive.[3] This kind of argument carried no weight, of course, with the radicals, who pressed on with the work of claiming what they regarded as their due, dismissing the accretions of centuries – monarchy, inherited privileges, rights of property, constitutional law – as indefensible encroachments on the liberty of the individual. In order to understand the view of society that Coleridge put forward in *The Friend*, and the principles which lay behind his later criticisms of current political trends, it will be necessary to look at the part he played in this debate.

Paine had substantiated his assertion that men were born equal by referring to the Genesis myth. At the Creation there was no such thing as a distinction of rank; and every child comes from God by a process which merely continues, and does not supersede, the Creation. Every child is therefore born with

---

[1] A. Cobban, *The Debate on the French Revolution*, p. 73.   [2] *ib.* pp. 339–40.
[3] *Reflections on the Revolution in France*, edited by Conor Cruise O'Brien, p. 151.

the same natural rights. From this follows his doctrine that 'every civil right grows out of a natural right'; we entrust our natural rights into a 'common stock' with the rest of the community, and we are bound to respect that community's laws only so long as we choose to relinquish our natural rights.[1] Godwin argued a superficially similar case, though he started from the opposite premise – that individuals possess no *a priori* rights. Society, which is nothing but an aggregate of individuals, can have no powers beyond what individuals consent to place in the 'common stock'. Therefore, 'if government be founded in the consent of the people, it can have no power over any individual by whom that consent is refused'.[2]

The theoretical debate, however, was of much less importance in the minds of the general public than the appalling threat of invasion from France, and the equally disturbing prospect of civil disorder. The propertied classes were afraid of anarchy, rather than of what we would now call socialism,[3] but the populace, for their part, accepted quite meekly Pitt's repressive legislation.[4] Internal faction and the invasion threat were linked, of course, in the thoughts of most men. Though the war – begun in 1793 – had not been at the start a war of ideologies,[5] it was soon being proclaimed as an ideological war by those who, like Burke, believed that Jacobinism threatened the peace and security of England, indeed of the whole Christian world, and held that the evil would not finally be cured until France was completely crushed. Burke's last published work urged the continuance of the war, not only because the French were the aggressors, but because 'the faction in France had assumed a form, had adopted a body of principles and maxims, and had regularly and systematically acted on them, by which she virtually had put herself into a posture which was itself a declaration of war against mankind.'[6] The debate on natural as against

---

[1] Thomas Paine, *The Rights of Man* (1792), Part I pp. 27, 80–1.

[2] William Godwin, *Enquiry concerning Political Justice* (2nd edition, 1796, 2 vols.) i pp. 165, 195.

[3] A. Cobban, *The Debate on the French Revolution*, introduction, p. 17.

[4] J. Steven Watson, *The Reign of George III, 1760–1815*, p. 361.

[5] Pitt's aims were limited to the restitution of part of the Netherlands to Austria, and the capture of some French territory in the West Indies. See J. Steven Watson, *The Reign of George III, 1760–1815*, p. 363.

[6] *Thoughts on the Prospect of a Regicide Peace*, p. 74.

constitutional rights therefore became inextricably intertwined with the controversy over the war with France. Coleridge lent his voice to the movement for peace, collaborating with Southey in an epic poem on Joan of Arc, writing verse in praise of Horne Tooke, and publishing poems in the *Cambridge Intelligencer* and the *Morning Post* which satirized the warmongers;[1] but he was disheartened with the Radical cause, and wrote no extended pieces of work on the 'natural rights' debate until he began to contribute articles to the *Morning Post* at the end of 1799, by which time his point of view had changed considerably from the 'democratic' position he adopted in *The Watchman*. 'Ode to the Departing Year' (1796) expresses grim forebodings of the destruction of Albion; but it ends with 'the deep Sabbath of meek self-content'.[2] Coleridge was very far from permanently giving up his concern with social and political institutions, however, as the articles written for the *Morning Post* show. They formulate a viewpoint which is avowedly anti-Jacobin, but preserves the vision of an organic and progressive society which he had learned to admire in Burke's thinking. Perhaps they also reflect the disillusion with Utopian systems of government that – as we learn from Coleridge himself – was general among liberal thinkers at the time. Writing of the year preceding the truce of Amiens,[3] he says

by the latter period the minds of the partizans, exhausted by excess of stimulation and humbled by mutual disappointment, had become languid. The same causes, that inclined the nation to peace, disposed the individuals to reconciliation. Both parties had found themselves in the wrong. The one had confessedly mistaken the moral character of the revolution, and the other had miscalculated both its moral and its physical resources.[4]

The 'moral character' of the Revolution was finally betrayed in 1804, when Napoleon proclaimed himself Emperor, and so 'struck a blow at English republicanism from which it has never recovered'.[5] But in 1799 radicals could still hope that genuine democracy might be established in France. Their hopes – which

[1] PW, i pp. 131, 150, 160, 211, 237.   [2] *ib.* p. 168.
[3] The truce of Amiens was signed on 27 March 1802.   [4] BL, i p. 123.
[5] E. P. Thompson, *The Making of the English Working Class* (revised edition, 1968), p. 495.

had already been severely battered by the French invasion of Switzerland, a country that remained a cynosure for English republicans even though it had never, in truth, been the haven of freedom they thought it to be – were pinned on the new Constitution which the government of Sieyès and Bonaparte presented to the French people at the end of 1799.[1] The *Morning Chronicle* 'extolled this constitution as the perfection of a wise and regulated liberty',[2] but Coleridge's analysis of it forced them to reconsider, for it showed that the democratic control which the proposed system theoretically allowed was in fact illusory. The Senate was to consist of 'eighty unremoveable senators, privileged to fill up their own vacancies';[3] these men were to be appointed by the Committees; but the Committees had been nominated by Sieyès and Bonaparte, and remained in their power. All decisions of the legislature – numbering three hundred – and all recommendations of the tribunate – numbering one hundred – were subject to the vote of the Chief Consul. The people were, indeed, to be asked to vote on the Constitution, but the sovereignty that was thus put in their hands would be instantly removed, once the Constitution came into operation; they would be exercising their 'natural rights' only to vote them away again, to invest them in a government which was oligarchic and self-perpetuating, and in which, moreover, there was no effective distinction between the functions of the legislature and the executive. Coleridge scornfully attacked the scheme as fraudulent, as leading inevitably to the corruption of all those who held office under it, and, not least, as 'betray[ing] a rooted contempt of the people, and a distrust of human virtue in general'.[4] Sieyès and Bonaparte had, he declared, no desire to see any real power exercised by the people. They were motivated by personal ambition alone, and had therefore arrogated to themselves, by a transparent piece of chicanery, ultimate authority over the whole of France. Not that the French people could look to Coleridge for sympathy. His contempt for them is undisguised: 'Γραῖοι ἀεὶ παῖδες: the French are always

---

[1] On Switzerland see Cestre, *La Révolution française et les poètes anglais*, p. 358.
[2] BL, i p. 147.
[3] *Essays on His Own Times*, edited by Sara Coleridge, i p. 185 (31 December 1799).
[4] EOT, i p. 188 (31 December 1799).

children, and it is an infirmity of benevolence to wish, or dread aught concerning them.' (The quotation is from Plato's *Timæus*, III, 22, where an Egyptian priest is made to say to Solon 'You Grecians are ever children; you have no knowledge of antiquity, nor antiquity of knowledge.'[1])

Coleridge is not, however, attacking the proposed Constitution because it contravenes democratic principles. The pith of his case against it is that it grants direct legislative powers to certain persons, and it is a recurring theme in Coleridge's political thought that personal power has no place in the well-governed state. The ancient Aristotelian doctrine that a country can be justly governed only by laws, and not by men, was attacked by Hobbes as a 'pernicious error', fostered in modern times by the theorizing of the scholastic philosophers; but to Coleridge it was no abstract theory but a practical axiom, the truth of which was demonstrated by the rise of every new demagogue both in England and in France. Indeed his distrust of the gifted leader, the man of talent who is swept to power by the impetus of popular acclaim, is a considerable factor in his opposition to democracy, and to Jacobinism in general; and he later argues, for this very reason, the precise opposite of Burke's case for continuing the war with France.[2] Paine had written in 1791, 'It appears to general observation, that revolutions create genius and talents; but those events do no more than bring them forward.'[3] Coleridge implicitly accepts this proposition, and it is to him a cogent reason for discouraging revolution, in particular by removing the threat to French – and English – security which the war represented. (His view has been endorsed by a historian of the period.)[4] He points out, however, that the new Constitution does not even have the limited advantage of a democracy in permitting men of genius and intellect, as time goes on, to work their way to positions of power, but in reality confers absolute authority on one man. Nor, of course, does it have the advantages of monarchy, where 'obedience is secured by

---

[1] *ib.* p. 184; see Bacon, *The Advancement of Learning*, edited by G. W. Kitchin, p. 38.

[2] See *Leviathan*, edited by M. Oakeshott, p. 448 (Part 4, chapter 46); EOT, i p. 223 (8 January 1800); and R. H. Williams, *Culture and Society*, p. 77.

[3] *The Rights of Man*, Part II p. 21.

[4] E. Halévy, *A History of the English People in the Nineteenth Century*, i p. 105.

superstition',[1] nor those of a government in which the ownership of property is a title to power. Now follows a passage which highlights Coleridge's disagreement with those who believed in the 'natural rights'. 'We are fortunate enough', he continues, 'to live in a country in which, with all its defects, the national character is made up, though in different quantities, by all these three principles, the influence of a court, the popular spirit, and the predominance of property.'[2] It is precisely because Coleridge abjures the notion of personal power that he can in this way declare 'the predominance of property' to be right and just. The argument is not one that it is easy for a modern reader to sympathize with, but an understanding of it is essential if Coleridge's case against 'natural rights' is to be clear. If a man owns no property, but by virtue of his talent, or genius, is elected to a position of responsibility in a government, there is nothing to prevent him from abusing his power, except his own integrity. He governs, that is, in his own person. If, on the other hand, he is the owner of property, he will be penalizing himself by bad government. His interests are identical with those of the state as a whole, and he can therefore be relied upon to safeguard the prosperity of those who elected him as conscientiously as he would defend his own household. 'Our nobles in England', Coleridge writes, 'from the largeness of their landed estates, have an important stake in the immediate prosperity of their country.'[3] They do not govern in their own persons; they are the representatives of the nation in a truer sense than the unpropertied man elected by popular vote, since their good is the nation's good, and their harm the nation's harm.

We have repeatedly pressed upon the attention of our readers the impracticability of all theories founded on *personal rights*; we have contended zealously, that the security and circulation of property, with political power proportioned to property, constitute a good government, and bring with them all other blessings, which our imperfect nature can, or ought to expect.[4]

This Coleridge affirmed in an essay on the peace negotiations of 1800; and for an example of the reverse of good government,

[1] EOT, i p. 181 (26 December 1799).   [2] *ib.* i p. 182.
[3] *ib.* i p. 185 (31 December 1799).   [4] *ib.* p. 224 (8 January 1800).

of irresponsible use of power by adventurers who lack the sobering curb of a substantial acreage to restrain their recklessness, he looked no farther than Paris:

'We have stated it as a necessary event, that the government of France will modify itself sooner or later into a government of property, and the war against France, by calling too many individuals without property into political importance, is the true cause of the delay of this event.'[1]

Not everyone, however, held 'personal power' to be an evil in the way that Coleridge did, nor were the French condemned in this respect by all British politicians. Soon after the peace of Amiens was made, the Whigs were in Paris fraternizing with Bonaparte and his ministers.[2] Fox in particular incurred Coleridge's displeasure for 'becoming the temporary courtier of Bonaparte, and the visitor and intimate of Talleyrand',[3] thus consummating the folly of having declared at the Whig club that he supported the doctrine of the Rights of Man – a declaration that was hardly consistent with his earlier opposition to universal suffrage, as Coleridge did not fail to point out.[4]

The mere fact that Coleridge criticized Fox, however, tells us little, in itself, about Coleridge's political position, for it would be wrong to envisage the debate as being conducted between two irreconcilable extremes of opinion, Coleridge siding with the upholders of the *status quo* against the Jacobins, and Fox and the Whigs campaigning for the immediate establishment of a parliamentary democracy resting on the Jacobinical doctrine of universal suffrage. No such clear-cut division existed, either in the House of Commons or in the arena of public debate. The word 'Jacobin' had indeed degenerated to the level of a mere term of abuse, and Coleridge tried to clarify the issues involved by stating what 'rights' the Jacobins laid claim to, and to showing exactly what opinions were being attributed to a man when his opponents designated him a Jacobin. 'Whoever builds a government on personal and natural rights, is so far a Jacobin. Whoever builds on social rights, that is, hereditary rank, property, and long prescription, is an Anti-Jacobin, even though he

[1] EOT, i pp. 224–5.
[2] J. Steven Watson, *The Reign of George III*, p. 410.
[3] EOT, ii p. 574 (9 November 1802).   [4] *ib.* p. 562 (4 November 1802).

should nevertheless be a republican, or even a democrat.'[1] Coleridge's own position in this dialectic is unequivocal; he held Jacobinism to be an 'absurdity' surely too blatant to deceive the British people.[2] On the other hand he certainly did not believe, any more than Rousseau did, that there could be only one just form of government for all ages and all nations. He dismissed 'the *rights* of man, as a creature of nature' as merely hypothetical; but the criterion he appealed to as the only true one – man's 'real and existing privileges, as a creature of society' – was not an absolute and inflexible one.[3]

In his attempt to consider society and the nation as a living whole, in which the interests of the various groups cannot be isolated from each other, and in which the political structure has to adapt to this interdependence so that it does not favour the interest of one group to the detriment of the rest, Coleridge was beginning to evolve his principles of political development; and it is by these principles that he defines for us what kind of relationship man should have to man in the society they share. For him, universal suffrage was no more the answer to this problem than universal despotism; if men possess disparate amounts of property, as is the case in England, then to grant every man an equal voice in the government is simply to give the man of small property a bigger proportionate say in the disposal of his neighbour's goods than the neighbour has in the disposal of his. If the right of property-ownership is recognized as valid for all, and that of political sovereignty is not, such is the logical conclusion. Coleridge phrases it thus: 'The great rule and law of [government by popular representation] is, that it shall recede from universal suffrage, as the state of property in the nation to be represented recedes from the subdivisions of Agrarian equality.'[4] Nations in which the land is divided nearly equally will resemble a 'pure democracy' in their representation. In America, for instance, 'the nature of the property permits, and, indeed, commands a much more extensive right of suffrage, than any wise man would wish in England or France'.[5] Such a right is a social right, however, a right established by the law of the country, and lasting only as long as the social conditions which gave rise to

[1] EOT, ii p. 548 (1802).   [2] *ib*. p. 550.   [3] *ib*. p. 499 (25 September 1802).
[4] *ib*. p. 496 (25 September 1802).   [5] *ib*. p. 498.

it are maintained, not a pre-existent right which is yielded up to a notional 'common stock' when a 'social contract' is formed. Similarly, property and hereditary rank – criteria by which political rights may be determined – are social rights, rights deriving from the very nature of the society in question, and established by 'long prescription'. This concept had been central to Burke's thought, for he too had held that the political rights of 'civil social man' could be derived only from society itself, and not vice versa.

As to the share of power, authority, and direction which each individual ought to have in the management of the state, that I must deny to be amongst the direct original rights of man in civil society; for I have in my contemplation the civil social man, and no other. It is a thing to be settled by convention.[1]

The modern historian, of course, rejects this way of speaking about societies, because of its apriorism. We cannot now conceive of societies as pre-existent to their conventions, but only as defined by, and indeed formed by, those conventions. De Tocqueville shows that he understands the difference between the two kinds of approach, at least as regards one province of law, when he writes: 'Je m'étonne que les publicistes anciens et modernes n'aient pas attribué aux lois sur les successions une plus grande influence dans la marche des affaires humaines... Ces lois...influent incroyablement sur l'état social des peuples, dont les lois politiques ne sont que l'expression.'[2] Here de Tocqueville makes civil law, in particular law of heredity, the formative factor, and political law a derivative phenomenon by which societies define themselves. Coleridge's argument, like Burke's, also presented political law as in some sense derivative, and Coleridge, moreover, saw that there was a causal connection between property-distribution and political structures; but he did not question, as de Tocqueville did, the basis in civil law of the distribution of property. This is undoubtedly a limitation; it gives Coleridge's vision of society an element of Burkean apriorism, and reduces to some extent the intrinsic value of his critique of those who would sweep away all the structures that had been evolved through centuries of English history, the men

---

[1] *Reflections on the Revolution in France*, edited by Conor Cruise O'Brien, p. 150.
[2] *De la Démocratie en Amérique* (13th edition, 1850), i p. 57.

who approved of the fragmentation that French society had undergone since the Revolution. '*Humists* in opinion, debauchees in conduct', he calls them; 'they have lost all power of sympathising with whatever exists in society.'[1] Yet what existed in society may have demanded a more radical examination than Coleridge at this time gave it.

Social rights can be violated from above, however, as well as disregarded by those who incline to philosophical scepticism and claim to question all laws. Bonaparte's treatment of Spain was an egregious instance of this. The Iberian peninsula was strategically very important to Bonaparte in the war with England; when, therefore, the Spanish queen denounced her son Ferdinand as illegitimate, a month after Ferdinand had forced the king to abdicate, Bonaparte took the chance to strengthen his hold on the peninsula by making the Spanish royal family give up the throne to Joseph Bonaparte. The people of both Spain and Portugal took up arms against the French: Wellesley was sent to Oporto to help the insurgents, and on 21 August 1808 the French forces were defeated at Vimieiro. Nine days later, following some questionable changes in the English high command, the notorious Convention of Cintra was signed. It permitted the French general, Junot, to take his army back to France without further penalty. The autumn and winter of 1808–9 saw Napoleon reassert his hold over northern Spain, and only the need to keep Austria at bay – and Sir John Moore's success in diverting part of the French forces away from Madrid – prevented him from bringing the whole peninsula under his control once more.[2]

Coleridge's 'Letters on the Spaniards', contributed to the *Courier* in the autumn of 1809, were intended to be read in conjunction with Wordsworth's tract on the Convention of Cintra.[3] Wordsworth had strongly opposed the idea that, as the country would be more efficiently administered, and material prosperity, therefore, would be greater, government by the French might improve the lot of the Spanish people. To deprive a nation of its political independence, as Bonaparte had done,

[1] From a *Morning Post* article of 12 December 1799, attributed to C by John Colmer, *Coleridge, Critic of Society*, appendix 'A', p. 194.
[2] J. Steven Watson, *The Reign of George III*, pp. 458–61.
[3] John Colmer, *Coleridge, Critic of Society*, p. 123.

was to undermine something much more important than its material wellbeing; it took away the human dignity of all its members, their moral free-agency; and, as Wordsworth phrased it, 'in the moral virtues and qualities of passion which belong to a people, must the ultimate salvation of a people be sought for'.[1] Coleridge adds to this the observation that support for Spain's freedom could not be (as we might say) a party issue, since it is not any question of 'natural rights' that is involved, but one of real 'social' rights that have been violated by Bonaparte's desire for the aggrandizement of France. The freedom of Spain is 'a cause, which, involving the most sacred *social* claims of mankind, neither bewilders us on the one hand with visionary speculations of *natural* rights; nor, like the former continental wars saddens us on the other with the uncomfortable thought, that *bad is the best*.'[2] Coleridge brought to bear on this question the thinking that played so large a part in the conception and content of *The Friend*, the first issue of which had appeared on 1 June 1809. The struggle of the Spanish people for liberty seemed to him a fine example of the assertion of man's free will in the face of brutal oppression; it had for him and for Wordsworth a deep moral significance. Where a people is conscious of its political identity – as was not the case, for instance, in most of Germany – it resents the yoke of the tyrant as an infringement of its moral freedom, and not merely of its political autonomy, for the former depends upon the latter. The power of the Spanish to resist Bonaparte is

the power of the insulted FREE-WILL, steadied by the approving CONSCIENCE, and struggling against brute force and iniquitous compulsion for the common rights of human nature, brought home to our inmost souls by being, at the same time, the rights of our betrayed, insulted, and bleeding country![3]

Coleridge's vision of society, then, already incorporates both the nation and the individual, and he fears for, and admires, the Spanish, not as 'a people', but as men. From Burke, Coleridge has learned that a civilized society is a product of history, and that the individual has therefore a duty to respect, and defend,

---

[1] *Political Tracts of Wordsworth, Coleridge and Shelley*, edited by R. J. White, p. 154.
[2] EOT, ii p. 594 (7 December 1809).   [3] *ib.* p. 612 (9 December 1809).

those social rights which custom and prescription have established, while he derives from the freedom of the political organism to which he belongs his right of free-agency in the moral
sphere. For a country to be justly governed it is by no means
necessary, as the Jacobins maintained, that every citizen should
have as of right an equal share in the government; when, as was
the case in England, property is unequally distributed between
the social groups, it is right that those with the greatest stake
in the well-being of the country should have a proportionate voice
in the government. Their landed interests guarantee that they
will not act irresponsibly, as might men of mere talent who own
no property. If every man performs his duties conscientiously,
and if there is no interference from outside, the whole will function in accordance with the best interests of all the parts. Jacobinism, in setting up postulative 'rights', destroyed this balance
of interests, and led inevitably to the supremacy of men of genius,
talent, and ambition, who could appeal to the masses for support,
but who, when in power, would put their own interests before
those of the nation as a whole.

In so far, then, as Coleridge's insights are based on what M.
Cestre calls 'la doctrine réaliste et historique',[1] they owe their
strength to the authority of Burke; but there is a sense in which
Coleridge is deeply opposed to Burke, as the passage last quoted
reminds us. Burke's feeling that social relations were in some
way sacred, since they had been appointed by God, just as he
appoints our familial relationships, was not endorsed by
Coleridge's more Protestant intelligence.[2] A clearer picture had
to be given of the evolving form of social institutions, and of the
'principle' behind those forms, which could not be just the absolute authority of God: God was surely the guide and critic of
human society, rather than its lawgiver.

3

Coleridge did not follow Burke in totally condemning the
philosophy that had inspired the French Revolution, even though
he was as repelled as Burke had been by many features of the

---

[1] *La Révolution française et les poètes anglais*, p. 445.   [2] See above, pp. 24–5.

Revolution itself. Supposing it had embodied, though in a degraded form, truths which still had value? In one light, Coleridge appears to us as the champion of the Revolution's principles against the English reaction:

Coleridge défend, envers et contre Burke, les grands principes de droit, de justice et de liberté. Au nom de la conscience universelle, il proclame qu'ils doivent dominer de haut l'empirisme incertain de la politique et éclairer de loin la marche hésitante de l'humanité. Soutenu par l'enthousiasme révolutionnaire purifié mais indestructible, il fait ainsi, aux choses du gouvernement, une féconde application de l'idéalisme moral et mystique qui est devenu à ses yeux l'essence de toute verité.[1]

It may be questioned, however, how much Coleridge's defence of liberty owed to the Revolution, or its principles; it seems to have had more in common with that recoil from French rationalism, and from Bonaparte, which a French historian has assured us encouraged a new attitude to liberty among the English from the turn of the century, as they 'now understood by liberty restraint self-imposed and freely accepted as opposed to restraint forcibly imposed by the Government'.[2] Coleridge had also, of course, experienced life in Germany, and Professor Colmer has argued that his knowledge of administrative practice there increased greatly his respect for the English system of government.[3] His idea of the state, and of the rights men should enjoy within it, bears a positive relation to all these factors, for they all operate in the realm of moral and sociological, rather than of purely political, thought, and it is characteristic of Coleridge's attitude to political man that he saw more than just material needs, and the delegation of power, at the root of the social organism. De Tocqueville wrote in 1835 that the accord which had always subsisted between men's ideas and their feelings had been shattered since the Revolution.[4] Coleridge felt strongly that there was a need to expound what was valuable in the ideas that had held men together, and to show the powerful that nothing but ideas, interfused with feelings, could ultimately sustain a society.

[1] Cestre, *La Révolution française et les poètes anglais*, p. 446.
[2] E. Halévy, *A History of the English people in the Nineteenth Century*, i p. 451.
[3] *Coleridge, Critic of Society*, p. 87.　　[4] See above, p 195.

THE SOCIAL STATE

This was not an easy task at a time when the spirit of philosophy was predominantly analytic. Hume, Voltaire, Condillac were too widely read, in Coleridge's judgment, and this overvaluation had led to an unjustifiable neglect of the great Renaissance philosophers – Bacon, Harrington, Machiavelli – of Spinoza, and above all of the Bible.[1] Scepticism, even if not intrinsically pernicious, could not be the foundation of any society, and if it met no healthy opposition would inevitably sap the resources of social cohesion.[2] Coleridge had never blamed the 'excesses' committed by the rioting crowds of Paris on the philosophy of their revolutionary leaders: 'the Light of Philosophy', he told his Bristol audience, 'when it is confined to a small Minority, points out the Possessors as the Victims, rather than the Illuminators, of the Multitude.'[3] Although the 'light' now had to come from a rather different kind of source, Coleridge remained constant to the principle that it is pointless to decry a philosophy for not providing what philosophy, as such, cannot provide. The very conditions which had shown the inadequacy of philosophy to govern and canalize the actions of the violent populace, however, also revealed that opinions and doctrine played a far greater part in inspiring them to resort to violence than 'personalities'. Coleridge took joy in deflating the vanity of the powerful by insisting on the essentially non-personal, or supra-personal, character of political events, recalling those early years of the Revolution to do so:

in the remotest Villages, every tongue was employed in echoing and enforcing the Doctrines of the Parisian Journalists... the public Highways were crowded with Enthusiasts, some shouting the Watchwords of the Revolution, others disputing on the most abstract Principles of the universal Constitution, which they fully believed, that all the Nations of the Earth were shortly to adopt... The more abstract the notions were, with the closer affinity did they combine with the most fervent feelings and the immediate impulses to action.[4]

Of course this assertion is by no means inconsistent with the statement that philosophy cannot control a mass movement, for abstract notions are not necessarily philosophical. They may,

[1] BL, i p. 38; *The Statesman's Manual* (1816), p. 18.
[2] See *Phil. Lects.*, p. 133 (Lecture III).
[3] *Lectures 1795*, p. 34 ('Conciones', Introductory Address).
[4] TF, ii p. 107 (no. 7: 28 September 1809); i p. 181.

211

indeed, breathe pure sophistry, and sophistry, as Coleridge points out in a passage written for the 1818 edition of *The Friend*, echoing the *Philosophical Lectures*, is divisive; it turns man's will into a means to some other end, whereas to the true philosopher will is the end, absolute in itself.[1] The multitude is swayed by abstraction, yet philosophy cannot guide it, and if sophistry prevails, men are inevitably subordinated to things. What shows men that the real object of their actions must be within the sphere of the truly human? – prevents them from turning themselves into mere means, and thereby into things? The answer is given in the same essay. 'As long as the spirit of philosophy reigns in the learned and highest class, and that of religion in all classes, a tendency to blend and unite will be found in all objects of pursuit, and the whole discipline of mind and manners will be calculated in relation to the worth of the agents.'[2] Those who were puzzled by Coleridge's apparently wild claims for Scripture might have been helped had they read this and learned that what Coleridge was arguing for was not so much Religion as the spirit of religion; not the extrapolation from a defunct society of laws for a living society, but the coming to consciousness of that living society according to the principles we have seen at work in the history of that dead society, and inherited from it. It can be said, then (to return to the question of Coleridge's search for the ideas that bound men together), that Coleridge had no intention of formulating a political proposition, or a putative structure, that men might subscribe to; the ideas he wished to draw his readers' attention to would be the living, energizing leaven by which alone a society could be sustained, not abstract propositions, arrived at deductively. They would not be the monopoly of a few enlightened leaders, but through the medium of the spirit of religion would be shared by every citizen. For this reason the essays on 'The Principles of Political Justice' in *The Friend* of 1809 (called in the 1818 edition 'On The Principles of Political Knowledge') move the focus of attention away from the political arena which Hobbes and Rousseau had pictured to their readers to the crucible of the individual mind.

The essence of Coleridge's case against Hobbes, in fact, is that he does not give a satisfactory account of the workings of the

---

[1] *ib.* i p. 444 (1818: Section the Second, Essay III).   [2] TF, i p. 444.

individual mind in its relation to the state; Hobbes ignores the very things that, for Coleridge, make man admirable. Their total divergence of views is predictable, given their quite different premises on the all-important question of free will. As we have seen, Coleridge admired the proof of their moral free-agency which the Spaniards gave by their struggle against Napoleon, and indeed *The Friend* makes Will not a concomitant, but a criterion of the fully human. Hobbes, on the other hand, dismissed the concept of free will as scholastic gibberish.[1] Like Coleridge, he was concerned to see what held men together in the state – very deeply concerned, since he had a horror of the turmoil which the Civil War had brought into a peaceful country – but the ligaments he could use had to be of a coarser material, for he denied that there was 'any such thing as absolute goodness, considered without relation. Seeing all delight is appetite, and presupposeth a further end, there can be no contentment but in proceeding . . . Felicity, therefore, by which we mean continual delight, consisteth not in having prospered, but in prospering.'[2] Coleridge gives the Will much more independence from the senses, and law, therefore, has to have sanctions that operate much more subtly. 'We can be subdued by that alone which is analogous in Kind to that by which we subdue: therefore by the invisible powers of our Nature, whose immediate presence is disclosed to our inner sense, and only as the Symbols and Language of which all shapes and modifications of matter become formidable to us.'[3] It is not fear, Coleridge insists, that substantiates laws, for the sword alone cannot compel obedience in the long term; it is a faculty which is innate in man, and which the greatest leaders appeal to by relying on open justice, and not coercion, to maintain discipline. Even where the head of the political state is a conqueror, he relies not on force, but on an oath of fealty to establish his subjects' obedience – an answer to Paine's contemptuous treatment of the British constitution as the legacy of Norman oppressors.[4] Coleridge

[1] See Basil Willey, *The Seventeenth-Century Background*, p. 100.
[2] Quoted by Willey, *ib.* pp. 100–1 (from *Human Nature*).
[3] TF. ii p. 101 (no. 7: 28 September 1809); i p. 172.
[4] *The Rights of Man*, Part I p. 36. James T. Boulton, in *The Language of Politics in the Age of Wilkes and Burke* (p. 142), speaks of a 'Norman Yoke' tradition in English radical politics.

examines the evidence which presented itself to his mind – his own knowledge of Sir Alexander Ball, and what was generally known, or thought to be known, about the practice of conquerors – and his enquiry leads him to 'the Spirit of LAW. . .the true necessity, which compels man into the social State, now and always, by a still-beginning, never-ceasing force of moral cohesion.'[1] The difference from Hobbes is radical, and is pointed up by the phrases 'true necessity', and 'force of moral cohesion'. Nothing is 'necessary' but what arises out of a man's own nature, as an individual and a free agent; if the State coheres it must be as the result of a moral choice, not of physical compulsion – in other words, because it is willed.

Once the autonomy of the individual, in the sense of his moral free-agency, is established, however, it must be decided what is his relation to the State; or rather, what the State is, as a function of his moral free-agency. The third and fourth essays in this series of *The Friend* turn to the system which, in Coleridge's phrase,

denies all rightful origins to Governments, except as far as they are derivable from Principles contained in the REASON of Man, and judges all the relations of men in Society by the Laws of moral necessity. . .according to archetypal IDEAS co-essential with the Reason, and the consciousness of which is the sign and necessary product of its full development.[2]

We should expect that such a system might win more respect from Coleridge than the Hobbesian system, and so, in a way, it does, but his use of its principles is wholly different from the use made of them by the 'natural rights' lobby. The Jacobins had, according to Coleridge, torn some of these principles from their contexts and misapplied them, blinded by the 'immorality' of the Hobbesian idea of political man;[3] but it was also patently obvious that societies could not be made to conform to 'the original laws of the pure Reason', as if they were all problems in geometry (something never actually claimed by Rousseau). There was all the more reason, therefore, to seek out what was inviolably true in the metapolitics of Rousseau, and save it from misapplication; 'Thus', (and here Coleridge again turns the whole drift of the argument inward)

[1] TF, ii p. 101 (i p. 171).   [2] *ib.* ii p. 105 (i p. 178).   [3] *ib.*

the dignity of Human Nature will be secured, and at the same time a lesson of Humility taught to each Individual, when we are made to see that the universal necessary Laws, and pure IDEAS of Reason, were given us, not for the purpose of flattering our Pride and enabling us to become national Legislators, but that by an energy of continued self-conquest, we might establish a free and yet absolute Government in our own Spirits.[1]

The total effect of Coleridge's critique of Rousseau is, indeed, to do exactly that; to establish the sovereignty of Reason as a faculty in the sphere of morality, which for Coleridge means the sphere of the individual's choices, while denying the part that Rousseau claimed for it in the political organism. Coleridge accepts that the faculty of Reason is the whole ground of the distinction between 'person' and 'thing', and the ground, there-fore, of all morality, law and justice; but Reason 'is not', he contends, 'susceptible of degree', and can strictly operate only in the realm of conduct. 'As the faculty of Reason implies Free-agency, Morality (i.e. the dictate of Reason) gives to every rational Being the right of acting as a free agent, and of finally determining his conduct by his own Will, according to his own Conscience.'[2] Reason alone cannot devise a course of action, any more than geometry alone can build a house. It can only weigh various courses of action against each other. It is pointless to demand that government be founded on Reason, seeing that no one man or group of men have ever been equipped with this faculty in its ultimate perfection. Coleridge will not, therefore, permit Rousseau to extrapolate from the individual's possession of Reason to its effective operation in the body politic. He will not permit Rousseau to add up each citizen's share in Reason, and so arrive at a total which will represent the prime mover of the political life of the community, because, as Rousseau himself says, the only lawgiver for the individual is Reason *per se*.[3] No man or group of men can supplant it, nor can it be treated as if it were quantifiable.

Reason...in any one Man, cannot even in the social state be rightfully

[1] TF, ii pp. 110–11 (no. 8: 5 October 1809); i p. 185. See *Phil Lects.*, p. 269 (Lecture IX).
[2] TF, ii p. 125 (no. 9: 12 October 1809); i p. 190.
[3] Coleridge may be recalling Godwin, who wrote in *Political Justice* (i p. 223) 'Reason is the true legislator.

subjugated to the Reason of any other. Neither an Individual, nor yet the whole Multitude which constitutes the State, can possess the Right of compelling him to do any thing, of which it cannot be demonstrated that his own Reason must join in prescribing it.[1]

Of course Rousseau had not exactly argued that the pressure of Reason could be crudely 'added up', and it was in elucidating this problem that he made the famous distinction between the 'volonté de tous' and the 'volonté générale'. Given a free interchange of arguments, the collective will of the people, the 'volonté générale', will invariably make itself clear. For Coleridge this is the crux of the matter: the distinction reveals the 'falsehood or nothingness of the whole system'.

For hence it follows, as an inevitable Consequence, that all which is said in the *Contrat social* of that sovereign Will, to which the right of universal Legislation appertains, applies to no one Human Being, to no Society or Assemblage of Human Beings, and least of all to the mixed Multitude that makes up the PEOPLE: but entirely and exclusively to REASON itself, which, it is true, dwells in every Man *potentially*, but actually and in perfect purity is found in no Man and in no Body of Men.[2]

Coleridge is implicitly rejecting, however, an important element in Rousseau's argument. 'Ce qui généralise la volonté est moins le nombre des voix que l'intérêt commun qui les unit', Rousseau had written,[3] not of course claiming that every man would understand equally well what 'l'intérêt commun' was, but nevertheless holding that every man would respect it as he respected his own interests, because the social contract obliged him to do so. This is wholly just, for the contract does not differentiate between citizens; they have the same obligations and the same rights.

Ainsi, par la nature du pacte, tout acte de souveraineté, c'est-à-dire tout acte authentique de la volonté générale, oblige ou favorise également tous les citoyens; en sorte que le souverain connaît seulement le corps de la nation, et ne distingue aucun de ceux qui la composent. Qu'est-ce donc proprement qu'un acte de souveraineté? Ce n'est pas une

[1] TF, ii p. 126 (no. 9: 12 October 1809); i p. 192.
[2] *ib.* ii pp. 127–8, i pp. 193–4.
[3] J-J. Rousseau, *Du Contrat Social*, edition of Garnier Frères, p. 255 (Book II, chapter IV).

convention du supérieur avec l'inférieur, mais une convention du corps avec chacun de ses membres: convention légitime, parce qu'elle a pour base le contrat social.[1]

Now for Rousseau the body politic has here a moral identity which Coleridge evidently does not recognize, though – as J. H. Muirhead shows[2] – later idealistic writers welcomed the concept of the 'volonté générale', since it could be seen as the expression of the 'permanent self' of the nation, and therefore as having authority, even though not all its acts are individually justifiable. For Coleridge, however, the idea that Will might express itself collectively was unconvincing. Rousseau does not, of course, wish to make the 'volonté générale' the arbiter of all moral questions, but he does argue that in its rightful sphere the 'acte authentique de la volonté générale' has moral authority, deriving from the social contract. Man is, however, both individual and citizen, and is himself subject, therefore, to the tension of conflicting wills: 'chaque individu peut, comme homme, avoir une volonté particulière contraire ou dissemblable à la volonté générale qu'il a comme citoyen.'[3] In this case, his will as a citizen must take precedence; if he subordinates it to his will as a private individual by disobeying the 'volonté générale' he has broken the social contract, and the community will be justified – morally justified – in disciplining him accordingly.

Coleridge has not recognized any such social contract, however, nor does he accept that in each individual there may exist two separate wills, which may come into conflict. There is no basis, therefore, on which the 'volonté générale' can have moral force, and no sense in which it can represent the voice of Reason. It cannot rightfully pronounce moral judgments, because a moral judgment is not a judgment on an act, but on the 'internal maxim' of that act, and that of course is outside the jurisdiction of any earthly authority. It cannot represent the voice of Reason, because it is contradictory to suppose that Reason never exists, in any one man, in absolute purity, and yet somehow asserts itself in the aggregate of men's wills.

Coleridge dismisses, then, the attempt to found society on Reason, although he succeeds in making some use of what

[1] ib.   [2] *Coleridge as Philosopher*, pp. 166–72.
[3] *Du Contrat Social*, p. 246 (Book I, chapter VII).

Rousseau says of Reason by speaking of it as the source of morality, and the proof of man's freedom.

That Reason should be our Guide and Governor is an undeniable Truth, and all our notion of Right and Wrong is built thereon: for the whole moral Nature of Man originated and subsists in his Reason. From Reason alone can we derive the Principles which our Understandings are to apply, the Ideal to which by means of our Understandings we should endeavour to approximate. This however gives no proof, that Reason alone ought to govern and direct human beings, either as Individuals or as States. It ought not to do this, because it cannot.[1]

The remainder of the essay is devoted to an analysis of the relationship between Reason and Understanding in the body politic, and in particular to showing that pure Reason cannot decide such questions as the distribution of property, or the extent of the franchise. It will be immediately obvious, however, that we are here in a quite different area of enquiry; we are once more looking at actual societies in their historical development, and Coleridge's observations begin to remind us of Burke's remark that 'Government is a contrivance of human wisdom to provide for human *wants*.'[2]

Yet is is precisely here, in the historical development of societies, that Coleridge looks for the principles which really hold the political organism together, imbuing men with an Idea of the state – principles not subscribed to consciously, as tenets of a political faith, nor formulated systematically by philosophers, but actually visible in the praxis of the community, and the very opposite, therefore, of abstract. Viewed in the 'spirit of Religion' – with faith that there is a final cause of human society, and that historical development is not directionless, but manifests the divine Will and purpose – our own history will appear, like that of Israel, as the progressive realization of an ideal, never coming fully to fruition but continually present, guiding and impelling, as 'something evermore about to be'.[3] Coleridge's three major political works were attempts to instil this point of view into a reluctant and often bewildered audience.

---

[1] TF, ii p. 131 (no. 9: 12 October 1809); i p. 199.
[2] *Reflections on the Revolution in France*, edited by Conor Cruise O'Brien, p. 151.
[3] Wordsworth, *The Prelude* (1805), edited by E. de Selincourt, p. 100 (Book vi, line 542).

To our basic question, 'what is the nature of the relationship that holds men together in the state?', they provide no definite answer in terms of politics or sociology, for Coleridge cannot define that relationship while the question of a final cause goes unanswered. The whole tenor of Rousseau's argument, no less than that of the utilitarian argument, is therefore alien to him. When he writes in *The Statesman's Manual* 'The perfect frame of a good man is the perfect frame of a state',[1] he is not falling back on a well-tried analogy, but stating a moral proposition of considerable importance. In the state, as in the good man, Reason, Religion and Will must be in their proper balance; when it is immanent in Reason and Religion 'the WILL appears indifferently, as wisdom or as love,' which are but 'two names of the same power.'[2] As in *The Watchman* and the Bristol lectures, Coleridge is arguing that political health will not be achieved simply by political reform, or by 'political' action of any kind; but whereas his aim in the 1790s was to purify the motives of the radical groups whose cause he had espoused, in later years he pressed for nothing less than a total change, initiated by the governing class, in the *'philosophic consciousness*, which lies beneath or (as it were) *behind* the spontaneous consciousness natural to all reflecting beings.'[3] For Coleridge, the common fault of the age was 'habitual unreflectingness', so that although the Bible was in theory readily accessible to every man, the impact it should have was nullified; theologians argued about 'historical evidences', while the people's moral sickness and their alienation from God – facts 'which no man can ascertain for another' – kept them in misery and blindness. 'As long as the principles of our gentry and clergy are grounded in a false philosophy, which retains but the name of logic, and has succeeded in rendering metaphysics a term of opprobrium, all the Sunday and national schools in the world will not preclude schism and Jacobinism in the middle and lower classes.'[4] Analytic philosophy could not supply the moral impulses on which the social state really depends. Societies cannot be maintained by one continuing process of rational deduction; they remain alive

[1] SM, p. vii.   [2] *ib.* p. ix.   [3] BL, i p. 164.
[4] Letter to Lord Liverpool (28 July 1817), printed in C. D. Yonge, *Life of Lord Liverpool* (300–7), p. 306.

only by the actual feelings of men towards each other, and by the idea which men share of the final cause of the social state. The only medium through which these feelings and this idea could be diffused and realized was religion, and that philosophy which took religious belief as its ground and its aim, for only religion is finally concerned with man as he actually is, in all his aspects. When we speak of the social state, it must be man in himself, the totality which only religion reveals to us, that we have in mind as the supreme end of political activity and theory.

In so far as they related to the 'objective' sphere, then, Coleridge rejected the insights of the rationalists; they seemed to treat men as mere units, as parts of a structure which was itself the only concern of the thinker. In so far as they related to the 'subjective' sphere, however – to the sphere of morality, the inner impulses and decisions of individuals – Coleridge adopted and used many of the rationalists' concepts, developing in this way an idea of 'liberty' which bore little outward resemblance to what the philosophers had proclaimed, but which had, undoubtedly, its own strength and its own logic.

4

It is its depth and religious intensity of concern, resulting in a conception of the 'final cause' of the social state, that gives Coleridge's most influential political essay its permanent value, in spite of the fact that the case it was to make for a change in the Catholic Emancipation Bills did not, in the end, need to be made. We can find in Coleridge's essay clear evidence of his desire for, above all, a new sense of purpose in the political life of the country. It is, he argues, the possession of this sense, of an idea of an 'ever-originating social contract' consisting in knowledge of the state's 'ultimate aim', which

constitutes the whole ground of the difference between subject and serf, between a commonwealth and a slave-plantation. And this, again, is evolved out of the yet higher idea of *person*, in contradistinction from *thing*, – all social law and justice being grounded on the principle, that a person can never, but by his own fault, become a thing, or, without grievous wrong, be treated as such: and the dis-

220

tinction consisting in this, that a thing may be used altogether and merely as the *means* to an end; but the person must always be included in the *end*.[1]

The distinction here drawn between 'person' and 'thing' is Kantian – indeed arguably it forms the climax of the Kantian philosophy. Its strength, therefore, derives from the argument that in man's remaining free to will the laws formed by his own reason, resides the essence of his humanity; the one thing which above all else distinguishes him from the rest of creation.[2] Coleridge uses this principle, adding the considerable weight of his political concern, as a statement about the relationship men have to the state, and to each other within the state. Whatever political structure a state is organized into, it will invariably be found extremely difficult for the governing body to treat the rest of the populace as persons, and very easy for it to treat them as quantifiable units. No citizen of the present century can have much cause to doubt that. Coleridge is making a statement which can hardly be called a political statement at all, or rather, its remoteness from most contemporary political dialectic shows how much the word 'political' has lost in meaning, since the notion of the 'polis' passed into obscurity. Distrusting, as we have seen, theories of the ideal State deduced from abstract principles, Coleridge felt that the test of any constitutional reform was whether it furthered the 'ultimate aim' of the state, which is the good of men as men, and not the health of the body politic considered as an aggregate of quantifiable 'things'. 'It is evident, that no specific scheme or constitution can derive any other claim to our reverence, than the presumption of its necessity or fitness for the general good shall give it.'[3] Mention of the 'general good' does not, of course, return us to the utilitarian argument; Coleridge's whole point is that a commonwealth flourishes by the moral as well as physical health of its subjects, and this means that they must enjoy moral free-agency, and due responsibility for themselves, including political responsibility. Since King Alfred's time, Coleridge believes, English history has been guided by the Idea of a Constitution, existing as a 'principle. . .in the minds and consciences of the persons, whose

---

[1] *On the Constitution of Church and State* (1830), pp. 7–8.
[2] R. D Miller, *Schiller and the Ideal of Freedom*, pp. 15–19.   [3] CCS, p. 6.

duties it prescribes, and whose rights it determines'.[1] No documentary evidence could be brought forward at any point to prove its existence, but when an appeal to a 'constitutional right' was made, 'it was no more than a *practical* way of saying, it is contained in the *idea* of our government, and it is a consequence of the "Lex, Mater Legum"'.[2] It had been a characteristic ploy of the Whigs to represent themselves as defending constitutional rights; after all, the Revolution of 1688 had resulted in the establishment, through the 'Declaration of Right', of constitutional limitations on the power of the Crown, and it was a fundamental Whig principle that these should be respected. According to the Whig writer of the 'Letters of Junius', the 'spirit of the Constitution' had indeed been alive in England even before 1688[3] – with 'a sort of uterine life', as Lord Carnarvon put it.[4] Radical criticism of the constitution came, in general, from outside the House, from the societies founded in the early 1790s to spread the gospel of Liberty on the French model; even those Members of Parliament who favoured reform criticized the letter, rather than what was felt to be the spirit, of the law, and men on both sides of the House tended to endorse Rousseau's judgment that the English were 'plus près de la liberté que tous les autres'.[5] In December 1792, Fox declared to the Commons 'Our Constitution was not made, thank God! in a day. It is the result of gradual and progressive wisdom.'[6] In his defence of Grey's proposals for parliamentary reform, too, Fox made the point that the Constitution was admirable precisely because it admitted of perpetual improvement.[7] Burke held a similar opinion; it was quite in keeping with the spirit of the Constitution to introduce reforms, provided they were, to use his own phrase, 'in the style of the building', and a Constitution that was passed on as it were by entail, from one generation to the next, would have the advantage of acquiring *'conformity to nature'*.[8]

[1] CCS, p. 12. [2] CCS, p. 29.
[3] J. T. Boulton, *The Language of Politics in the Age of Wilkes and Burke*, pp. 13, 22.
[4] In a speech in the House of Lords. See *Notes, Theological, Political, and Miscellaneous*, pp. 184–5.
[5] J. Steven Watson, *The Reign of George III, 1760–1815*, p. 324; J-J. Rousseau, *Du Contrat Social*, 244 (Book I, chapter VI).
[6] A. Cobban, *The Debate on the French Revolution*, p. 132. [7] *ib*. p. 109.
[8] *Reflections on the Revolution in France*, pp. 375, 121.

There was room for some disagreement as to what rights this admirably flexible constitution actually established, however. Richard Price, for instance, had appealed to the 'Declaration of Right' as proof that the people had a *de facto* right to choose their own governors, while Burke answered him by explaining that the Declaration had in fact removed that right, once and for all.[1] Nevertheless, Coleridge's view that the Constitution had been 'self-evolving' was far from original. What *was* new in Coleridge's claims was the thesis that, by reason of being self-evolving, the Constitution had guaranteed the people a greater degree of real freedom, including of course moral freedom, than would have been possible in a democracy.

For little less than a century and a half Englishmen have collectively, and individually, lived and acted with fewer restraints on their free-agency, than the citizens of any known Republic, past or present. The fact is certain. It has been often boasted of, but never, I think, clearly explained. The solution of the phenomenon must, it is obvious, be sought for in the combination of circumstances, to which we owe the insular privilege of a self-evolving Constitution.[2]

We have seen, however, that for Coleridge the moral freedom enjoyed by a people is not something it is possible to find separated from the political freedom they enjoy as a nation.[3] What Burke speaks of as 'long prescription' is a factor, not merely in the evolution of political structures, but in the moral development of a people – their development as persons, rather than as units in a political mechanism. A system where the 'will of the people' is the predominant power does not, in Coleridge's view, favour this development, any more than an absolute monarchy, for in both cases 'nothing is left obscure, nothing suffered to remain in the Idea, unevolved and only acknowledged as an existing, yet indeterminable Right'.[4] We are led to an interesting paradox, which plays across all Coleridge's writings on politics; it is clearly apparent in what M. Cestre says in arguing that Coleridge 'resta consciemment et délibérément fidèle à l'idéal proclamé par les hommes de 1789'. 'Interprétant à la lumière de cet idéal, la Constitution britannique – code sacré de la tradition – il y découvrit les principes mêmes de progrès

---

[1] *ib.* pp. 104, 107.   [2] CCS, pp. 106–7.
[3] See above, p. 208.   [4] CCS, pp. 107–8.

qu'avaient invoqués les rationalistes français.'[1] If there is a single unifying element in Coleridge's political thought, it is surely to be found in this crux. Coleridge could not finally answer the Jacobins' case in their own terms, nor were the principles of progress he discovered in the British Constitution of the same kind, strictly speaking, as the principles of progress formulated by the rationalists. Indeed, it may be questioned whether Rousseau's vision, in particular, was progressivist at all, for he saw that a state could go beyond 'maturity' into an era of stagnation, where it became as intractable as any human being in his old age.[2] The dialectic in which such an observation moves is far indeed from that of Coleridge's thought, as is apparent from the criticisms of Rousseau made in *The Friend*. 'Progress' in the state, regarded as a political progress, is meaningless to Coleridge; the only sense in which a state can be really said to progress is by the greater self-awareness, the 'increase of consciousness', of each of its citizens.[3] For this reason, Coleridge's answer to the claimants of natural rights, and to the Utilitarians (whose practical conclusions were in many ways similar to the Jacobins' in spite of the difference in their starting-point),[4] is his plea that 'the subjects of Christian Governments should be taught that neither historically or morally, in fact or by right, have men made the State; but that the State, and that alone, makes them men.'[5]

5

It will be useful to consider in this light the contributions made by Coleridge to contemporary political controversy, for they will all be found to bear on some aspect of the distinction between person and thing by which Coleridge defines his conception of relationships within the state, and to adumbrate a vision of the

---

[1] *La Révolution française et les poètes anglais*, p. 474
[2] *Du Contrat Social*, p. 265 (Book II, chapter IX).
[3] 'Theory of Life', in *Miscellanies, Æsthetic and Literary*, p. 372.
[4] See Leslie Stephen, *The English Utilitarians*, vol. I p. 302.
[5] Letter to Lord Liverpool, C. D. Yonge, *Life of Lord Liverpool* (300–7), p. 305. It is interesting that in C's eyes a revolution, far from being the opportunity for rejuvenation that Rousseau held it to be, was anathema because it causes 'a depravation of the national Morals' (*Lay Sermon* (1817), p. 104.)

political organism where the final cause is not, in the accepted sense of the term, political, but moral and spiritual. One example is the emphasis laid in *Church and State* on the idea of property as trusteeship. If the supreme consideration in the resolution of political and economic problems is to be that a state consists of persons, not things, it by no means follows that power and property are to be looked on as personal possessions. Coleridge attacked the French Constitution of December 1799, as has been shown, for its neglect of the property criterion, and its resultant tendency to favour personal power, to the detriment of the idea of trusteeship, to which the responsible landowner is committed. He now develops the theory of property as trusteeship by referring to the practice of the Hebrew, Celtic, Gothic and Scandinavian tribes, in each of which 'Property by absolute right existed only in a tolerated alien'.

Even in that species of possession, in which the right of the individual was the prominent relative character, the institution of the Jubilee provided against its degeneracy into the merely *personal*; reclaimed it for the state, – that is, for the *line*, the *heritage*, as one of the permanent units, or integral parts, the aggregate of which constitutes the STATE, in that narrower and especial sense, in which it has been distinguished from the *nation*.[1]

By the same kind of title the 'barons' of England hold their land; their tenure provides, in Coleridge's well-known scheme, for the 'permanency' of the nation, while the merchants and manufacturers provide for its 'progressiveness, and personal freedom'.[2] Coleridge nevertheless had to recognize that Hebrew practice could not be equated in every respect with that of modern England. In the Hebrew nation, wealth did not qualify its owners for political responsibility in the way that landed property did; Hebrew culture discouraged trade, and all enterprises of a purely financial kind. Coleridge did not wish to deny, however, that monied property brought with it the same kind of responsibility for national well-being that was incumbent on the landed gentry; merchants as well as landowners, as he saw it, were capable of 'that proprietorship to which a certain portion of political power belongs as its proper function' – of becoming,

[1] CCS, p. 39. [2] *ib.* pp. 42–3.

that is, trustees much as the landowners were. A more round-about argument had to be used, however, to show in what sense the test of property-ownership could be valid for the entrepreneur. Coleridge makes his point by implicitly criticizing that alternative political system which would produce talented but unpropertied statesmen. If our candidates have to be rich, rather than merely intelligent, we ensure that there is 'at least a strong probability, that intellectual power will be armed with political power, only where it has previously been combined with and guarded by the moral qualities of prudence, industry, and self-control.'[1] This argument from 'moral qualities' was very much Coleridge's own; it was, for instance, quite extraneous to the view of 'trusteeship' propounded by Burke. Burke was, of course, making a point similar to Coleridge's 'permanence and progression' theory when he argued that ability was a 'vigorous and active principle', while property was 'sluggish, inert, and timid'. As he did not recognize the connection between ability and prudence on which Coleridge rested part of his case, however, Burke's conclusion was rather different. Property 'can never be safe from the invasions of ability', Burke wrote, 'unless it be, out of all proportion, predominant in the representation'.[2]

Burke was thinking in particular of one supposed advantage of the large landed estate – that it guarantees security to smaller masses of property. The large landowner is, in his view, a kind of guardian, his estate forming 'a natural rampart about the lesser properties in all their gradations'.[3] Burke's argument was based on the theory of government developed by Adam Smith, who follows Locke's principle that 'government has no other end but the preservation of property'. 'All the inferior shepherds and herdsmen', Smith wrote, 'feel that the security of their own herds and flocks depends upon the security of those of the great shepherd or herdsman.'[4] Coleridge does not give this argument much prominence; security of tenure was not his major concern, for where the idea of trusteeship is fully operative, land-grabbing should be eliminated.

Smith also believed, however, that the landed class in the modern state had a stake in their country's prosperity – a belief

[1] CCS, pp. 97–8.   [2] *Reflections on the Revolution in France*, p. 140.
[3] *ib.*   [4] *The Wealth of Nations*, ii p. 236.

Coleridge shared – and he also argued that the interest of 'those who live by rent' is 'strictly and inseparably connected with the general interest of the society'.[1] He differed radically from Coleridge, though, in his attitude to the monied class, for he held that those who live by profit are *not* disciplined by any identification of their interest with that of the nation, since profit 'does not, like rent and wages, rise with the prosperity, and fall with the declension, of the society'.[2] The operations of the East India Company gave him ample proof that good administration is not by any means identical, or even consonant, with good trading practice.[3] It seems clear that Coleridge, in fact if not in intention, was applying to the case of manufacturers and traders a theory of trusteeship suitable (at least in the eyes of Adam Smith, and Burke) to the case of the landed class only. Coleridge distinguished, however, between the City and the 'real' employers of labour. Indeed in the year when *Church and State* was published Coleridge was voicing doubts about the 'stock-jobbing and moneyed interest', which he knew had 'more than once prevailed in our foreign councils over national honour and national justice'.[4] The Spirit of Commerce could be a force for good in the national life, but it needed a bridle, and neither Canning (about whom Coleridge had been speaking) nor the landed interest nor, in the end, any merely political powers could supply this need. The manufacturers, on the other hand, were still in many parts of England identified more closely in the public mind with the landowning than with the monied classes; it was their ambition to be respected on equal terms with the local squire, and, even more, for their children to marry into landowning families, so uniting a newly-amassed fortune with a name and a property that had links with the past.[5] There was consequently less reason than we might at first assume for discriminating between the capitalist and the landowning classes, as regards their political responsibility – in spite of what Smith had written to show that trade and government should not be mixed.

In arguing that it was of supreme importance to recognize the supra-personal nature of political power, Coleridge added to the

[1] *ib.* i p. 276.   [2] *ib.* i p. 277.
[3] *ib.* ii p. 154.   [4] *Table Talk*, 4 July 1830.
[5] E. Halévy, *A History of the English People in the Nineteenth Century*, i pp. 283–4.

theory of Smith and Burke his conviction that all property is owned in the name of the people, a conviction illustrated by the analogy with the practice of Hebrew tribes, and reinforced by his abhorrence of personal political power in any form – for he believed also that neither King, Lords nor Commons enjoyed their rank in any other name than that of the people. The writer of the strongly Whiggish 'Letters of Junius' – which were much read and admired by Coleridge[1] – made a similar point: 'The power of the King, Lords and Commons is not an arbitrary power. They are the trustees, not the owners of the estate. The fee-simple is in US.'[2] Coleridge emphasized that the monarch merely represented, and did not possess, the power of the nation and its laws:

the Crown in its legislative character represents the Nation, its ancient Laws and Customs, ante-Parliamentary as well as Parliamentary, and on his solemn oath alone...does the Commonwealth depend for the continuance of its super-Parliamentary Rights: while as the Executive Power, the Crown is the Agent and Trustee for all, chosen by the Nation, not elected by the Estates.[3]

For Coleridge all political power and all interests in the large masses of property therefore had the same basis of trust; neither the monarch, or the 'barons', nor even the *parvenus* in the House of Commons enjoyed their power by any other title than that of their responsibility to the people.

6

Though he was to envisage for them a political role of some importance, Coleridge was far from idealizing the manufacturers, and his criticisms of them reveal a deep distrust of the economic philosophy of the time. Adam Smith argued that their function was to increase the real wealth of the country by enabling labour to be 'mixed' with raw materials, so producing goods which were of greater value than their constituent parts; the motive for investment in activity of this kind was, and could only be, that of

[1] See James T. Boulton, *The Language of Politics in the Age of Wilkes and Burke*, p. 17.
[2] *ib.* p. 19.   [3] *Notes, Theological*, p. 213.

profit. The landowner similarly provides for labour, on a large scale, to be 'mixed' with natural produce, and undertakes to support the labourer on condition that the returns from the land he works show a profit. '[The labourer's] maintenance is generally advanced to him from the stock of a master, the farmer who employs him, and who would have no interest to employ him, unless he was to share in the produce of his labour, or unless his stock was to be replaced to him with a profit.'[1] The interests of employer and employee are, in both cases, at odds. It is in the interest of the labourer, obviously, that his wage should be as high as possible; it is in the employer's interest that the wages he pays should be as low as is compatible with 'common humanity', which means, in effect, that they should enable the labourer to bring up a family so that a continual supply of labour is ensured.[2] With Hobbes, Smith holds that 'a man's labour also, is a commodity exchangeable for benefit, as well as any other thing';[3] and if the demand for labour should decrease, the supply will, in the natural course of things, adjust itself, since fewer children will survive if workers' families have to live in poverty. 'It is in this manner that the demand for men, like that for any other commodity, necessarily regulates the production of men; quickens it when it goes on too slowly; and stops it when it advances too fast.'[4] 'The demand for labour', in short, 'regulates the subsistence of the labourer.'[5]

Burke took over this doctrine from Smith, as he had taken over the doctrine of property as a guarantee of security. 'Labour', he wrote, 'is a commodity, and, as such, an article of trade. . . subject to all the laws and principles of trade.'[6] The most important element in Smith's argument, however, was his defence of a free market in commodities and manufactured goods. When Burke resolutely opposed all restriction of free trade, according to the principles established by Smith, he was doing more than bringing Smith's thought to bear on the economic practices of country in an academic way; he was speaking for the landowners

[1] Adam Smith, *The Wealth of Nations*, edited by E. Cannan (2 vols.), i p. 73.
[2] *ib.* pp. 73–6.
[3] *Leviathan*, edited by M. Oakeshott, p. 161 (Part 2, chapter 24).
[4] *The Wealth of Nations*, i p. 89.   [5] *ib.* ii p. 392.
[6] From *Thoughts and Details on Scarcity*; see A. Cobban, *The Debate on the French Revolution*, p. 409.

and farmers of England, who felt, like him, that the laws of commerce were virtually laws of nature – immutable, and indeed God-given.[1] Fox also favoured the 'spirit of competition'; but it was not only the Whigs who profited from Smith's work. Pitt had ratified a trade agreement with France, just before the Revolution, on the theory that France would prove a better trading partner than America, and this theory had first been propounded by Smith.[2] Between 1803 and 1813 the working classes, who naturally feared and hated the doctrine of *laissez-faire*, found that the rights they had enjoyed under archaic statutes, such as the Elizabethan apprenticeship laws, were gradually eroded and replaced by a system of 'free competition' in labour. There appeared to be no legal means of redress; court cases brought against the employers by the unions either failed, or won only nominal damages.[3] In Europe the picture was similar, except that the 'physiocratic' doctrines that influenced continental economic practice differed from the principles laid down by Smith chiefly in that the latter included manufactured goods in his estimate of real wealth, whereas the physiocrats only counted produce actually extracted from the soil.[4]

In spite of his continued opposition to both Smith and the physiocrats, Coleridge was very far from holding trade, and far less agriculture, to be intrinsically evil. Long before writing of the mercantile class as one of the forces of 'progression' in the state, he had stated his belief that it was through the exercise of trade, and the resultant intercourse between nations, that Europe had become civilized. It was the worst of Napoleon's many crimes, in his view, to attempt to reverse all the good that had been done by strangling European trade, so as to weaken England's economic strength:

that in order to gratify his rage against one country, he made light of the ruin of his own subjects; that to undermine the resource of one enemy, he would reduce the Continent of Europe to a state of barbarism, and by the remorseless suspension of the commercial system, destroy

---

[1] E. Halévy, *A History of the English People in the Nineteenth Century*, i p. 232; and Cobban, p. 410.

[2] Halévy, i p. 192; J. Steven Watson, *The Reign of George III*, p. 288.

[3] E. P. Thompson, *The Making of the English Working Class*, pp. 595–6.

[4] *The Wealth of Nations*, ii p. 183; Leslie Stephen, *History of English Thought in the Eighteenth Century*, ii p. 261; A. Goodwin, *The French Revolution*, pp. 19–20.

the principal source of civilization, and abolish a *middle class* through-out Christendom; for this, Sir, I declared him the common enemy of mankind![1]

It is especially easy for the modern reader to distort this view-point into the still more questionable doctrine that trade is intrinsically good, and that anything which favours increase of trade is therefore to be welcomed. Coleridge did not hold, and could not have held, such a view, as he had always in mind the difference between material prosperity and national well-being. He knew, in short, that the availability of fine lace and French wines meant nothing to a family who could not afford to buy bread. This is clear in the comments he made on a debate between Lord Liverpool and Lord Grenville, as to whether the blockade on French ports should be lifted. The position of France at the end of 1799, just after Bonaparte had made himself consul, was weak, for she had suffered severe losses at sea, and the Allies had had useful successes in Italy. The British fleet was in a position to support an invasion of her south-eastern shores.[2] Lord Liverpool was in favour of using Britain's advantage to secure a monopoly of world trade, by ensuring that the ports of France stayed closed. Grenville opposed him, arguing that the ports should be allowed to open, not only on grounds of humanity, but also because it would in fact favour Britain's commercial interests. Coleridge, however, put his weight squarely behind the humanitarian argument. He wrote: 'Let us not forget that commerce is still no otherwise valuable than as the means to an end, and ought not itself to become the end, to which nobler and more inherent blessings are to be forced into subserviency.'[3] Coleridge did not leave the question of the benefits of trade in these somewhat vague terms, however. As in his thought on political responsibility, he directed his readers' attention to the actual consequences for the individual of theories of trade. In the same essay, he issued a warning that all was not right with the country's economic system, if the working popula-tion could be habitually referred to as 'the labouring poor'. These

[1] EOT, ii pp. 647-8 (21 December 1809). The term 'middle class' was at this time of quite recent coinage. See Asa Briggs, *The Age of Improvement*, pp. 65, 170.
[2] J. Steven Watson, *The Reign of George III*, p. 380.
[3] EOT, i p. 274 (1 February 1800).

words were a facile generalization of a reality that appalled him. The arguments of those who looked on labour as a commodity, and on the employer as having, therefore, no other interest in the employee than as a source of profit, were in his eyes wholly pernicious. Provisions and money will, he concedes in an essay of 1800, 'find their level', but 'O God! what scenes of anguish must take place while they are *coming to a level*?'[1] The doctrine really did treat men not as persons but as things – as the quantifiable units of a labour force – and it thereby violated Coleridge's deepest instincts. For it was no mere philosophical cavil that led Coleridge to reject vehemently the kind of economic relationship envisaged by the free-trade theorists, and to argue consistently for the kind that was defined for him by the term 'person', and by its necessary consequence, the treatment of men as ends in themselves, and not merely as means. (A modern reader will wish to question why it should be necessary for men to be treated as means at all; this need not, however, obscure for us the essential difference between Coleridge's account of the employer and worker relationship and Adam Smith's.) 'The distinction between Person and Thing', Coleridge wrote in *The Friend*,

consists herein, that the latter may rightfully be used, altogether and merely, as a *Means*; but the former must always be included in the *End*, and form part of the final Cause. We plant the Tree and we cut it down, we breed the Sheep and we kill it, wholly as *means* to our own *ends*. The Woodcutter and the Hind are likewise employed as *Means*, but on an agreement of reciprocal advantage, which includes them as well as their Employer in the *end*.[2]

The very essence of Coleridge's long-standing disagreement with Smith and the physiocrats was, precisely, a disagreement about final causes. Smith had attacked all interference with a free market on the general ground that

it retards, instead of accelerating, the progress of the society towards wealth and greatness; and diminishes, instead of increasing, the

---

[1] EOT, ii p. 456 (8 October 1800). The phrase in question was actually used (in a rather different sense) by Godwin (*Political Justice*, ii p. 516; and see Leslie Stephen, *History of English Thought in the Eighteenth Century*, ii p. 237), though it seems to have been most often associated in C's mind with the doctrines of Adam Smith.

[2] TF, ii p. 125 (no. 9: 12 October 1809); i p. 190.

real value of the annual produce of its land and labour. All systems either of preference or of restraint, therefore, being thus completely taken away, the obvious and simple system of natural liberty establishes itself of its own accord.[1]

This kind of view was reflected by Burke, when he wrote that it was 'generally pernicious to disturb the natural course of things, and to impede, in any degree, the great wheel of circulation which is turned by the strangely directed labour of these unhappy people [that is, of the French peasantry]'.[2] The fourteenth essay of the series on 'Political Justice' in *The Friend* takes issue with the physiocrats over just this point. 'They worship a kind of non-entity under the different words, the state, the whole, the society, etc.' Coleridge asserted; it was a system which 'would blend men into a State by the dissolution of all those virtues which make them happy and estimable as Individuals'.[3] The system was vitiated by the criterion of 'productivity', according to which, for instance, a vine-dresser is only usefully employed when he is at work in the vineyard – producing 'liquor that will disease the bodies, and debauch the souls of an hundred'[4] – while all the time he may spend in the acquisition of knowledge, or in the improvement of his moral and intellectual qualities, and of those of his family, is time wasted. Something non-human, something entirely conjectural and abstract, has been substituted for real human happiness and fulfilment – happiness that cannot be dismissed as the goal of a selfish individualism, since it will surely 'overflow into countless channels, and diffuse itself through the rest of the Society'.[5]

It was in the *Lay Sermon* of 1817, however, that Coleridge expressed himself most fully on the subject of economic relationships. England after the death of George III seemed to be facing a proletarian revolution, whose objectives became avowedly political but which was instigated by an economic crisis. In January 1816 the price of a quarter of wheat was 53s 6d: by December of that year it had risen to 103s. Agricultural wages were subsidized from poor relief (a practice that had been started in 1795) so that they could be kept low, while the price

---

[1] *The Wealth of Nations*, ii p. 208.
[2] *Reflections on the Revolution in France*, edited by Conor Cruise O'Brien, p. 271.
[3] TF, ii p. 326 (no. 24: 15 February 1810); i p. 299.
[4] *ib.* p. 327, i p. 300.   [5] TF, ii p. 327 (i p. 300).

of corn had been artificially maintained by high exporting in order to protect the interests of landowners and merchants, until July 1816, that is, when workers at Ghent sabotaged British exports. A severe fall in the already low standard of living among the working classes led to widespread discontent. There were strikes, rioting and machine-breaking, and the ringleaders were savagely punished.[1] Coleridge was involved in the anti-Corn Law agitation, to the extent of making a speech in that cause at Calne in 1815, and it was the events of these years that led him to ask whether 'all the great component interests of the State' were really 'adequately represented' in Parliament.[2] He saw that what was needed was for politicians to stop allowing their preoccupation with a 'healthy' market to determine their treatment of the labourer, and in particular to see that wages were raised to a just level. For it was a monstrous affront to human dignity that men who did a fair day's work should have to be supported from poor relief. Did not agriculture, after all, have the same end as that of the state? Yet the Spirit of Commerce was now the dominant power in British agriculture; it had far overstepped its proper bounds, and would have to be restrained and purified by concern for the real welfare of the nation. While Commerce is supreme, the 'ladder of society' is broken, and 'the Hope, which above all other things distinguishes the free man from the slave, is extinguished'.[3] In other words, the relationship of employer to worker is vitiated, since the profit motive becomes all in all, and the interest of the worker in the conditions of his employment, the opportunity it gives him to better himself and his family, intellectually and in other ways, is wholly neglected. What should benefit both employer and employee becomes entirely one-sided, and mutual antagonism is the result. Asa Briggs points to Coleridge's use of the 'ladder' metaphor as a typical example of the view of society as a permanent hierarchy, which he holds to have been the common one in Coleridge's lifetime.[4] For Coleridge, however, the idea

[1] E. Halévy, *A History of the English People in the Nineteenth Century*, i pp. 248–9, ii pp. 10, 29; E. P. Thompson, *The Making of the English Working Class*, pp. 347–84.
[2] *Letters*, iv pp. 549, 554 (nos. 957, 959: 10 March 1815 and 13 March 1815).
[3] LS, p. 131.
[4] *The Age of Improvement*, pp. 9–10.

was essentially dynamic, not static. 'The Ideal of a Government', he wrote in 1831, 'is that which under existing circumstances most effectually affords Security to the Possessors, Facility to the Acquirers, and *Hope* to all – Poverty, whatever can justify the designation of "the Poor" ought to be a transitional State.'[1] A more critical account of the 'ladder' as a model of society is given by Raymond Williams, however: he points out that it allows for the advancement of individuals, as individuals, but suggests nothing that may help the poor as a class. Indeed, it rather implies that a relatively poor class must always exist, so as to provide the lower rungs of the ladder.[2]

Though Coleridge did not take the step of advocating direct government control over wages, he did argue that it was the state's duty to protect its 'inalienable and untransferable Property', the 'health, strength, honesty and filial love of its children', from the claims of commercial necessity, should these become excessive; if the economic system became injurious to the people's welfare, the state must withdraw from it all artificial aids.[3] But this was the limit of the government's right to interfere in private concerns. Under normal circumstances, the landowner would naturally pay his workers a just wage; to do so was part of his responsibility, his position of trust. It was still possible for Coleridge to believe that the Spirit of Commerce could be of real benefit to the nation as a whole, provided it was duly regulated by the state where it conflicted with the interests of the people.

This proviso was of no small significance, however, in an age dominated by the doctrines of Adam Smith, and in which current economic realities bore out the theory of a fixed 'real wage' that Ricardo, Smith's disciple, and Malthus had formulated.[4] Coleridge had to establish, therefore, against all the weight of an economic theory from which both Whigs and Tories had learned, that the government had a duty to correct the balance of the economy where necessary. In order to do so, he used the *argumentum ad hominem* to attack the notion that the economy should be allowed to find its own 'level'. 'It would be less

[1] Notebook 50, fol. 46.   [2] R. H. Williams, *Culture and Society*, pp. 331–2.
[3] LS, p. 118.
[4] E. Halévy, *A History of the English People in the Nineteenth Century*, p. 246.

equivocal and far more descriptive of the fact to say, that Things are always *finding*, their level: which might be taken as the paraphrase or ironical definition of a storm...But Persons are not *Things* – but Man does not find his level. Neither in body nor in soul does the Man find his level!'[1] The importance of the 1817 *Lay Sermon* lies precisely here. Coleridge's refusal to deal in abstractions, and his sense of a living and suffering population to whom the ratio of wage levels to the price of corn can make all the difference between hunger and a sufficient meal, sustain and impel the whole argument. The result is that he represents the nation's needs as something calculable, not in terms of share prices or the balance of payments, but as a function of those qualities which make men happy and responsible individuals, and which cannot be quantified by the economist, any more than Reason can be quantified by the political theorist. Coleridge, like Burke, thought and wrote always with the conviction that, where political structures are in question, only 'man in the concrete' mattered,[2] and it may be that he owed to Burke, in some measure, his ability to transmit this feeling to his readers; but he also had something that Burke lacked, and which was characteristic of Dissenting rather than of Anglican or Catholic thought. This was the sense of men as individuals answerable to God alone, and of the correspondingly great moral importance of 'popular enlightenment' in the national life.[3] Yet there was a crucial qualification to be made to the arguments of the Dissenters before Coleridge could adopt them. In the circulars which he wrote in support of Peel's Bill to shorten the working hours of child factory workers, Coleridge again brought to his readers' imaginations the stark reality of poverty, and the real suffering that was caused by the 'adjustment' of the 'system'; but he also appealed to another quarter to establish the government's right to 'interfere', and in doing so touched on this qualification – the total dependence of our 'rights', and even of our moral free-agency, on the Constitution, and in particular on the kind of spirit that the Constitution enshrines (more by what it does not than by what it does say). Coleridge's reference to it in *Two*

[1] LS, p. 101.
[2] J. T. Boulton, *The Language of Politics in the Age of Wilkes and Burke*, p. 76.
[3] *ib.* p. 91.

Addresses, in close conjunction with the kind of *ad hominem* argument that he used in the second *Lay Sermon*, shows, too, that for him the two lines of thought were not separable. Fair treatment of every sector of the 'commonwealth' in economic matters – the fulfilment, that is, of the trust reposed in the land-owner and the employer of labour – is not a separate issue from the defence of the 'liberty of the subject'. The difference between a 'subject' and a 'serf', of which so much was to be made in *The Constitution of Church and State*, is a moral as well as an economic difference. Coleridge carried his point by questioning the basis of the Smithite's insistence on a free market in labour.

It is our duty to declare aloud, that if the labour were indeed free, the employer would purchase, and the labourer sell, what the former had no right to buy, and the latter no right to dispose of; namely, the labourer's health, life, and well-being. These belong not to himself *alone*, but to his friends, to his parents, to his King, to his Country, and to God.[1]

When the employer buys labour, he does this within the frame-work of a mutually interdependent community (the unbroken 'ladder of society', as Coleridge put it in the *Lay Sermon*), and he must recognize that the labourer has certain rights which must not be encroached on. The basis of these rights is the 'principle and spirit' of the Constitution. It is, Coleridge argues, the physiocrats, and their disciples the engineers of the French Revolution, who have really established a 'free market' in labour, since they have shattered the 'ladder' that rendered it a duty incumbent on the employer to treat his employees as per-sons. They have swept aside constitutional law, and for the happiness of the individual they have substituted the criterion of 'productivity'. England, like Holland and parts of Germany, has by contrast a Constitution that in no way favours those who object to interference with a 'free market'. If an actual precedent for such interference is needed, apprenticeship law can be cited, but it is not necessary to argue as if the law specified what rights of the employee are to be respected. The principle that he is a free subject, and not a serf, is sufficiently established, not as an

---

[1] *Two Addresses on Sir Robert Peel's Bill* (April 1818), edited by Edmund Gosse (privately printed, 1913), p. 21.

a priori truth, but as a condition of the society in which he lives. 'The *principle* of *all* constitutional law is to make the claims of each as much as possible compatible with the claims of all, as individuals, and with those of the common-weal, as a whole: and out of this adjustment, the claims of the individual first become *Rights*.'[1] Such rights are conditional, not absolute, however. Coleridge makes an implied comparison, again, with physiocratic doctrine. 'English subjects...pretend to no *rights* that do not refer to some duty, as their origin and true foundation.'[2] Far from being a concession to the manufacturers, this is in context an argument on behalf of the workers; they will fulfil their obligations to society, the argument runs, unless the 'ladder' is broken – as it may be by the 'Spirit of Commerce' – in which case duties, together with rights, are swept aside, and the situation reverts to pure chaos.

This argument was to some degree undercut, of course, by the very fact that legislation had become necessary; that some manufacturers could still oppose Peel's Bill on the ground that two or three hours a day could make no difference at all to the life of a child factory worker. Sophistry had debased the minds of the employing classes, just as it had debased the Jacobins. 'Generalities', Coleridge wrote, 'are apt to deceive us. Individualize the sufferings which it is the object of this Bill to remedy: follow up the detail in some one case with a human sympathy: and the deception vanishes.'[3] Such deception was not merely a matter of faulty epistemology, as Coleridge well knew. As a young radical, Coleridge had had sharp things to say about the kind of false sensibility which weeps over the sorrows of Werther, and regards the slave-trade with equanimity. 'Benevolence impels to action', he wrote sternly, 'and is accompanied by self-denial.' His tone in 1818 was rather less fiery. 'Something else is wanted here, the warmth to impel, and not the knowledge to guide.'[4] The difference in tone surely indicates not so much a change of convictions, as a realization of the magnitude of the problems that had to be faced, if there were to be any serious attempt to bring about, by a major change in attitudes rather than through a violent revolution, a society in which men were really treated as

---

[1] *Two Addresses*, p. 19.   [2] *ib.* p. 21.   [3] *ib.* p. 25.
[4] *The Watchman*, p. 140 (no. IV: 25 March 1796); *Two Addresses*, p. 26.

persons, not as things. The 'enlightened self-interest', the 'good sense and humanity' of the commercial class, had apparently not induced them to abolish the slave-trade of their own accord; nor were these qualities very greatly evident in the attitude of manufacturers to the use of child labour. Coleridge does not conclude, however, that the evil is inherent in the system, and the stance he takes on this issue is, in our time, peculiarly susceptible to misunderstanding, particularly since we know that his youthful views were rather different. He had told the radicals at Bristol, 'Our object is to destroy pernicious systems not their misguided adherents. Philosophy imputes not the great evil to the corrupted but to the system which presents the temptation to corruption. The evil must cease when the cause is removed.'[1] Coleridge's understanding of men and their motives, of philosophy, of religion, above all, had changed greatly between 1795 and 1818; moreover, between those two dates – in 1803 – a new enemy had appeared, and was spreading sophistry among the upper classes. 'Is it not lamentable', Coleridge was to say, '...that the monstrous practical sophism of Malthus should now have gotten complete possession of the leading men of the kingdom!' Malthus's doctrine was a 'lie in morals', and a licence to men's cruellest and most selfish inclinations.[2] Yet even men who admired Malthus and defended their selfishness with Malthusian sophistry were not to be thought of as beyond the range of the moralist's voice. Nor did their abuse of capitalism amount, in Coleridge's eyes, to a condemnation of capitalism itself.

Coleridge's opposition to the predominant religious mood of his day was total; the Bible was read, he believed, in entirely the wrong spirit; religious observances, in utter contradiction to the teaching of Christ, had become divorced from the conduct of life's affairs; and the 'something, not ourselves, that makes for righteousness', in Arnold's phrase, had been lost from the national life. The age was, by Coleridge's standard, very far from being an age of faith. The *argumentum ad hominem* was to him much more, therefore, than a trick of rhetoric. 'We must learn to act nationally...as Christians', Coleridge wrote in the

[1] *Lectures 1795*, pp. *18–19* ('A Moral and Political Lecture': part of a passage omitted *from* 'Conciones ad Populum'.)
[2] *Table Talk*, p. 170.

second *Lay Sermon*, and he went on to insist that every man must also '*act personally and in detail* wherever it is practicable'.[1] There was no need for such an overt appeal, in a sense: after all, something was in this case being done, and it was Coleridge's primary purpose to vindicate the Bill that Sir Robert Peel had introduced, not to stir his readers into taking action themselves. Nevertheless, the second Address ends with an exclamation of faith that is far more than mere pious sentiment. 'Praise be to God, who never fails to supply what is wanting to us, as long as we are in earnest in doing *our* best, the Powers of the Christian World *have* united.'[2] God cannot be expected, that is, to reform the factories on his own; not a statement that betrays complacency in religious belief, whether we wish to condemn it as hypocritical, or welcome it as courageous. Yet the very fact that Coleridge turns here, as in the *Lay Sermon*, to the sphere of religion for his final word shows that he looked for no social or political solution, far less a revolutionary solution, to the problems of social and political injustice. If the evil is not 'inherent in the system', then neither will it be eradicated merely by a change in the system. The injunction to 'act nationally...as Christians' certainly presupposes a Christianity in which social concern figures at least as prominently as 'private' morality. But that is also to presuppose Christianity itself. Social justice, whatever our definition of the phrase, will never be achieved until it is uniformly desired, and our desires, or the motives behind our actions, are exactly what the state, with all its machinery of law and economic structures, cannot determine.

7

A further issue to which the distinction between Law and Religion is fundamental is that of 'social' as against 'natural' rights. It has been pointed out that one reason for the lack of major political turbulence in the England of the late eighteenth and early nineteenth centuries was the success of the Dissenting churches in channelling discontent and unrest into religious sentiment, so diverting men's potentially revolutionary sympathies

[1] LS, pp. 132–4.   [2] *Two Addresses*, p. 28.

away from their natural target, the secular authorities. So far were the Nonconformists from regarding themselves as outright enemies of the secular authorities that in a manifesto produced in 1811 they could point to 'the beneficent influence exercised by the Nonconformist sects during the previous half-century, "in raising the standard of public morals, and in promoting loyalty in the middle ranks, as well as subordination and industry in the lower ranks of society".'[1] This goes some way towards explaining what Professor Colmer holds to be a failure on Coleridge's part, his inability to recognize that the basing of political demands on religious tenets, the kind of argument that Paine and Cartwright used, was an integral part of English Dissenting tradition, not an importation from the doctrines of the French 'physiocrats'.[2] If, by 1811, the Dissenters had lost so much of their old political orientation, there was at least some reason for Coleridge's 'failure' in this respect. Yet it is undeniable that Coleridge's thought as regard the 'natural rights' debate tends the same way as the message of those Dissenting churches which encouraged the populace to regard their misery as a symptom of religious, rather than of political, alienation.

The argument that Major Cartwright put forward was somewhat different from Paine's in the detail, but its general conception was similar. Cartwright (as quoted by Coleridge in *The Friend*) pointed out that 'the equality and dignity of human nature in all men, whether rich or poor, is placed in the highest point of view by St Paul'. He then went on to quote I Corinthians VI.3: 'Know ye not that we shall judge angels? how much more things that pertain to this life?' The opponent of universal suffrage was, Cartwright concluded, an enemy of God himself. Coleridge regarded this passage as conclusive proof that Cartwright's claims were identical with those of Rousseau, and Coleridge had already 'confuted' Rousseau, as has been shown, by accepting that all he said of Reason was true in so far as it related to 'private' morality, but denying his right to introduce such principles without modification into the sphere of government and legislation. Yet Cartwright's arguments, in spite of

1 E. Halévy, *A History of the English People in the Nineteenth Century*, i pp. 424, 431; ii p. 75.
2 *Coleridge, Critic of Society*, p. 105.

their similarity to Rousseau's, could not be treated with the same leniency. 'The tendency of [Cartwright's] writings', Coleridge affirmed, 'in my inmost conscience I believe to be perfectly harmless'; but 'the tendency of one good man's writings is altogether a different thing from the tendency of the system itself, when seasoned and served up for the unreasoning multitude'.[1]

Coleridge was therefore driven to expose what he regarded as the basic fallacy of Cartwright's system; its 'confusion of political with religious claims', amounting to a

transfer of the rights of Religion *disjoined* from the austere duties of Self-denial, with which religious rights exercised in their proper sphere cannot fail to be accompanied, and not only disjoined from Self-restraint, but *united* with the indulgence of those Passions (Self-will, love of Power, etc.) which it is the principal aim and hardest Task of Religion to correct and restrain – this, I say, is altogether different from the *Village Politics* of Yore, and may be pronounced alarming and of dangerous tendency by the boldest Advocates of Reform not less consistently, than by the most timid Eschewers of popular Disturbance.[2]

Coleridge was by no means the first to make this kind of attack upon the 'natural rights' lobby. Burke too had argued that 'metaphysic rights entering into common life, like rays of light which pierce into a dense medium, are, by the laws of nature, refracted from their straight line...In proportion as they are metaphysically true, they are morally and politically false.'[3] Burke was simply using metaphor to expound a view substantially similar to Coleridge's doctrine of Reason and Understanding. A metaphysical truth can be a moral and political falsehood, if we regard the principles of pure Reason as bearing only indirectly on the sphere of conduct, of 'common life'. Burke's use of the term 'moral' differed, admittedly, from Coleridge's, for Burke used the word in the context of a purely objective view of conduct, whereas for Coleridge 'the object of morality [was] not the outward act, but the internal maxim of our actions'.[4] This does

[1] TF, ii pp. 136, 137, 138 (no. 10: 19 October 1809); i pp. 207, 209, 211.
[2] *ib.* ii p. 140 (no. 10: 19 October 1809); i p. 214.
[3] *Reflections on the Revolution in France*, p. 153.
[4] TF, ii p. 128 (no. 9: 12 October 1809); i p. 194.

not materially affect the comparison, however. For both writers, the practical details of government – apportionment of land, and of the 'social rights' on which political sovereignty depends – were things to be settled by the Understanding, not by the pure Reason. Government was first formed for the protection of property (a point on which Adam Smith, Burke and Coleridge all agreed), but it was impossible to 'deduce the Right of Property from pure Reason'. In a revealing footnote to this remark, Coleridge added in 1818 'I mean, practically and with the inequalities inseparable from the actual existence of Property. Abstractedly, the Right to Property is deducible from the Free-agency of man. If to act freely be a Right, a *sphere* of action must be so too.'[1]

There can be few better indications of the degree to which Coleridge's convictions, particularly his conviction that the social state was not an end in itself, led him to make statements which to the political philosopher appear wholly specious and false. Coleridge's presentation of man as an amenable[2] creature demands always that we consider what he calls the subjective sphere, where Reason, morality (in the Coleridgean sense) and the Will operate, as well as the objective sphere of conduct, action and history. Such a view should not be confused with those of the Christians whom Rousseau represents as being concerned solely with the spiritual world. Coleridge desired the proper management of the material bases of life; but only in order that man's subjective faculties might be more fully developed. He was not indifferent to the 'material world', but regarded it merely as a *means*; persons and the personal were the *end*. It was the same problem that bedevilled the Dissenting churches and encouraged them to grow less and less concerned with changing the objective reality of the disparity of wealth, and more and more preoccupied with the salvation of men's souls, no matter what privations they might have to suffer in order to sustain the level of 'civilization'. It was a problem that became more acute for the liberal mind as the nineteenth century wore on. But it was philosophically still possible for Coleridge to argue that the hire was worthy of the labourer provided his work served the final cause

[1] TF, 1 p. 200 (footnote added in 1818 text).
[2] That is, responsible.

of the social state – the moral, intellectual and spiritual development of men as individuals, including that of the labourer himself, of course. The radicals of Coleridge's time, however, saw no value in this kind of distinction between 'objective' and 'subjective' worlds. They did indeed 'confuse' political with religious claims, in so far as they saw that a politics which undermines the avowed purpose of religion made as little sense as that superstitious kind of religion which denied that politics was a subject worthy of serious consideration. But the spearhead of protest was now no longer Dissent, but included a politically oriented section of the working class;[1] and their doctrines therefore invited denunciation by churchmen and statesmen as 'ungodly'. (For example, the two Committees appointed under Lord Liverpool's administration to report on 'revolutionary plots', following the supposed attempt on the Regent's life in January 1817, drew special attention to the 'irreligious' doctrines spread by the radicals, especially the democrats of the London political clubs).[2] In one way, Coleridge's distinction between the inner world of spirit and the outer world of conduct, though it helped to preserve against the attacks of the Utilitarians many important ideas about man's capabilities, also perpetuated a source of potential conflict which other writers (among whom Blake was perhaps the most notable) were doing their best to eradicate.

To Blake, the idea of a 'subjective' sphere which could be spoken of in terms not applicable to the historical reality – even when one was simply the opposite 'pole' of the other – was anathema.

> The whole creation will be consumed and appear infinite and holy, whereas it now appears finite and corrupt.
> This will come to pass by an improvement of sensual enjoyment.
> But first the notion that man has a body distinct from his soul is to be expunged.[3]

Blake saw, too, that it was specious to consider the material world purely as a 'means', denying that the organization of the material was of more than secondary importance. The day's

---

[1] See the chapters on the 1810s and 1820s in E. P. Thompson, *The Making of the English Working Class.*
[2] E. Halévy, *A History of the English People in the Nineteenth Century,* ii pp. 23–30.
[3] *Poems and Prophecies,* pp. 48–9.

labour cannot be treated as a mere chore; it binds man's spirit as viciously as other forms of oppression, and its effect is not annulled by any 'freedom' enjoyed during the hours of darkness. The human spirit, before it can procreate, has to be encircled with fires of prophecy from the god of a material universe. Los, forced to work by day, finds that his labour binds him with a succession of girdles, which

> falling down on the rock
> Into an iron Chain,
> In each other link by link lock'd.[1]

8

In *Leviathan*, Hobbes divides laws into 'natural laws', which are eternally valid, and 'positive laws', or those which 'have been made laws by the will of those that have had the sovereign power over others'. Of 'positive' laws, some are human, and some divine. Hobbes argues that a sovereign cannot demand our wholehearted acceptance of 'divine positive laws' as proceeding from supernatural revelation, since no man can be expected to judge whether another is truly the vehicle of divine Will; but the sovereign can legitimately demand our obedience to such laws, for we are in this respect bound by the same duty that we owe to the sovereign as head of the civil commonwealth. That is, we are bound to obey divine positive laws, but not bound to believe them.[2] This doctrine was repugnant to Coleridge, not only because it divorced belief and act, but because the recent example of Ireland showed how dangerous was any attempt by a civil authority to bring the rule of law into the sphere of religious profession. Coleridge wrote in a letter to the *Courier* of September 1811,

It is not yet definitely settled, what are the things of Cæsar, and what of God: we still want a complete table of all those points, with which the magistrate has no right to interfere, as well as of those which the teacher of religion may be rightfully prevented from meddling with... why need I refer to past History? Ireland is at this moment before our

---

[1] William Blake, The Book of Urizen, v 11, 3 (*Poems and Prophecies*, p. 88.)
[2] *Leviathan*, edited by M. Oakeshott, pp. 186–7 (Part 11, chapter 26).

eyes, the immediate object, if not of our alarm, yet of our just solici-
tude, and deepest interest.[1]

He goes on to refute Hobbes's system, on the ground that it
split inward conviction from its outward manifestations; if the
people are not permitted to express their faith where it conflicts
with the dictates of the monarch, then, even though they may
think what they will, their faith will inevitably die. 'The same
law, therefore, which obliges me to retain, must likewise oblige
me to express and communicate my faith.'[2] For the sake of an
outwardly stable commonwealth, Hobbes had sacrificed the
spiritual integrity of the individual, and all possibility of a
sincere faith.

Coleridge did not carry his analysis beyond this brief confrontation with Hobbes – in spite of a 'To be continued' at the
foot of the letter, a promise which was not fulfilled – but in
Church and State he again took up the question of the relation of
the monarch to the Church. The Catholic Emancipation Bill
which was the occasion of Coleridge's essay came at the end of a
long history of attempts to change the law relating to Catholics.
As early as 1800, Pitt had made such an attempt, and had been
forced to resign when it was blocked by George III. Similar
opposition had met the attempts of the 'Ministry of all the
talents' to throw Army and Navy posts open to Catholics in 1807.
In general, the advocates of Catholic Emancipation belonged to
the anti-war faction in British politics, which was discredited
after Waterloo and the restoration of monarchical government
in France, while the supremacy of the orthodox Tories was, for
the time being at least, assured. And although Ireland was torn
by rioting in 1820 and 1821, the grievances of the Irish labouring
class had more to do with the inequality of wealth than with the
cause of freedom of beliefs, or even that of their country's political status. Irish Catholics, unlike English Catholics, had since
1793 possessed the right to vote, but, unwilling to stand up
against their Protestant landlords, they dutifully returned the
landlords' anti-Emancipation nominees to Parliament. Canning,
though personally in favour of Emancipation, did not wish to risk
his position by flouting the united opposition of the Court, the
Evangelicals, and the English middle and lower classes, who

---

[1] EOT, iii pp. 927–8 (26 September 1811).   [2] *ib.* iii p. 932.

were united in their contempt for the Irish, though their opposition to Emancipation had political rather than theological grounds. They dreaded the prospect of an English Parliament being swamped by Irish demagogues and revolutionaries, for the franchise in Ireland was far closer to being a 'democratic' franchise than was that of England. Yet in 1825 the Whigs did succeed in carrying (by 247 votes to 230) a motion to discuss the issue of Catholic Emancipation, though, to reassure the English electorate, they considerably tempered their Bill by proposing, with O'Connell's approval, that the franchise in Ireland should be narrowed, and that the state should take over responsibility for paying the Irish Catholic clergy. But they could not overcome the opposition of the Court. Their Bill, though passed by the Commons, was thrown out by the Lords, following a speech by the King's brother, the heir-apparent, affirming that it was and would remain the King's duty, by virtue of his Coronation oath, to defend the Established Church. Canning took this as a warning from the King, and persuaded the Whigs not to raise the issue again, at least until after the election of 1826. In that election, however, O'Connell managed to swing the balance of the representation in Parliament much more in favour of the Emancipationists, by persuading the free tenants in Ireland to vote for Emancipation candidates. Nevertheless a Whig motion of 5 March 1827 was defeated, though only by four votes. The Emancipationists strengthened their hand, however, by securing the repeal of the Test and Corporation Acts, which had discriminated against Dissenters (though by long-established custom Dissenters who infringed the Acts had been granted an annual amnesty, so that repeal was simply the recognition of a *de facto* principle of tolerance).[1]

But it was O'Connell who precipitated the crucial change of policy by standing against Vesey Fitzgerald, the government's candidate, in a by-election which had to be held in County Clare in May 1828. The purpose of the by-election was to enable Wellington, the new Prime Minister, to appoint Fitzgerald to his Cabinet; but Fitzgerald decided to withdraw, as support for O'Connell was obviously overwhelming. Though, being a

---

[1] E. Halévy, *A History of the English People in the Nineteenth Century*, ii pp. 139–40, 218–20, 223–4, 240, 249, 263–6.

Catholic, O'Connell was technically ineligible, to declare the election void would have been to incite all Southern Ireland to open rebellion. In June and July the situation worsened, although O'Connell dissuaded his countrymen from embarking on civil war. Wellington secured Peel's reluctant support for an appeal to the King, who finally yielded; the Speech from the Throne which opened the session of 1829 contained a promise to 'review' the position of the King's Roman Catholic subjects; and in March 1829 three Bills were introduced and given Royal assent. One suppressed the Catholic Association; one raised the franchise qualification in Ireland from a freehold of the value of two pounds annually to a freehold of the value of ten pounds annually; and the 'Emancipation Bill' itself granted Catholics the right of suffrage, the right to sit in Parliament, and the right to hold office under the Crown.[1]

Yet feeling among the Protestant majority in England still ran high, though they feared more the threat to their political supremacy than the endangering of the nation's spiritual health.

[The Protestants] were afraid of the Catholic Church because they regarded her as a State within the State, whose members owed allegiance to a foreign monarch; and the danger presented by the admission of Catholics into Parliament appeared all the more serious because the Church of England was so strictly bound to the State and unconditionally subject to the authority of Parliament.[2]

Though an attempt to ensure protection for the Anglican Church by extorting 'securities' from the Catholics had to be abandoned for the sake of speed, the Bill accordingly included a requirement that Catholics must undertake to respect the Established Church, to recognize the Protestant succession, and to repudiate any interference by the Pope in the government of the country.[3]

The tract that Coleridge was preparing, however, and which he published in 1830, laid most emphasis on the responsibility that the King still had towards the Established Church, responsibility, not for its doctrines, as Hobbes would have wished to argue, but for protecting it against the state, that other pole of the 'magnet' which the King's person represented. Before he is

---

[1] E. Halévy, *A History of the English People in the Nineteenth Century*, ii pp. 268–72.
[2] *ib.* p. 275.
[3] *ib.* p. 277.

declared supreme head of Church and State, Coleridge pointed out, the monarch has to take an oath binding him to veto

> any measure subverting or tending to subvert the safety and inde-
> pendence of the National Church, or which exposed the realm to the
> danger of a return of that foreign usurper, misnamed spiritual, from
> which it had with so many sacrifices emancipated itself. . . it is no addi-
> tional power conferred on the king; but a limit imposed on him by the
> constitution itself for its own safety.[1]

The King does not thereby become the fountainhead of the doctrine and ministry of the Church; his authority is not personal, any more than his authority over the state is personal. He takes the oath as the representative, and not the possessor, of the nation's power. Nor does the nation, when the coronation oath is administered, 'decide for the King's conscience and reason' on matters of doctrine. The oath is meant simply to ensure the autonomy of the National Church. It was found necessary to do this after the reigns of Henry VIII, Edward VI, Queen Mary and Queen Elizabeth, when the people had been forced to change their religious beliefs with each successive new monarch.

Can we wonder that the nation grew sick of parliamentary *Religions*? or that the Idea should at last awake and become operative, that what virtually concerned their humanity, and involved yet higher relations, than those of the citizen to the state, duties more awful, and more precious privileges, while yet it stood in closest connection with all their *civil* duties and rights, as their indispensable condition and only secure ground – that this was not a matter to be voted up or down, off or on, by fluctuating majorities![2]

Yet there would seem to be a contradiction inherent in this view. The advantage of Hobbes's system is that it considerably simplifies the process by which we justify the punishment of malefactors. If a man disobeys the will of the monarch, no matter what reasons he may give for doing so, we are justified in punishing him, as long as the will of the monarch is held to be identical with 'morality' – in the non-Coleridgean sense of 'rule of outward conduct'. If, however, we admit that there are 'duties more awful, and more precious privileges' than are involved in our relation to the state, we seem to be faced with the possibility of a conflict between the demands of conscience on the one hand,

[1] CCS, pp. 120–1.   [2] CCS, pp. 117–18.

and those of social expediency on the other. Coleridge's answer would be essentially the same as the one he gave in *The Friend* to the same difficulty: the state has no concern with morality as such. Against an article on 'Liberty of Conscience' in the *Encyclopædia Londiniensis,* which included the sentence 'With Religion, Christian governments have no further concern than as it tends to promote the practice of virtue', Coleridge wrote 'No! If this were once admitted, even the Inquisition might be defended. Not the practice of *virtue*, but the peace of Society and the Legality of the Individuals, are the objects of Law; these secured, we may safely trust to Religion, Education, and Civilization for the rest.'[1] Coleridge returns to the idea that the real work of rendering a recalcitrant people virtuous must be done from the inside, by an influence which works on their motives and their conscience. For to say that government is not concerned with 'the practice of virtue' is not to say that Religion does not serve the ends of the state – its true ends, that is, which are to be found in the subjective as well as in the objective sphere. It is through the medium of Religion that 'the morality which the state requires in its citizens for its own well-being and ideal immortality' is embraced by the people; Religion is 'the centre of gravity in a realm, to which all other things must and will accommodate themselves.'[2]

It is difficult for a modern reader not to assume here that Coleridge is in fact asking for the nation to neglect law, science, economics – everything that does not have overt theological or eschatological significance. Coleridge believed, however, that theology was, as a matter of historical fact, the ground and basis of all science, and of what we may loosely term 'culture'; and, moreover, that science, morality and 'culture' themselves return to theology in the end. To put it another way, theology did not in Coleridge's eyes exclude 'humanism', and the 'humane sciences', but was indeed their foundation, both historically and in essence: '*educing*, i.e. eliciting, the latent *man* in all the natives of the soil, [it] *trains them up* to citizens of the country, free subjects of the realm'.[3] The aim of the National Church, therefore, is not a kind of solemn national piety, but what Coleridge calls 'civilisation with freedom', a state of society in

[1] *Notes, Theological,* p. 220.   [2] CCS, p. 71.   [3] *ib.* pp. 49–50.

which every citizen has both opportunities and incentives to reach a higher and still higher stage of perfection, not only spiritually but intellectually; improving his faculties of discrimination and judgment in science, literature and the arts, as well as achieving self-knowledge and self-discipline in accordance with the teaching and example of the moralist, the philosopher and the divine. No less than Arnold – though Arnold perhaps lacked that belief in the 'final cause' of human society which was the backbone of Coleridge's social writings[1] – Coleridge believed that the attainment of 'freedom' was possible only through the continuing pursuit of the ideal of 'cultivation', which was Hebraic rather than Greek, and moral rather than æsthetic.

Coleridge's distrust of Catholicism, or more specifically, his conviction that the autonomy of the National Church stood in danger, now that Catholics were to be permitted to hold seats in Parliament, was not a matter of doctrinal difference only, nor was it identical with that feeling which Halévy represents as being prevalent among English Protestants of the time, that the Irish Catholics were a major political threat to the stability of the nation. Were it so, the essay on *Church and State* would have taken a very different form. Coleridge believed that Catholicism merged into one all-powerful body two essentially distinct institutions: the earthly *imperium*, which can judge only the 'objective facts' of outward conduct, and those spiritual descendants of the Church Fathers to whom is entrusted the all-important, positive function of '*educing*...the latent *man* in all the natives of the soil'. In short, Catholicism destroyed what was, for Coleridge, the very essence of human society; instead of providing a milieu in which man could develop his gifts and faculties, it overlaid on all men's lives a system of prohibitions, of purely negative exhortations, with respect to this world, and of purely outward, 'objective' observances, with respect to the world to come.

9

Since the state, and therefore man himself, is a product of history, man, far from being the degenerate descendant of a once noble

[1] See R. H. Williams, *Culture and Society*, pp. 118, 128.

race, is coming closer, century by century, to his final perfection. This 'perfection' is to be understood rather in religious than in 'humanistic' terms, though the best phrase for it is Coleridge's own – 'the Divine Humanity'; since only religion can unite 'Idea in the Subject' with 'Law in the Object'.[1] There is a further point to be made, however, concerning the place of Religion in the state. It is the only area of human experience that can be shared by all sections of the community. It is only through Religion, indeed, that true community exists.

We have seen that Coleridge described Religion as 'the centre of gravity in a realm'. In the same passage in *Church and State* he contrasts it with science – including philosophy – which cannot, he declares, be popularized, only 'plebified'.[2] The fear of such 'plebification', of the evil and anti-religious effects on the populace of the promulgation of half-understood philosophies, had been with him for a long time. In 1802, he had criticized Fox for failing, in his *History of England*, to correct by judicious admonishments the idea of man presented in the works of the deists, and others, 'those sophists, who have developed the vices of individuals, in order to enfeeble the virtues of the species, who have exhibited the depravity of a singularly corrupted age, as the means, not of deterring us from their vices, but of alienating our understanding from the best impulses of our own best affections.'[3] Fox's portrait of eighteenth-century England overemphasized the elegant and cultured aspect of the period; he ignored the many evils, and the 'actions disgraceful to our country and to human nature' which marred it.[4] Coleridge insisted that scepticism was the effect, and not the cause, of the moral depravity of the age. Man continues to grow in self-knowledge only so long as he is true to the 'principles of action' that may be discovered in his past, and in the instincts which that past has built into him. Deism and scepticism, far from being steps towards a deeper understanding of man as he 'really is', were aberrations – aberrations which did not result from over-zealousness in the cause of truth, but were the fruit of a period of unparalleled licentiousness. Their spirit lived on in the

---

[1] TF, i p. 497, note 2. [2] CCS, p. 71.
[3] EOT, ii p. 571 (4 November 1802).
[4] *ib.* ii p. 570.

philosophy of Coleridge's own time, with, he believed, dire consequences to the nation as a whole.

It was in the *Lay Sermons* of 1816 and 1817 that Coleridge's
opposition to both scepticism and deism was most forcefully
stated. The joint effect of these two schools of thought had been
to separate religion and religious observance further and further
from the cross-currents of everyday life, leading inevitably to
the fragmentation of society, since it was Religion alone that
checked the divisive effects of the 'Spirit of Commerce'. Even if
all question of 'atonement' were left aside, Religion could still
be seen to have a salutary effect, merely in the way it occupied
men's minds. 'It is well known', Coleridge wrote,

that Poetry tends to render its devotees careless of money and outward
appearances, while Philosophy inspires a contempt of both as objects
of Desire or Admiration. But Religion is the Poetry and Philosophy of
all mankind; unites in itself whatever is most excellent in either, and
while it at one and the same time calls into action and supplies with the
noblest materials both the imaginative and the intellective faculties,
superadds the interests of the most substantial and home-felt reality to
both, to the poetic vision and the philosophic idea.[1]

What Coleridge says here has, however, wider implications than
can be accounted for simply by mentioning his desire for a
counterbalance to the commercial spirit. One characteristic of
the 'subjective–objective' distinction was that it posited a unified
stream of experience, which is viewed from two different stand-
points, rather than two wholly different kinds of experiences.
This passage reintroduces the same element in Coleridge's
thought, and exemplifies the tendency of all his later writings
on Religion to present the aim and object of Christian faith as
being '*another* world, not a world *to come* exclusively, but likewise *another world that now is*'.[2] Religion 'superadds the interests of the most substantial and home-felt reality to...the
poetic vision and the philosophic idea'. It was Coleridge's constant theme in writing about the Old Testament that it recorded
the real lives and the real experiences of men and women, and
of the nation they belonged to; he argues in the *Confessions* that
Scripture meets and completes the subjective experience of the

[1] LS, pp. 87–8.
[2] CCS, p. 136; and see *Letters*, vi p. 596 (no. 1537: 27 July 1826) and note.

individual with an 'objectiveness, a confirming and assuring outwardness' which enables the 'insulated Self' to be transcended, re-absorbs it into history, into the stream of human *praxis*.[1] Given the unity of experience that this would produce – a unity in which every action has the intense personal importance that a poet in Coleridge's era would often seize upon, yet also the general significance which is what finally matters to the philosopher – it becomes easier to see why Coleridge felt that the 'spirit of Religion' might change the outlook of an entire people. Yet it was precisely this sense of actuality, of history as a humane rather than as an abstract study, that had been lost from the literature of Coleridge's own time.

In nothing is Scriptural history more strongly contrasted with the histories of highest note in the present age, than in its freedom from the hollowness of abstractions . . . The histories and political economy of the present and preceding century partake in the general contagion of its mechanic philosophy, and are the *product* of an unenlivened generalizing Understanding... [The contents of the Sacred Book] present to us the stream of time continuous as Life and a symbol of Eternity, inasmuch as the Past and the Future are virtually contained in the Present. According therefore to our relative position on its banks the Sacred History becomes prophetic, the Sacred Prophecies historical... In the Scriptures therefore both Facts and Persons must of necessity have a two-fold significance, a past and a future, a temporary and a perpetual, a particular and a universal application. They must be at once Portraits and Ideals.[2]

To gain some sense of the importance which this reading of Old Testament history had for Coleridge, we need only turn to the tenth 'Essay on the Principles of Method' in the 1818 edition of *The Friend*. It centres on the Epistle to the Hebrews, and especially on the eleventh chapter of the Epistle, which illustrated the nature of faith by citing examples from Old Testament history. 'Now faith is the substance of things hoped for, the evidence of things not seen. For by it the elders obtained a good report. Through faith we understand that the worlds were framed by the word of God, so that things which are seen were not made of things which do appear.'[3] Essay X shows how the history of the patriarchs can be read as the history of an educational process,

[1] CIS, pp. 79–80.   [2] SM, pp. 34–6.   [3] Hebrews XI, 1–3.

whose first beginnings – 'the very first lessons in the Divine School'[1] – took place in Old Testament times, but which is still not completed, so that the Christian, far from being instantly recompensed for his selflessness (as Warburton would have it) can expect no immediate reward, but like the Israelites must *endure*, AS SEEING HIM WHO IS INVISIBLE'. Hebrews XI concludes: 'And these all, having obtained a good report through faith, received not the promise: God having provided some better thing for us, that they without us should not be made perfect.'[2] Yet it must again be emphasized that it was not some new form of piety that Coleridge found in his reading of Old Testament history, nor was it piety that he advocated in the modern world. 'The aim, the method throughout', he wrote in Essay X, 'was, in the first place, to awaken, to cultivate, and to mature the fully *human* in human nature.'[3] The plea that he made in *The Statesman's Manual* was an attempt to further the same process in contemporary society. England, or rather England's politicians, seemed to Coleridge to have lost all faith in the possibility of 'cultivation'; they sacrificed men, and human fulfilment, to an illusory ideal of commercial strength, productivity and prosperity. By contrast with the politician's preoccupations, Christianity demanded a return to reality – the reality, that is, of human needs, spiritual, intellectual and emotional, as well as material.

In the long run, moreover, atheism was inevitably divisive, since it vitiated all causal relations. The whole concept of causality is meaningless, Coleridge would argue, unless we accept the existence of a First Cause. But that was exactly what the atheist had to deny, and when the main theological controversy of the age was between atheism and the rationalistic depersonalized Christianity of the Anglican divines, it was no wonder that societies began to fragment. The sense of causality could have effective life only in a faith which worshipped an eternal and omnipresent, yet personal, God. Only, therefore, if the Scriptures were read in the spirit of true faith, and the existence of the living God affirmed, could there be any legitimate basis for earthly power. If causality is denied, earthly authority becomes a mere arbitrary institution, with no real

[1] TF, i p. 501.   [2] Hebrews xi, 39–40.   [3] TF, i p. 500.

power to bind and loose. Only when a First Cause is affirmed, as it was in Jewish culture, has the authority of an earthly government any firm basis, or its ministers any true responsibility. For the appeal to causality works in two ways; the theocentric government may be able to invoke divine wisdom as its justification, but it must also be answerable, as no Gentile government could be, to divine judgment on its actions and motives. Hence Jewish history remains important for a Christian government; it is only in the Scriptures that 'the *Jus divinum*, or direct Relation of the State and its Magistracy to the Supreme Being, [is] taught as a vital and indispensable part of all moral and of all political wisdom, even as the Jewish alone was a true theocracy.'[1] It follows from the existence of this 'direct Relation...to the Supreme Being', indeed, that the social state must have such a final cause as Coleridge describes, and were it not so, the state would be nothing more than a slave-plantation, an estate-agency and labour-market; a single pole, if such a thing could exist, of the magnet.

Precisely because Religion is both a personal, subjective experience and the manifestation of a historical process, it drives us constantly back to reality, not away from it. It gives general truths the immediacy that imaginative literature, and especially poetry, strives for, and on the other hand imbues even men's daily lives, their 'little, nameless, unremembered, acts'[2] with a significance far beyond themselves. 'Both Facts and Persons must of necessity have a two-fold significance, a past and a future, a temporary and a perpetual, a particular and a universal application.' For, corresponding to the historical progression of the race towards greater perfection and a higher degree of 'cultivation', there is the fact of the spiritual progression of individuals. Impossible in a religion which is characterized by superstition, or by mere token assent, not proceeding from the heart, such a progression is the chief demand of that faith which can 'employ and actuate the understandings of men, and combine their affections with it as a system of Truth gradually and progressively manifesting itself to the Intellect'.[3] Coleridge even

1 SM, p. 40.
2 Wordsworth, *Poetical Works*, edited by E. de Selincourt, p. 164.
3 LS, pp. 92–3.

thought it necessary to take Wordsworth severely to task over
these lines in the 'Ode: Intimations of Immortality':

> Thou, whose exterior semblance doth belie
>   Thy Soul's immensity;
> Thou best Philosopher, who yet dost keep
> Thy heritage, thou Eye among the blind,
> That, deaf and silent, read'st the eternal deep,
> Haunted for ever by the eternal mind, –
>   Mighty Prophet! Seer blest!
>   On whom those truths do rest,
> Which we are toiling all our lives to find,
> In darkness lost, the darkness of the grave.[1]

Surely Wordsworth did not mean to imply, Coleridge asks, that
a human being could earn the titles of 'Mighty Prophet' and
'Seer blest' by any other means than those of 'reflection. . .
knowledge. . .conscious intuition. . .or. . .any form or modification of consciousness'?[2] His concern was, perhaps, understandable in view of the fact that the idea of growth in
self-knowledge was central to his own moral thought, and indeed
was the basis of the Essays on the Principles of Method which he
inserted in the third edition of *The Friend*: but it was also of the
greatest significance for his thinking on the social state as a
whole, as indeed he made clear in those Essays. One of the most
important reasons for his interest in education, as he understood
it, was that he held it to be 'the *nisus formativus* of social man. . .
the appointed PROTOPLAST of true humanity'. 'Never', he
insists,

can society comprehend fully, and in its whole practical extent, the
permanent distinction, and the occasional contrast, between cultivation and civilization; never can it attain to a due insight into the momentous fact, fearfully as it has been, and even now is exemplified in a
neighbour country, that a nation can never be a too cultivated, but may
easily become an overcivilized, race: while we oppose ourselves
voluntarily to that grand prerogative of our nature, A HUNGERING
AND THIRSTING AFTER TRUTH, as the appropriate end of our intelli-
gential, and its point of union with, our moral nature.[3]

This emphasis on the education of the individual, as of the race,
and the distinction between 'cultivation' and 'civilization', is

---

[1] *Poetical Works*, p. 461.   [2] BL, ii p. 112.   [3] TF, i pp. 494–5 (Essay IX).

perhaps the most important single strand in all that Coleridge writes of the relation of man to the social state. The strength which it lends to his argument in *Church and State* is beyond doubt. 'We must be men in order to be citizens', Coleridge was to write in that essay, in one of his finest expositions of the idea of a final cause in the social state; and he pleads for recognition of the fact that true civilization and the perfection of the social state will never be achieved until it can be founded in *'cultivation*, in the harmonious development of those qualities and faculties that characterize our *humanity'*.[1]

It was a plea that at least one citizen of the despised 'neighbour country', a man with a sense of history no less acute than Coleridge's own, echoed, though unconsciously, in an analysis he gave of the sickness which bedevilled French society.

Je comprends que [les partisans de la liberté] vont se hâter d'appeler la religion à leur aide, car ils doivent savoir qu'on ne peut établir le règne de la liberté sans celui des mœurs, ni fonder les mœurs sans les croyances; mais ils ont aperçu la religion dans les rangs de leurs adversaires, c'en est assez pour eux: les uns l'attaquent, et les autres n'osent la défendre.[2]

As the second quotation that heads this chapter is intended to emphasize, Coleridge too, if his own representations are correct, was living in a society where 'chacun perd de vue l'objet même de ses poursuites'; and it was in the hope of bringing back into view the real purpose of the struggle that Coleridge pleaded the cause of Religion in his two *Lay Sermons*.

10

Coleridge's 'National Church' is not identical with the Christian Church. As Hooker had separated the duties which are incumbent upon all men from those which only Christian believers must observe, so Coleridge was careful to separate the 'National Church', which serves the final cause of the whole social state, from the body of believing Christians; and here again the subjective–objective distinction is vital.

[1] CCS, p. 44.   [2] Alexis De Tocqueville, *De la Démocratie en Amérique*, i p. 13.

Opposites, as we have seen, can only be things of the same kind, as the two poles of a magnet are of the same kind. The Christian Church is not, like the National Church, opposite to the state; it is a kingdom not of this world.

> The Christian Church is not a KINGDOM, REALM, (*royaume*), or STATE, (*sensu latiori*) of the WORLD. . .nor is it an Estate of any such realm, kingdom or state; but it is the appointed Opposite to them all, *collectively* – the *sustaining, correcting, befriending* Opposite of the world! the compensating counter-force to the inherent and inevitable evils and defects of the STATE, *as* a State. . .The true and only contraposition of the Christian Church is to the world. Her paramount aim and object, indeed, is *another* world, not a world *to come* exclusively, but likewise *another world that now is.*[1]

We move into another dimension of the subjective–objective distinction, and in doing so we are faced with a division of mind that was of immeasurable importance to the nineteenth century, and retains a high degree of importance even in our own time, though its influence is greatly diminished. If we are now liable, as I have suggested, to attribute Coleridge's change of political attitude to hypocrisy rather than to faith it is in large part because the 'world. . .to the concerns of which alone the epithet spiritual, can be applied' is now known or believed to be illusory. For Coleridge that world was indeed extremely real, and yet the value of Coleridge's political thought is precisely that it does *not* assume the existence of an infrangible divide between the spiritual and the material, between the sphere of worship and that of *praxis*. The spiritual world is not a hereafter but 'another world that now is'. Coleridge's position here represents an astonishing advance on the dialectic of eighteenth-century argument on this point; some divines, like Warburton, had identified the claims of religion so closely with worldly duties that they made religion virtually synonymous with civil obedience, whereas others divorced religious observance totally from political and civic life, making it entirely a matter of inner belief, much in the way Hobbes had in *Leviathan*.[2] Priestley wrote in a letter to Burke, 'Religion has naturally nothing at all to do with

---

[1] CCS, pp. 132–3, 136.
[2] See the account of Warburton and of 'Later Theology' in Leslie Stephen, *History of English Thought in the Eighteenth Century*, i, pp. 292–393.

COLERIDGE AND THE IDEA OF LOVE

any particular form of civil government; being useful to all persons, the rich as well as the poor, but only as individuals.'[1] This leaves us with a religion quite divorced from public life, from *praxis*; but Coleridge's view could inspire the exhortation, 'We must learn to act nationally as Christians.'[2] Priestley makes the world of the spirit something contrary to the world of action, and, as Coleridge remarks, 'contraries cannot be opposites'.[3] As the institutions of the civilized world, by their very nature, can deal solely with material things, neglecting the subjective, only the kingdom of the spirit, he argues, can be a *'befriending* Opposite', a 'counterforce', to such institutions. Without this kingdom, life becomes a matter of mere outward things; with it, the subjective, the mind and the spirit, have a home and a goal, as well as the body.

Relevant here is the comparison that Professor Passmore draws between the millenial hopes of some Christian thinkers (of whom Cudworth and Priestley are examples) and the Augustinian conception of a 'City of God'. Both ideas have in view the creation of a perfected society, but the millenialist looks to Christ's Second Coming as the condition of such a society's coming into being, whereas for Augustine and his followers the City of God is a historical reality, the glory of which is that it represents and foreshadows on earth the true Eternal City.[4] The City of God stands in opposition to the city of the worldly. In this respect Coleridge is close to the spirit of Augustinianism; Christianity (as he emphasizes in the *Confessions*) is *historical*, as well as spiritual. There were indeed those 'with whom the Christian religion is wholly objective, to the exclusion of all its correspondent subjective'[5] and without the 'light of the Spirit' religion became, indeed, a mere sham; but the historical church, the presence of an actual community of people who were ἔκκλητοι, those called out of the world, was also essential to Christianity. In this part of *Church and State*, Coleridge was concerned to show that the Church of Christ is not esoteric, but lives by witness, as well as belief.

In the once current (and well worthy to be re-issued) terminology of

[1] A. Cobban, *The Debate on the French Revolution*, p. 437.
[2] LS, pp. 132–4.   [3] CCS, p. 136.
[4] John Passmore, *The Perfectibility of Man*, p. 145.   [5] CIS, pp. 77–8.

our elder divines, [the Christian Church] is objective in its nature and purpose, not mystic or subjective, *i.e.* not like reason or the court of conscience, existing only in and for the individual...A city built on a hill, and not to be hid – an institution consisting of visible and public communities.[1]

Yet the very fact that the prime concerns of these communities are founded in, and return to, an idea of 'the spirit' – that their ultimate purpose is the incorporation of men into 'the spiritual and invisible church' – means that the presence of the Church in a nation is never inconsistent with the government's exercise of 'secular' authority according to its own designs. It is here that some of the worst dangers of Coleridge's approach become apparent. The Church, he writes, asks only for protection and 'to be let alone', but these it asks 'only on the ground, that there is nothing in her constitution, nor in her discipline, inconsistent with the interests of the state'.[2] Shortly afterwards Coleridge further develops this point by stating, 'the nisus, or counter-agency, of the Christian Church is against the evil *results* only, and not (directly, at least, or by primary intention) against the defective institutions that may have caused or aggravated them'.[3] Such an argument is perhaps an intrinsic part of any defence against Erastianism, but it is easy to see how it could be perverted to justify all kinds of hypocrisy. If it is once admitted that the church cannot meet the state on its own ground; that the best of secular administrations cannot obviate the evils inherent in the human condition; that the state has done all it needs to do so far as the moral health of its citizens is concerned if it simply allows them 'free-agency'; that the Church has no right to attack 'directly' the defective institutions of the social state; then what is to stop the Church from appearing to condone the most vicious abuses? Furthermore, making the National Church and the Christian Church between them the main repositories of spiritual or subjective values, when the Christian Church is denied the right to intervene 'directly' in political matters, carries with it the danger that the state (in Coleridge's use of the term) may have been defined too negatively, as a purely 'objective' institution, with no power or right to take into account the subjective sphere of existence. Such an

---

[1] CCS, p. 135.   [2] *ib.* p. 134.   [3] *ib.* p. 137.

institution will sooner or later begin to act as if this sphere did not exist.

The potential dangers are even more manifest in a note that Coleridge appended to a copy of the letter written by 'Vindex' to Viscount Goderich about the government's conduct towards the colonies.

Let every remedy be applied according to its specific Power. The Gospel is a remedy for corruptions in the will, and darkness in the Reason, (whence proceed the only dangerous errors in the understandings) of Persons, of Individuals. It was not intended as a *direct* remedy for *Things* – and Institutions, States of Society, etc., are *Things*, and therefore excluded from a *Spiritual* agency.[1]

This argument could well be taken by the unscrupulous as an assurance to the faithful that their commitment in no way obliged them to oppose the secular authorities even when these authorities blatantly ignored Christian principles. Coleridge cannot have intended this conclusion to be drawn from his argument ('We must learn to act nationally as Christians'), but it is a limitation in his case that he sees no possibility of a confrontation between the Church, as the body of committed Christians, and the state, when such a direct confrontation might very often be the only way in which the bearing of Christian principles on national politics could be brought to the notice of governments. As Coleridge himself observes,

Lords, Knights, and Burgesses...Men perfectly competent, it may be, to the protection and management of those interests, in which, as having so large a stake they may be reasonably presumed to feel a sincere and lively concern...are not the class of persons most likely to study, or feel a deep concern in, the interests here spoken of, in either sense of the term CHURCH.[2]

To trust to a 'spiritual' agency working on the minds and motives of such men is very like naïve idealism, especially when (a further limitation, we may feel) they are encouraged to regard the institution to which they belong as more a 'Thing' than an organic part of the community. The division of mind here formed also vitiates certain areas of controversy in which the decision of the private citizen is likely to have the highest

[1] *Notes, Theological*, p. 222.   [2] CCS, p. 118.

THE SOCIAL STATE

importance. *'War'*, Coleridge writes, 'is not forbidden by the Gospel, but only the Passions, whence alone come Wars among men',[1] an observation scarcely very helpful to the believing Christian who wishes to know whether Christianity forbids him to fight for his country. We may be tempted here to feel that caution has softened the prophet's sternness to the point of complete ineffectuality. But it should be emphasized that the issue we have been examining is not, 'Should there be opposition between the Church and the world?' but 'What form should such opposition take?' Coleridge is clear that this kind of opposition did and should exist, and from the perspective of eighteenth-century theological argument this admission can be seen as an advance of no small significance. Something of the force that Coleridge's appeal to a 'spiritual' agent did have, moreover, can be gauged from the fact that even a man of the intellectual rigorousness of J. S. Mill could argue that a philosophy such as that propounded by Coleridge was capable of liberalizing 'the great mass of the owners of large property, and of all the classes intimately connected with the owners of property'.[2] If we wish to commend Victorian liberalism for its high estimation of the powers of rational argument, a great deal of the credit we are to apportion must undoubtedly go to Coleridge, and to those whom he influenced most.

[1] *Notes, Theological*, p. 222.
[2] F. R. Leavis, editor, *Mill on Bentham and Coleridge*, p. 168.

Epilogue

It is to be hoped that this examination of Coleridge's thought on the social state has conveyed some impression of the development which Coleridge's thought underwent between the 1790s and the publication of *Church and State* in 1830. It was a development that affected not incidental or secondary concerns only, but the very roots of his political philosophy; yet throughout his work we can see certain issues and principles emerging, changing, perhaps, in their relative importance, but never wholly lost to sight.

Some indication of the extent of this development is given by a comment which he made on the abortive 'Pantisocratic' scheme, some fifteen years after it had collapsed, and by a much later note which outlined a philosophy of society diametrically opposed to the whole principle of the Pantisocratic venture. The comment on Pantisocracy occurs in the eleventh issue of *The Friend*.

I was a sharer in the general vortex, though my little World described the path of its Revolution in an orbit of its own. What I dared not expect from constitutions of Government and whole Nations, I hoped from Religion and a small Company of chosen Individuals, and formed a plan, as harmless as it was extravagant, of trying the experiment of human Perfectibility on the banks of the *Susquehannah*; where our little Society, in its second Generation, was to have combined the innocence of the patriarchal Age with the knowledge and genuine refinements of European culture...Strange fancies! and as vain as strange! yet to the intense interest and impassioned zeal, which called forth and strained every faculty of my intellect for the organization and defence of this Scheme, I owe much of whatever I at present possess, my clearest insight into the nature of individual Man, and my most comprehensive views of his social relations, of the true uses of Trade and Commerce, and how far the *Wealth* of Nations promotes or impedes their true *welfare* and inherent *strength*.[1]

[1] TF, ii pp. 146–7 (no. 11 : 26 October 1809) ; i pp. 223–4.

264

It is an assertion which is perhaps vulnerable to attack from many quarters; but before condemning Coleridge for revealing only self-righteousness, or worse, in his contempt for 'the pitfalls of sedition', it would be as well to examine the note in which he writes of the ethical dilemma faced by the refugee from any existing society. For though, as we have seen, Coleridge recognized no 'social contract', he did recognize the implications for the political philosopher of the axiom in ethics, 'So act that thou mayest be able to *will*, that thy *maxim* should be the *law* of all rational beings.'[1] The axiom sprang to Coleridge's mind after he had read, in Algernon Sydney's works, the statement 'Ten men may as justly resolve to live together, frame a civil society, and oblige themselves to laws, as the greatest number of men that ever met together in the world.'[2] Unless society itself has been dissolved, or the ten men are victims of shipwreck, Coleridge reflected, 'the arrangement would be hollow as to its ground, and pernicious as to its consequences; and would justify manifold and contradictory *imperia in imperio*... To form a society, on the maxim that no duties are owing to society, is to will the conditions of connexion and dissolution by the same act.'[3] There is thus no possible foundation on which a future society may be built by any group of men who have seceded from an existing society; for – remembering always that in Coleridge's eyes, 'rights' were not absolute but were conditional on the acceptance of 'duties' – the denial of their duty to the existing society, provided that society was doing its duty by them, must entail the repudiation of all such duties to any hypothetical future society, and hence of all social rights, if we wish to be constant to the laws of ethics. The proviso that society must do its duty by the individual is, of course, crucial; and here Coleridge reaffirms his belief that the social state must be guided by the idea of a final cause. We may wish to accept that it might be legitimate for such a group of men to secede unilaterally from the old society, and set up a new one at the risk of losing themselves in the 'labyrinth' of self-determination. But, in that case,

we must suppose them not born in a formed society capable of maintaining them, needing their services, and yielding them due protection,

[1] *Notes, Theological*, p. 190.   [2] *ib.* p. 189.   [3] *ib.* p. 190.

and their rightful share of the fruits of society, such as education, and the other means and opportunities of developing their bodily, moral, and intellectual faculties, which is the final cause of human society; because human faculties cannot be fully developed but by society and a man *per se* is a contradiction; he is only *potentially* a man, not *actually*. Persecution in religion, and the absolute withholding of all withhold-able knowledge, renders society to the injured persons not society, and does not so much dissolve their duties as preclude them.[1]

This is indeed a far cry from the Utopianism of the Pantiso-cratic era; but the passage states succinctly, if without any great refinement of style, the first principle of all that Coleridge wrote on man's relation to the social state, following his disillusion-ment with Pantisocracy. In a way that is typical of his best writings on politics, it offers itself to polemicists of both the right and the left; yet it stands in no danger of becoming a mere empty slogan. Indeed, its use is a means of testing the serious-ness of any political debate, for, if used thoughtfully, it must force both sides to examine closely the principles from which they are arguing, and the ends they have in view. But it has one further characteristic, one which it shares with the whole canon of Coleridge's political thought, and also, in a sense, with the Bible as Coleridge expounded it. It demands the rejection of the abstract and theoretical, and a return to realities. Perhaps for that very reason, it is unlikely that any polemicist, politician or propagandist will ever dare to use this or any other extract from Coleridge's political works; but it would be a healthy exercise for all polemicists to call to mind J. S. Mill's courageous prayer, 'O Lord, enlighten thou our enemies.' If general enlightenment as to ultimate aims forms any part of our purpose in stimulating political debate – if our desire is for serious thought, and not for effective propaganda – then Coleridge's writings on politics provide a valuable and highly demanding testing-ground.

In particular, it can be said that the desire to escape the cor-ruptions of an existing community by creating a smaller one, protected from its parent community either by geographical isolation or by doctrinal barriers, is not new, and there are many ways of justifying this kind of active utopianism; but the men and women who abhor the particularly insidious ways in which

[1] *Notes, Theological*, pp. 190–1.

modern industrial society vitiates human relationships are still faced with the dilemma that Coleridge described. If they remain within society, and manage to avoid compromising their ideals, their message is still liable to be affected by the trivialization which is one of the worst features of the society they oppose. If they succeed in creating a separate community, then the more successful it is, the more it diverts from the parent community the forces which should be working for change.

In asserting, in the introduction to this book, that Coleridge's ideas must finally be judged by their 'value', I did not intend that any or all of them (for instance, the judgment of persons by what they are, rather than what they do: the assertion that love is an act of the will: the substitution of 'consciousness of the other-than-self' for Kant's 'pure apperception') should emerge as absolutely, unconditionally valid. Literary research should not produce reach-me-down dogmas; if it does, it has failed. The important question is whether our society has resolved the conflicts with which Coleridge concerned himself, or whether it has merely made us forget about them.

Eventually, change may be forced upon us. Successive ecological crises will encourage a new sense of dependence on the natural world. Smaller, more cohesive communities may have to be evolved, to avoid too rapid a depletion of natural resources, and if this happens a new kind of importance will attach to human relationships, if only because in a technologically simpler society human interdependence will once again be a matter of daily life instead of mere theory. The other alternative is perhaps too obvious to mention: the destruction and fragmentation of every community, as the nations quarrel over dwindling resources of food and energy. If we escape this, and the accompanying regimentation of society in the interests of 'efficiency', it will no longer be possible to forget the real issues of the interhuman.

Bibliography

Abrams, M. H. *The Mirror and the Lamp* (New York, 1958).

Arnold, Matthew. *Culture and Anarchy*, edited by J. Dover Wilson (London, 1946).

Babbitt, Irving. *On Being Creative and Other Essays* (Boston, 1932).

Bacon, Francis. *The Advancement of Learning*, edited by G. W. Kitchin (London, 1861).

Bald, R. C. (editor). *Literary Friendships in the Age of Wordsworth* (London, 1932).

Bate, W. J. *Coleridge* (London, 1969).

—— *From Classic to Romantic* (Cambridge, Mass., 1946).

Baudelaire, Charles. *Les Fleurs du Mal*, edited by A. Adam (Paris, 1961).

Beer, J. B. *Coleridge the Visionary* (London, 1959).

—— Review of Norman Fruman's *Coleridge, the Damaged Archangel*, in *Review of English Studies*, vol. xxiv, no. 95 (August 1973), pp. 346–53.

Berkeley, George. *The Principles of Human Knowledge*, edited by T. E. Jessop (London, 1942).

—— *Works*, edited by A. A. Luce and T. E. Jessop, 9 vols. (London, 1948–57).

Bewley, E. M. 'The Poetry of Coleridge' ('Revaluations', xii), *Scrutiny*, vol. viii, no. 4 (March 1940), pp. 406–20.

Blake, William. *Poems and Prophecies*, edited by Max Plowman, revised by Geoffrey Keynes (London, 1963).

Blunden, E., and Griggs, E. L. (editors). *Coleridge – Studies by Several Hands* (London, 1934).

Boulton, J. T. *The Language of Politics in the Age of Wilkes and Burke* (London, 1963).

Briggs, A. *The Age of Improvement, 1793–1867* (London, 1960).

Brown, J. A. C. *Freud and the Post-Freudians* (London, 1961).

Browning, Robert. *Poetical Works* (London, 1964).

Burke, Edmund. *Reflections on the Revolution in France*, edited by Conor Cruise O'Brien (London, 1968).

Burke, Edmund. *Thoughts on the Prospect of a Regicide Peace, in a series of Letters* (London, 1796).

Burnet, J. *Early Greek Philosophy*, fourth edition (London, 1948).

Byron, George Gordon, Lord. *Poetical Works* (London, 1959).

Calleo, D. P. *Coleridge and the Idea of the Modern State* (New Haven, Connecticut, and London, 1966).

Carlyle, Thomas. *English and other Critical Essays*, 2 vols. (London, 1915).

—— *Heroes and Hero-Worship* (London, 1912).

Cestre, C. *La Révolution française et les poètes anglais* (Paris, 1906).

Cobban, A., editor. *The Debate on the French Revolution* (London, 1950).

—— *A History of Modern France*, 3 vols. (London, 1961). Vol. I: *The Old Régime and the Revolution, 1715–1799*.

Coburn, K., editor. *Coleridge: A Collection of Critical Essays* (Englewood Cliffs, New Jersey, 1967).

—— 'Coleridge and Wordsworth and "the Supernatural",' *University of Toronto Quarterly*, vol. xxv, no. 2 (January 1956), pp. 121–30.

Colmer, J. *Coleridge, Critic of Society* (London, 1959).

Cornford, F. M. *Principium Sapientiæ: the Origins of Greek Philosophical Thought* (London, 1952).

De Quincey, Thomas. *Reminiscences of the English Lake Poets*, edited by John E. Jordan (London, 1961).

De Tocqueville, Alexis. *De la Démocratie en Amérique*, thirteenth edition, 2 vols. (Paris, 1850).

Eliot, Thomas Stearns. *Collected Poems* (London, 1963).

Enscoe, G. *Eros and the Romantics* (The Hague and Paris, 1967).

Erikson, Erik H. *Childhood and Society* (London, 1965).

Fruman, Norman. *Coleridge, the Damaged Archangel* (London, 1972).

Gérard, A. 'The Systolic Rhythm: The Structure of Coleridge's Conversation Poems', *Essays in Criticism*, vol. x, no. 3 (July 1960), pp. 307–19.

Godwin, William. *Enquiry concerning Political Justice*, second edition, 2 vols. (London, 1796).

—— *Caleb Williams*, edited by David McKraken (London, 1970).

Goodwin, A. *The French Revolution* (London, 1966).

Green, Joseph Henry. *Spiritual Philosophy, founded on the teaching of S. T. Coleridge*, edited by J. Simon, 2 vols. (London, 1865).

Halévy, E. *A History of the English People in the Nineteenth Century*, 7 vols. (London, 1949). Vol. I: *England in 1815*, translated by E. I. Watkin and D. A. Barker. Vol. II: *The Liberal Awakening, 1815–1830*, translated by E. I. Watkin.

Harding, D. W. *Experience into Words* (London, 1963).

COLERIDGE AND THE IDEA OF LOVE

Harper, G. M. 'Coleridge's Conversation Poems', *Quarterly Review*, vol. 244 (April 1925), pp. 284–98.

Haven, Richard. *Patterns of Consciousness* ([Amherst, Massachusetts], 1969).

Hobbes, Thomas. *Leviathan*, edited by M. Oakeshott (Oxford, [1946]).

Hooker, Richard. *Of the Laws of Ecclesiastical Polity*, with an introduction by Christopher Morris (London, 1969). Volume I: Books I – IV.

House, A. H. *Coleridge: The Clark Lectures 1951–52* (London, 1969).

Hume, David. *A Treatise of Human Nature*, edited by L. A. Selby-Bigge (London, 1968).

Jackson, J. R. de J., editor. *Coleridge: the Critical Heritage* (London, 1969).

Jaeger, W. *The Theology of the Early Greek Philosophers: The Gifford Lectures 1936*, translated from the German MS. by E. S. Robinson (London, 1967). (First published 1947 by the Clarendon Press, Oxford.)

James, William. *The Varieties of Religious Experience: a study in human nature: The Gifford Lectures 1901–1902*, thirty-sixth impression (London, 1928).

Johnson, Samuel. *Rasselas, Prince of Abyssinia*, edited by A. J. F. Collins (London, 1962).

Kant, Immanuel. *Critique of Pure Reason*, translated by Norman Kemp Smith (London, 1970). (First published 1929.)

—— *Critique of Practical Reason*, translated by T. K. Abbott (London, 1963). (First published 1873.)

Keats, John. *Letters*, edited by M. Buxton Forman, fourth edition, with revisions and additional letters (London, 1952).

Kierkegaard, Søren. *The Last Years: Journals 1853–1855*, translated by R. Gregor Smith (London, 1968). (First published 1965.)

—— *Purity of Heart is to Will One Thing*, translated by Douglas Steere (London, 1961).

Knight, G. W. *The Starlit Dome* (London, 1941).

Knights, L. C. 'Taming the Albatross', *New York Review of Books*, 26 May 1966. p. 12.

Körner, S. *Kant* (London, 1955, reprinted 1970).

Lindsay, J. I. 'Coleridge Marginalia in Jacobi's *Werke*', *Modern Language Notes*, vol. L (1935), pp. 216–24.

Locke, John. *An Essay Concerning Human Understanding*, edited by A. S. Pringle-Pattison (London, 1924, reprinted 1969).

Lovejoy, A. O. 'Coleridge and Kant's Two Worlds', in *Essays in the*

BIBLIOGRAPHY

History of Ideas (Baltimore, 1948), pp. 254–76.

—— 'Kant and the English Platonists', in *Essays Philosophical and Psychological: In Honor of William James* (New York and London, 1908).

McFarland, T. *Coleridge and the Pantheist Tradition* (London, 1969).

McKenzie, G. M. *Organic Unity in Coleridge* (Berkeley, California, 1939).

Mill, John Stuart. *Bentham and Coleridge*, edited by F. R. Leavis (London, 1950).

Miller, J. H. *The Disappearance of God (Five Nineteenth Century Writers)* (London, 1963).

Miller, R. D. *Schiller and the Ideal of Freedom* (London, 1970). (First published 1959 by the Duchy Press, Harrogate.)

Milton, John. *Samson Agonistes* (London, 1671).

—— *Poems*, edited by B. A. Wright, revised edition (London, 1966). (First published 1956.)

Muirhead, J. H. *Coleridge as Philosopher* (London, 1930).

—— 'Coleridge – Metaphysician or Mystic?' See under 'Blunden, E., and Griggs, E. L., editors'.

Nietzsche, Friedrich. *Thus Spoke Zarathustra*, translated by R. J. Hollingdale (London, 1961).

Orsini, G. N. G. *Coleridge and German Idealism* (Carbondale, Illinois, 1969).

Paine, Thomas. *The Rights of Man*, 2 vols. bound as one (London, 1792).

Passmore, John. *The Perfectibility of Man* (London, 1970).

Prickett, S. *Wordsworth and Coleridge: The Poetry of Growth* (London, 1970).

Raysor, T. M. 'Coleridge and Asra', *Studies in Philology*, vol. xxvi (July 1929), pp. 305–24.

Robinson, Henry Crabb. *Blake, Coleridge, Wordsworth, Lamb, &c.*, edited by Edith J. Morley (London, 1922).

Rousseau, Jean-Jacques. *Du Contrat Social* (Paris, 1962).

Schelling, Friedrich Wilhelm Joseph von. *Werke* (Stuttgart und Augsburg, 1856–60).

Schrickx, W. 'Coleridge and F. H. Jacobi', *Revue Belge de Philologie et d'Histoire*, vol. xxxvi no. 3 (1958), pp. 812–29.

Shaffer, E. S. 'Iago's Malignity Motivated: Coleridge's Unpublished "Opus Magnum"', *Shakespeare Quarterly*, vol. xix no. 3 (Summer 1968), pp. 195–203.

Smith, Adam. *The Wealth of Nations*, edited by E. Cannan, 2 vols. (London, 1961).

Stephen, Leslie. *The English Utilitarians*, 3 vols. (London, 1900).

271

—— History of English Thought in the Eighteenth Century, 2 vols. (London, 1962). (First published 1876.)
Stirling, James Hutchinson. Jerrold, Tennyson and Macaulay, and other Essays (Edinburgh, 1868).
Stoll, E. E. 'Symbolism in Coleridge', Publications of the Modern Language Association of America, vol. LXIII (March 1948), pp. 214–33.
Storr, A. The Integrity of the Personality (London, 1963).
Tate, A., editor. T. S. Eliot, the Man and the Work (New York, 1968).
Thompson, E. P. The Making of the English Working Class (London, 1970). (First published 1963; revised edition first published 1968.)
Trilling, L. The Opposing Self (London, 1955).
Warren, R. P. 'A Poem of Pure Imagination', Kenyon Review, vol. VIII, no. 3 (Summer 1946), pp. 391–427.
Watson, G. G. Coleridge the Poet (London, 1966).
Watson, J. S. The Reign of George III, 1760–1815 (vol. II of the Oxford History of England, edited by Sir George Clark) (London, 1960).
Watson, Lucy E. Coleridge at Highgate (London, 1925).
Wellek, R. Immanuel Kant in England, 1793–1838 (Princeton, New Jersey, 1931).
Whalley, G. Coleridge and Sara Hutchinson and the Asra Poems (London, 1955).
—— 'The Mariner and the Albatross', University of Toronto Quarterly, vol. XVI, no. 4 (July 1947), pp. 381–98.
Wheelwright, P. Heraclitus (Princeton, New Jersey, and London, 1959).
White, R. J., editor. Political Tracts of Wordsworth, Coleridge and Shelley (London, 1954).
Whyte, L. L. The Unconscious before Freud (London, 1967). (First published 1962.)
Willey, B. Darwin and Butler – Two Versions of Evolution (The Hibbert Lectures 1959) (London, 1960).
—— The English Moralists (London, 1964).
—— Nineteenth Century Studies (London, 1964). (First published 1949.)
—— The Seventeenth-Century Background (London, 1964). (First published 1934.)
Williams, R. H. Culture and Society, 1780–1950 (London, 1958).
Woodring, C. 'Christabel of Cumberland', Review of English Literature, vol. VII, no. 1 (January 1966), pp. 43–52.

BIBLIOGRAPHY

Wordsworth, Dorothy. *Journals*, edited by E. de Selincourt, 2 vols. (London, 1959.)

Wordsworth, William. *Early Letters of William and Dorothy Wordsworth*, edited by E. de Selincourt (London, 1935).

—— *Poetical Works*, edited by Thomas Hutchinson, revised by E. de Selincourt (London, 1967). (First revised edition published 1936; reset and reprinted 1950.)

—— *The Prelude (Text of 1805)*, edited by E. de Selincourt (London 1966). (First published 1933; revised by Helen Darbishire in 1960).

Yarlott, G. *Coleridge and the Abyssinian Maid* (London, 1967).

Yeats, William Butler. *Collected Poems* (London, 1967). (First edition first published 1933; second edition, with additional poems, 1950.)

Yonge, C. D. *The Life and Administration of...Lord Liverpool*, 3 vols. (London, 1868).

Index

capitalism, 239; *see also* property; trade
Carlyle, Thomas, 157
Carnarvon, Lord, 222
Cartwright, Major, 241
Catholic Emancipation Bills, 220, 246–8
Catholicism, *see* Roman Catholic
  Church
Cestre, C., 197, 201, 209–10, 223–4
childhood, 37, 86–8, 94, 145, 160–1,
  188
Christ, 62, 114, 118, 132, 138–9, 160,
  239, 260
Christian Church (as opposed to
  National Church), 258–63
Christianity, 4, 24, 32–3, 41, 45–6, 58,
  60–1, 82, 93, 101–2, 115, 124, 135,
  149–50, 158, 160, 162, 167–9,
  218–19, 239–40, 253, 260; *see also*
  dissent; Protestantism; Revelation;
  Roman Catholic Church
Church Fathers, *see* patristic writings
Cintra, Convention of, 207
Clevedon, Somerset, 48, 53
Cobban, Alfred, 21, 157, 199
Coburn, Kathleen, 9, 42, 58
Coleridge, Berkeley (C's son), 15, 26,
  87
Coleridge, Derwent (C's son), 15,
  67–8, 87, 128
Coleridge, Edward (C's nephew), 128,
  131, 154
Coleridge, George (C's brother), 14
Coleridge, Hartley (C's son), 15, 52,
  86, 127
Coleridge, Samuel Taylor: able to
  pray, 131; and opium, 80, 122–3;
  and Pantisocracy, 2, 7, 10, 41, 264–6;
  as conversationalist, 28, 31; as
  'German metaphysician', 129; as
  poet, 43–78, 80–93; as 'Satyrane',
  19, 79–80; as scientist, 35; at Highgate, 125–8; children, 11, 15;
  dependence on friends, 6, 80;
  family, 14, 87; friendship with Davy,
  35; with Sara Hutchinson, 6, 9, 12,
  13, 26, 32–3, 35, 39, 84, 90, 94, 122,
  127; with Poole, 6, 8, 13–15; with
  Southey, 6, 41; with Wordsworth,
  6–11, 107, 122, 127, 148; marriage,
  9–11, 16, 26–7, 127; 'oneversazioni',
  126; solitude, 27, 79–80, 122;
  spiritual incompleteness, 122–3;

Aids to Reflection, 27, 29, 130–2, 140,
  145, 151, 154–5, 164, 167–8; *Anima
  Poetæ*, 6, 27, 30, 102, 106, 132, 133;
  Biographia Literaria, 10, 19, 32,
  33, 36–7, 43, 84–5, 133, 137, 148,
  163, 173, 175, 179–80, 184, 200–1,
  211, 257; 'The Blossoming of the
  Solitary Date Tree', 78; 'Christabel',
  44, 66–74, 78; *Confessions of an
  Inquiring Spirit*, 128, 162, 253, 260;
  'The Dungeon', 55–6; 'The Eolian
  Harp', 44–8, 50, 57, 78; *Essay on
  Faith*, 93, 121, 128, 133, 185, 188–
  92; *Essay on Marriage*, 155–8;
  Essays on His Own Times, 201–5,
  208, 231–2, 246, 252; 'Fears in
  Solitude', 51–5, 65; *The Friend*, 7,
  13, 27, 29, 36, 41–2, 79, 91, 93–5,
  101, 103–5, 111, 114–6, 123, 192,
  208, 212–18, 224, 232–3, 242–3,
  252, 254–5, 257, 264; 'Frost at
  Midnight', 52, 54; 'Idly we suppli-
  cate the Powers above', 127; 'Kubla
  Khan', 28; *Lay Sermon*, 152, 224,
  233–6, 240, 253, 256, 260; *Lecture
  on the Prometheus of Æschylus*, 139–
  40; *Lectures 1795*, 23–5, 48, 61, 93,
  167, 211, 219, 239; *Letters*, 7–9,
  10–12, 14, 16, 20–1, 26–31, 34–6,
  95, 101–2, 106–7, 114–18, 122,
  127–8, 131, 139, 143–6, 148, 154,
  156–8, 160, 162, 166, 168; 'Letter
  to Lord Liverpool', 219, 224; 'Lines
  written in the Album at Elbingerode', 15; *Literary Remains*, 93, 121,
  128, 133, 185, 188–92; *Miscellaneous
  Criticism*, 95–6, 112, 148, 161;
  Notebooks, 9, 13, 16–21, 25, 28, 30–1,
  33, 35–43, 81–9, 93–4, 96–7, 99,
  102, 109, 111–14, 122–4, 167, 187;
  Notebooks (unpublished), 37, 81,
  83–5, 88–94, 101–2, 106, 108–10,
  114, 116, 122–4, 125, 127–8, 132,
  138–9, 149, 155, 158–60, 186,
  193–4; *Notes, Theological*, 222, 228,
  250, 262, 265; 'Ode: Dejection', 10,
  15, 74–8, 127, 150; 'Ode to the
  Departing Year', 49–51, 200; *On
  the Constitution of Church and State*,
  154, 197, 221–8, 237, 246–53,
  252–3, 258, 260–2; 'On the Philosophic Import of the Words